Also by Thomas Gilovich

How We Know What Isn't So: The Fallibility of Human Reason in Everyday Life

Heuristics and Biases: The Psychology of Intuitive Judgment (with Dale Griffin and Daniel Kahneman)

Social Psychology (with Dacher Keltner and Richard Nisbett)

Also by Gary Belsky

23 Ways to Get to First Base: The ESPN Uncyclopedia (with Neil Fine)

Should You Really Be a Lawyer? The Guide to Smart Career Choices Before, During & After Law School (with Deborah Schneider)

ESPN The Magazine Presents Answer Guy: Extinguishing the Burning Questions of Sports with the Water Bucket of Truth (with Brendan O'Connor and Neil Fine)

On Second Thought . . . 365 of the Worst Promises, Predictions, and Pronouncements Ever Made

Why Smart People Make Big Money Mistakes...
and How to Correct Them

Lessons from the Life-Changing
Science of Behavioral Economics

GARY BELSKY & THOMAS GILOVICH

SIMON & SCHUSTER PAPERBACKS
NEW YORK   LONDON   TORONTO   SYDNEY

Simon & Schuster
1230 Avenue of the Americas
New York, NY 10020

This Simon & Schuster trade paperback edition January 2010

SIMON & SCHUSTER and colophon are registered trademarks of Simon & Schuster, Inc.

For information about special discounts for bulk purchases,
please contact Simon & Schuster Special Sales at 1-866-506-1949
or business@simonandschuster.com.

The Simon & Schuster Speakers Bureau can bring authors
to your live event. For more information or to book an event
contact the Simon & Schuster Speakers Bureau at 1-866-248-3049
or visit our website at www.simonspeakers.com.

Designed by Jaime Putorti

Manufactured in the United States of America

10 9 8 7 6

Library of Congress Cataloging-in-Publication Data
Belsky, Gary.
    Why smart people make big money mistakes and how to correct them : lessons from
the life-changing science of behavioral economics / by Gary Belsky & Thomas Gilovich.
      p. cm.
      1. Finance, Personal—Psychological aspects.   2. Finance, Personal—
Decision making.   3. Investments—Decision making.   4. Consumers—
Attitudes.   5. Economics—Psychological aspects.   I. Gilovich, Thomas.   II. Title.
HG179.B375   2009
332.024—dc22   2009041637

ISBN 978-1-4391-6336-8
ISBN 978-0-7432-0442-2 (ebook)

CONTENTS

INTRODUCTION:
WHY SMART PEOPLE MAKE BIG MONEY MISTAKES   **1**
An introduction to the life-changing science of behavioral
economics.

1 NOT ALL DOLLARS ARE CREATED EQUAL   **21**
How "mental accounting" can help you save, or cost you money.

2 WHEN SIX OF ONE ISN'T HALF A DOZEN OF THE OTHER   **45**
How "loss aversion" and the "sunk cost fallacy" lead you to
throw good money after bad.

3 THE DEVIL THAT YOU KNOW   **77**
How the "status quo bias" and the "endowment effect" make
financial choices difficult.

4 NUMBER NUMBNESS   **105**
"Money illusion," "bigness bias," and other ways that ignorance
about math and probabilities can hurt you.

5 DROPPING ANCHOR   **131**
Why "anchoring" and the "confirmation bias" lead you to
make important money decisions based on unimportant
information.

6 THE EGO TRAP   **155**
"Overconfidence" and the price of thinking that you know more
than you do.

7 **HERD IT THROUGH THE GRAPEVINE**   183
   *"Information cascades" and the danger of relying too much on
      the financial moves of others.*

8 **EMOTIONAL BAGGAGE**   209
   *The role of emotions in decision making: what we don't know
      about how we feel.*

CONCLUSION: NOW WHAT?   235
   Principles to ponder and steps to take.

POSTSCRIPT: PSYCHIC INCOME   253

ACKNOWLEDGMENTS   257

INDEX   261

Why Smart People Make
Big Money Mistakes...
and How to Correct Them

WHY SMART PEOPLE MAKE BIG MONEY MISTAKES

This is an optimistic book, written by a pair of realists. Optimistic, because this project rests on the belief that ordinary individuals can enhance life's enjoyment by understanding—and altering—the way they deal with their money. Realistic, because your authors know that correcting money-related behavior is like tinkering with a golf swing or getting along better with in-laws: It may take a while, and for every fix there's a danger that you'll create a new set of problems. Still, our purpose here is straightforward, and we are confident of its merits.

This remains true ten years after the first edition of our work was published, a decade during which this book's underlying research received significant attention beyond academia. Over that same span of time, we witnessed what can safely be called a major upheaval in global financial markets and individuals' personal finances. Both of these developments connect directly to our reasons for writing—and now updating—this book: We have always believed that by identifying the psychological causes behind many kinds of financial decisions, you can change your behavior in ways that will ultimately put more money in your pocket and help you keep more of what you have. Ten years on, many more people agree with us, and still more are interested in any kind of knowledge or advice that will assist them in navigating the treacherous waters of financial decision making. As it happens, we think we can help.

How do we plan to accomplish this feat? For starters, the insights and strategies we offer in this book arise from many wellsprings, not least our experiences as a psychologist and as a journalist specializing in personal finance. We're also spenders, savers, borrowers, and investors like you, with firsthand knowledge of the mistakes we'll be discussing. But underpinning most of this book is a field of research called "behavioral economics," which has flourished in intellectual arenas for the better part of four decades and has recently become very trendy. We might even say "hot," to the extent that anything having to do with economics can be called that. But regardless of what you might think about a subject once you learn that journalists and politicians have suddenly warmed to it, know this: Behavioral economics, which brings together tools and insights from economics and psychology, truly can explain why and how people make seemingly irrational or illogical decisions when they spend, invest, save, and borrow money.

It can, in other words, provide answers to the question implied in our book's title: Why do smart people make big money mistakes?

It's an especially apt question to ask these days, when confusion about money—how we earn it, spend it, waste it—may be more prevalent than at any period in memory. Instability in the banking business and the securities industry in recent years has shaken many people's belief in the wisdom of their savings and investment strategies, not to mention the institutions they thought were safeguarding their nest eggs. This new uncertainty has joined forces with long-felt anxiety about stocks, bonds, 401(k) accounts, annuities, and IRAs to create widespread befuddlement when it comes to the choices we make at the car dealer, department store, brokerage, or bank. Indeed, whether we're dealing with the stock market, real estate market, or supermarket, we all commit financial follies that cost us hundreds or thousands of dollars every year. Yet in the main, we are blissfully ignorant of the causes of most of our monetary missteps and clueless as to how we might correct them.

- Why, for example, do so many investors sell stocks just *before* the share prices skyrocket? And why do those same investors keep a tight grip on falling stocks far too long?
- Why do mutual fund investors put their money into the latest hot funds, when those same portfolios, over time, routinely lag behind the overall stock or bond markets?
- Why do so many Americans maintain savings accounts earning negligible interest even as they carry credit card balances that rack up hundreds or thousands of dollars a year in finance charges?
- Why are many of us willing to spend so much more for a product bought on credit?
- Why do business owners and executives spend ever-increasing amounts of money on failing products or money-losing divisions?

- Why do so many employees turn down free money from their employers (in the form of matching contributions to their retirement accounts)? And why do so many of those who accept these corporate gifts invest them so unwisely?
- Why do so many people have such low deductibles on their insurance policies?

The answers to these pervasive and puzzling questions can be found in behavioral economics. But before we throw you headfirst into this amazing science, let us take you on a quick tour of its history. By examining how economics came to be linked with psychology in the study of decision making, you'll be that much better prepared to grasp how behavioral economics can help improve your finances—and many other kinds of life choices, too.

A (MERCIFULLY) BRIEF HISTORY OF ECONOMICS

There's an old joke that if you laid every economist in history end to end, they still wouldn't reach a conclusion. But in fact, economists have been describing the way money and mankind interact for quite a while, often with impressive (if dubious) certainty. In 1848, for instance, British economist and philosopher John Stuart Mill wrote in his *Principles of Political Economy:* "Happily, there is nothing in the laws of value which remains for the present or any future writer to clear up; the theory of the subject is complete." Mill's forecast aside, economics has long drawn some of the world's greatest minds, who have developed many theories to explain how people (and groups of people, like companies and countries) allocate available resources to achieve desired goals. These thinkers have ranged from the fourth-century

(B.C.) Greek philosopher Plato (one of the first to recognize the economic basis of social life) to the renowned eighteenth-century Scotsman Adam Smith (an early and insightful observer of economic markets) to the twentieth-century Englishman John Maynard Keynes (who revolutionized the way we look at the economy as a whole).

Whatever the prevailing theory, economic study has traditionally been informed by a few core assumptions. The most significant are that humans are fundamentally rational and ultimately efficient when it comes to money. Put simply: We know what we want, what we want is for our own good, and we know (or will figure out) the best way to get it. In short, people make rational, consistent, and self-interested decisions.

But of course, while most people are often self-interested, very few are consistently so, and even fewer are perfectly rational. What is consistent about the man who thinks saving $5 is sufficiently worthwhile to drive twenty minutes to a discount grocery store, but who throws away hundreds of dollars a year on the gas-guzzling car used for the trip? What is rational about the woman who owns a favorite singer's CD, yet still buys individual downloaded songs from that album online? On the other hand, where's the self-interest in giving money to charity or taking a friend out to dinner? To be fair, economists don't confuse self-interest with selfishness. Most economic theories assume that people can find value in things that do not necessarily enhance their material well-being. They concede that humans can be motivated by nonfinancial concerns like love or generosity or convenience.

Nonetheless, the notion of rational and consistent self-interest requires a belief that people donate to Oxfam, buy a Prius, or invest in Amazon based on some consistent calculation of value. That is, we assign a value to the good feeling that generosity or self-sacrifice brings—as well as to the loss of buying or investing power that donating money entails—and we make decisions accordingly. To be sure, economists know that these calculations are not always made consciously. But it is a tenet of conventional economics that such an evaluation of benefits and costs occurs, if only on a subconscious and experiential plane. On one level or another, traditional theory holds, we make decisions because of a consistent and sensible pursuit of satisfaction and personal fulfillment, of getting the most out of life with our current and future resources.

As you might imagine, such a dogged insistence on rationality, self-interest, and consistency as the driving forces behind financial decisions has often put economists in a quandary: How to explain seemingly irrational human behavior as the result of the rational pursuit of self-interest? Consider, as just one example, our habit of tipping. If you think about it, tipping is about as irrational as can be: folks routinely giving away money without a clear obligation to do so, to people they'll likely never see again, in places they'll never revisit, for a level of service that may not have even pleased them. Marketing professor Michael Lynn, after reviewing a great many studies of tipping published over the years, found that exceptional service increased the average tip by less than 2 percent, which means that a lot of non-exceptional service is consistently being rewarded.

Not surprising, right? Everybody tips because, well, we just do. For economists, though, explaining why that is has always been tough. It's not enough to say that the self-interest in tipping is the guarantee of good service. Tipping comes *after* the meal, so that would only explain why people might tip in neighborhood restaurants or other eateries to which they are certain they will return. It does not explain why, as several studies have shown, travelers will tip their waiter at, say, a California Pizza Kitchen in Chicago when they know it's unlikely they'll ever eat there again. Where's the self-interest in that? Nor is it sufficient to explain tipping as simply the result of goodwill—a heartwarming decision by the vast majority of Americans (people don't generally tip in many countries) that being nice to service people is worth about 15 percent of whatever we spend. If that were the case, we'd all be tipping gas station attendants, cashiers, and bank tellers.

So why do Americans tip? No one knows for certain, but the economist Russell Roberts, author of *The Price of Everything* and other novels about economics, has some interesting thoughts on the matter. He notes that people frequently use social heuristics—rules of thumb—when interacting with each other, without conscious acknowledgment, as a way to make life a more pleasant experience. For example, most of us agree to wait our turn in line at the car wash rather than bang fenders with one another to get there first. Roberts theorizes that Americans have an unspoken rule of thumb about dining at restaurants: We all want to eat out, and we all want the experience to be pleasant. (If being served cold food by a grouch was the goal, we could just stay home.) And because diners are better judges of service than restaurant managers could ever be, a social rule of thumb evolved over time: Servers should be paid low wages that are supplemented by tips. Problem solved: Restaurant managers leave the difficult job of policing their staff to patrons—allegedly, the word *tip* has its origins in eighteenth-century England, where coffeehouse patrons were asked to put coins in a box labeled "To Insure Promptness." The problem today, of course, is that people often tip without thinking. According to one survey, only 54 percent of respondents said they based their tip on the quality of service; 30 percent tip out of pity; and roughly 10 percent say they tip because it's expected. So the next time you have lousy service at a restaurant, don't blame the server—blame previous customers who didn't uphold their end of the social contract by refusing to tip when the service was poor.

But even if you have a different take on the matter, the tipping mystery is a minor example of how traditional economists struggle to merge assumptions of rationality, self-interest, and consistency with aspects of human behavior that most mortals would identify as central to money decisions: guilt, fear, regret, compulsiveness, addiction, bad habits, ego, and peer pressure, to name just a few. It's ironic that most of history's greatest economists failed to recognize the influence of commonplace human characteristics on money decisions, given that most businesses exploit these frailties routinely. The modern fashion industry, for example, rests almost solely upon the public's seemingly irrational willingness to pay more than they would otherwise need in order to clothe themselves with items whose only unequivocal appeal is that very skinny, very pale people look good wearing them. Similarly, economic theory was essentially at a loss—even if economists wouldn't admit it—to explain why people stampede to invest in the stock of companies (or to get rid of their shares) for no better reason than that other investors are doing the same.

Why, traditional economics has been pained to explain, do people routinely make decisions that are not rational, self-interested, or consistent? Answering that question is essential to the task of trying to help people utilize their resources more efficiently—that is, help people get more bang for their bucks.

The solution, or at least the firm beginnings of a solution, began to crystallize some forty years ago, when a new breed of researchers took on the task. Many of these newcomers were psychologists, not economists. Nonetheless, they were the pioneers of behavioral economics. As is the case with many achievements of broad scope, it's difficult to pin medals for the creation of behavioral economics on one or two chests, but we won't get many arguments if we begin the telling of this tale at Hebrew University in Jerusalem, Israel, in the late 1960s. There, two psychologists—Amos Tversky and Daniel Kahneman—were discussing the way Israeli aviation instructors had been motivating pilots during training. The flight instructors, who were taking a class that Kahneman taught at Hebrew U, took exception to a point their professor was making, essentially the idea that rewards are a more effective teaching tool than punishments. Rather, the officers found that when a pilot was praised for a good flight he tended to do worse the next time in the air, while pilots who were criticized after a poor performance routinely did better the next time they flew.

Readers familiar with statistics probably recognize the flaw in the instructors' conclusion and theory of motivation. In the nineteenth century, the British scientist Sir Francis Galton introduced a concept called "statistical regression." He explained how in any series of uncertain events that tend to fall around an average or mean—imagine taking two dozen swings at a tennis ball, for instance—any extraordinary single event will likely be followed by one closer to average. So a really bad forehand will generally be followed by a slightly better one, and a really great backhand will likely be followed by one that isn't so crisp. That's how probabilistic events play out, and it's why exceptionally tall people tend to have children who are not as tall and why exceptionally short people tend to have children who are not quite so short. Kahneman recognized that any single performance by a pilot—good or bad—would likely have been followed by a flight that moved closer to that pilot's long-term average. So the pilots who were criticized for a poor flight were more likely to do better the next time *regardless* of what their instructors did, while those who had received compliments were statistically more likely to do worse on their next flight. Not knowing this, the officers had concluded that the criticism was helping their pilots perform better and the praise was somehow making their performance suffer.

Kahneman noted the flaw to the instructors—presumably enhancing the self-esteem of future generations of Israeli fighter pilots—but the real significance of this episode was that it prompted him and Tversky to begin thinking more about human judgment and decision making in various arenas of life. What was remarkable about the flight instructors' experience was that events seemed to conspire against the correct conclusion. Subpar flights *did* tend to follow praise, and superior flights *did* tend to follow criticism. And unless a flight instructor knew about regression ahead of time, the logical conclusion was that punishment worked and rewards didn't. In what other areas of life, the two psychologists wondered, were proper conclusions hard to see because of faulty intuitions or the fiendishly complicated nature of the information available? Tversky seized upon one such instance and put it to work in one of the classic experiments on human judgment. Take the test yourself:

Imagine that two bags are filled—out of your sight— with the same number of poker chips. In one bag, two-thirds of the chips are red and the remain-

der are white. In the other bag, the proportions are reversed—one-third of the chips are red and the remaining two-thirds are white. Your task is to guess which is the bag with mostly red chips and which is the bag with mostly white chips. You're asked to grab a handful from bag A—say, five chips—and many handfuls from bag B—say, thirty chips. As it happens, four of the five chips you pulled from bag A are red, while twenty of the thirty chips you pulled from bag B are red. Which bag would you guess has more red chips?

If you're like most people, you probably reasoned that bag A has the most red chips because 80 percent (four out of five) of the chips you picked were red, while in bag B a less convincing 66 percent (twenty out of thirty) of those you chose were red. But you would have been more justified in your answer if you had guessed bag B. Reason: Statistics tells us that the larger the sample (thirty chips versus five), the more reliable the conclusion or outcome.

So what does this have to do with the way people handle money or, really, make any meaningful life choices? Quite a lot, actually. Consider how often folks make decisions based on small, statistically insignificant, or inconclusive samples—say, an investor in Boston who sees a long line at a new fast-food chain and decides to buy the company's newly issued stock, only to discover when the stock's price falls that those lines reflected slow service. Or an investor who buys a mutual fund because it beat the market over the past year—and then finds herself owning a fund that goes on to underperform the average. Or a traveler who avoids airplanes after a terrorist incident, ignoring the fact that cars are a more dangerous way to get from one place to another.

(Sadly, that's what happened in the year after the 2001 attack on the World Trade Center in New York. More Americans opted for car travel over plane travel, and the number of automobile-related deaths in the United States spiked significantly.)

More specifically, Tversky and Kahneman's experiments were important to the field of economics because they made it clear that people's judgments and decisions are not always fully rational. While this may seem as earth-shattering as proving that the sun rises in the morning, the act of scientifically validating common sense was in this case quite significant, for several reasons. Not the least was that Kahneman and Tversky (and many others who followed) were able to start describing and classifying many of the tricks that people use to simplify and solve some of the difficult problems of judgment and choice that confront them. Kahneman and Tversky referred to these simplifying procedures as "judgmental heuristics"—mental shortcuts (or rules of thumb) that most people rely on reflexively. Such guidelines might be instinctive (a long line at a restaurant probably means business is good) or societally reinforced (it's a good idea to stretch your budget when buying a house), but in either case, they are sometimes misleading. Long lines at a restaurant can mean that the service is slow or that other competing restaurants are closed; home prices don't rise as fast or as much as Americans think, and even when they do, such levels are rarely sustainable (as we have seen in recent years). So there is often no financial justification for buying more house than you can afford in the hope that price hikes will reward you later.

We should point out that heuristics, judgmental and otherwise, have been essential to human evolution (regardless of whether you think we evolved over six thousand or six million years). In order to get through life, humans have to make thousands of decisions every day. Some of these decisions are decidedly conscious (say, where to go in the morning) and some are completely mindless (say, which muscles do you twitch to take your next step). But whatever their nature, that's a whole lot of choices to make and still get stuff done during the day. And so human brains come with decision-making shortcuts—heuristics—that make deciding easier.

Most heuristics, of course, work very well; humanity's rise from a small number of nomadic beings competing with animals for resources to the fruitfully multiplied food-chain toppers we are today proves that. But if 99 percent of our heuristics work just fine now, some of them, all logic tells us, have surely become obsolete as life's needs and society's demands have evolved. You'll see examples of these soon enough, but in some ways, behavioral economics can be fairly described as the study of obsolete heuristics; the study of rules of thumb that were useful to our ancestors on the savannah or in the jungles but often get in our way today. Consider one of the more basic judgmental heuristics, called "representativeness." Demonstrated decades ago by Kahneman and Tversky, representativeness is a rule of thumb that tells us that we can infer a lot of information about an object, a being, a pattern of behavior, or a set of results based on their similarities to other such objects, beings, patterns, or sets. Back in the day, our ancestors might have decided (in a hurry) between staying in a clearing to gather berries or running away based on the similarity between a newly encountered member of the cat family and the lions they knew to avoid. Today, representativeness might tell you to avoid investing with people who promise Bernard Madoff–like investment returns (a good result for most of us), but it might also tell you to avoid the stock market altogether (a less good result for most people).

In any event, Tversky and Kahneman were joined by other researchers—psychologists and economists—and this group of curious men and women essentially created the body of work called behavioral economics. The two Israelis, by the way, eventually migrated to the United States and became ambassadors of their field—Kahneman at Princeton University in New Jersey, and Tversky at Stanford University in Palo Alto, California. In 2002, Kahneman won the Nobel Memorial Prize in Economics for research he and Tversky produced in the late 1970s (which we'll get into in Chapter 2). Sadly, Tversky, who earned Israel's highest honor for bravery during his military career, died of cancer in 1996 at age fifty-nine. He once said that all he really did was use scientific methods to explore aspects of human behavior already known to "advertisers and used-car salesmen." In reality, behavioral economics has become a significant force in academia, business, and economic policy. President Barack Obama's administration (not to mention his campaign to reach the White House) has been heavily influenced in its early stages by a number of leading lights in behavioral economics, including University of Chicago professor Richard Thaler, whose book *Nudge* (coauthored with law professor Cass Sunstein) is a virtual manual for using the science in public policy. More on their thoughts later, but Thaler has long been a frequent guest on Capitol Hill, lecturing to Congress about behavioral economic biases and how they affect savings habits.

Despite these inroads, however, there's one realm where behavioral economics has yet to achieve the prominence it deserves: the minds of typical consumers, savers, borrowers, spenders, and investors. That's who this book is for. We've distilled four decades of academic research—the labors of Kahneman, Tversky, and dozens of others, including one of this book's authors—into an easy-to-navigate guide to the workings of our money mind-sets.

THE METHOD TO OUR MADNESS

Like many endeavors, the writing of this book posed a variety of interesting problems. Some were small, such as how to refer to ourselves in a book whose tone is meant to be that of a conversation at a cocktail party. That's easy when we're a unified front—"We hope you recommend this new edition to lots of people"—but more difficult when the voice is specific to one or the other of us: "I'm a professor of psychology at Cornell University" is something only Tom can say honestly, while Gary alone would be correct in noting, "I was a writer at *Money* magazine and have been lecturing about behavioral economics for ten years." This is an important issue, since we bring our individual experiences to the table for your edification—the anecdotes we'll use to highlight poor decision making come from real life—and it strikes us as misleading to use the phrase "a friend of ours" or "someone we know" when only one of us knows the person in question. Our solution, then, is to refer to ourselves in the third person when appropriate, as in "This solution was Gary's idea." Forgive us, on such occasions, if we sound a little self-absorbed.

We also worried about expectations, specifically the assumptions of readers who may be accustomed to a certain tone and approach from the kind of self-help guides that are now ubiquitous in bookstores. So, for the record: We have tried to avoid the trappings of most pop psychology books. That is, despite the fact that Tom is a psychologist, there will be no attempt between these covers to psychoanalyze *you*. There will be no theorizing, for example, that a tendency to rack up staggering Visa card balances is the result of having been breast-fed for too long or too briefly, or that the impulse comes from your genes. There will be no attempts,

SELF HELP OR HURT?

While we're discussing self-help books, we want to mention a study by psychologist Joanne Wood. She wanted to see how useful it is to articulate positive things about ourselves. In other words, is "The Power of Positive Thinking" (to borrow the title of Norman Vincent Peale's famous self-help tome) a real phenomenon? In her study, participants were tested for self-esteem (there are reliable ways to do this), then asked to spend a few minutes writing any thoughts or feelings they had at that moment. Half, though, were randomly asked to say to themselves "I am a lovable person" whenever they heard a bell ring. Then, right after their thinking/writing time, everyone was asked to answer questions that would indicate their level of optimism and mood. (Example: "What is the probability that a thirty-year-old will be involved in a happy, loving romance?") The results? People with high self-esteem who repeated the "lovable person" mantra were more optimistic than those who didn't. But participants with low self-esteem who intoned those five words felt less optimistic than those who didn't. Wood's conclusion: *People with a negative self-image are reinforced in that belief when they try to will their way out of it.* We have two other conclusions: 1) Some self-help books may do more harm than good; and 2) We won't have you try to convince yourself that you're a "savvy shopper" or "canny investor." We'll just try to offer strategies to help no matter what you think.

moreover, to identify an inner child, inner investor, or pretty much inner anything. That's not to say we oppose these sorts of books out of hand. But to the extent that you seek to discover some Freudian cause of your individual psychological tendencies with regard to money, you'll find our virtual couch wanting.

Although we expect to help you avoid getting into debt by showing how credit cards cheapen money—to cite one example in this book—we have little hope of illuminating the reason that you *in particular* fall prey to that tendency. Our focus in this book is on patterns of thought and behavior that lead most people—people *in general*—to get less out of their financial choices than they should.

That focus is not always easy to maintain, in part because some concepts of behavioral economics can appear to contradict each other at times. This is not surprising, given the way the human mind works. But we don't want readers of one chapter to throw up their hands in dismay when the next chapter seems to be saying something quite opposite. An example? In Chapter 7, we'll talk about herding, which is the tendency many people have to rely too much on the opinions or actions of others, as when investors buy or sell a stock simply because the company is recommended or dismissed by a stockbroker or because everyone else is buying or selling it. On the flip side, Chapter 6 focuses on people's tendency toward overconfidence, which causes them to have more faith than they should in the reliability of their own judgment or experience. How can we reconcile these two concepts? We can't. Sometimes people make mistakes because they behave like sheep, and sometimes they err because they behave like mules. The critical task is to identify which tendency is harming us in what circumstance and then try to break the habit. People are overconfident in predictable ways in predictable contexts, and they follow one another in predictable ways in predictable contexts. And that predictability is useful. It allows us to know when to look out for one sort of mistake and what to do about it.

Which brings us to the last of our structural problems. Many readers would doubtless prefer that we promise to fix what ails them, with no qualifications or caveats. This we cannot do. But we hope that such an admission inspires trust and respect rather than dismissal. There is no single magic pill we can prescribe to eliminate all the mental money maladies from which you may suffer. But one of the reasons we chose to update the book was that in the years since we wrote it, we've come across even more useful and practical advice (some of it ours, some from others) that we think will help you eliminate troublesome behaviors. Some of these curatives are practical—involving, for instance, simple record keeping, deadline setting, or investing in stock market index funds. Other solutions are more conceptual—instances in which we will try to change the way you frame a problem that will make your choices clearer. And some, to be honest, are profound combinations of the two approaches, including one, which we'll explore in Chapter 2, that we think can dramatically affect your ability to save for the future. Whichever the case, we'll offer these remedies at the end of each chapter, under the heading "How to Think and What to Do." Then we'll summarize and add to them in the conclusion, called "Now What?," which is expanded in this edition.

More important, though, we share a firmly held conviction that knowledge is the best medicine. If this book achieves its goal, it will provide numerous occasions when you'll smile (or frown) in recognition of a money trap that has snared you in the past (it certainly has for each of us). That moment—that exposure of a particular mental blind spot—can do as much for your financial health as even the most helpful bit of advice that any financial adviser can give you.

1

NOT ALL DOLLARS ARE CREATED EQUAL

By the third day of their honeymoon in Las Vegas, the newlyweds had lost their $1,000 gambling allowance. That night in bed, the groom noticed a glowing object on the dresser. Upon inspection, he realized it was a $5 chip they had saved as a souvenir. Strangely, the number 17 was flashing on the chip's face. Taking this as an omen, he donned his green bathrobe and rushed down to the roulette tables, where he placed the $5 chip on the square marked 17. Sure enough, the ball hit 17 and the 35–1 bet paid $175. He let his winnings ride, and once again the little ball landed on 17, paying $6,125. And so it went, until the lucky groom was about to wager $7.5 million. Unfortunately the floor manager intervened, claiming that the casino didn't have the money to pay should 17 hit again. Undaunted, the groom taxied to a better-financed ca-

sino downtown. Once again he bet it all on 17—and once again it hit, paying more than $262 million. Ecstatic, he let his millions ride—only to lose it all when the ball fell on 18. Broke and dejected, the groom walked the several miles back to his hotel.

"Where were you?" asked his bride as he entered their room.

"Playing roulette."

"How did you do?"

"Not bad. I lost five dollars."

This story has the distinction of being the only roulette joke we know that deals with a bedrock principle of behavioral economics. Indeed, depending on whether or not you agree with our groom's account of his evening's adventure, you might have an idea why we considered a different title for this chapter: "Why Casinos Always Make Money." The usual answer to that question—casinos are consistently profitable because the odds are always stacked in management's favor—does not tell the whole story. Another reason casinos always make money is that too many people think like our newlywed: Because he started his evening with just $5, he felt his loss was limited to that amount.

This view holds that his gambling winnings were somehow not real money—or not his money, anyway—and so his losses were not real losses. No matter that had the groom left the casino after his penultimate bet, he could have walked across the street and bought a brand-new BMW for every behavioral economist in the country (and had enough left over to remain a multimillionaire). The happy salesman at the twenty-four-hour dealership would never have asked if the $262 million belonged to the groom. Of course it did. But the groom, like most amateur gamblers, viewed his winnings as a different kind of money, and he was therefore more willing to make extravagant bets with it. In casino-speak this is called playing with "house money." The tendency of most gamblers to fall prey to this illusion is why casinos would make out like bandits even if the odds weren't stacked so heavily in their favor.

The "Legend of the Man in the Green Bathrobe," as the above tale is known, illustrates a concept that behavioral economists call "mental accounting." This idea, first proposed by the University of Chicago's Richard Thaler, underlies one of the most common and costly money mistakes: the tendency to value some dollars less than others and thus waste them. More formally, mental accounting refers to the inclination to categorize and handle money differently depending on where it comes from, where it is kept, or how it is spent. To understand how natural, and tricky, this habit can be, consider the following scenarios. Here, as in similar mental exercises you'll find throughout this book, try to answer each of the following questions as realistically as possible. The more honest your responses, the more you'll learn about yourself.

> *Imagine that you've bought a ticket to the Super Bowl or a hit Broadway play. At the stadium or theater you realize you've lost your ticket, which cost $150. Do you spend another $150 to see the game or performance?*

> *Now imagine the same scenario, but you're planning to buy the $150 ticket when you arrive. At the box office, you realize you've lost $150 somewhere in the parking lot. Still, you have more than enough in your wallet to buy the ticket. Do you?*

If you're like most people, you probably answered no to the first question and yes to the second, even though both scenarios present the same dilemma: a loss of $150 and the subsequent prospect of spending another $150 to be entertained. The reason for this odd inconsistency is that for most people, the first scenario somehow translates into a total entertainment cost of $300—two actual tickets, each costing $150. This might be too much, even for a Super Bowl or hit play. Conversely, for most people, the loss of $150 in cash and the $150 cost of the ticket are somehow separated mentally into two independent categories. They are unfortunate but unrelated. This type of thinking—treating two essentially equal $150 losses in very different ways because they occur in different manners—is a classic example of mental accounting.

The notion of mental accounts is absent in traditional economic theory, which holds that wealth in general, and money in particular, should be fungible: That is, $100 in roulette winnings, $100 in salary, and a $100 tax refund should have the same significance and value to you, since each C-note could buy the same number of downloads from iTunes or the same number of burgers at McDonald's. Likewise, $100 kept under the mattress should invoke the same feelings or sense of wealth as $100 in a bank account or $100 in U.S. Treasury securities (ignoring the fact that money in the bank, or in T-bills, is safer than cash under the bed). If money and wealth are fungible, there should be no difference in the way we spend gambling winnings or salary. Every financial decision should result from a rational calculation of its effect on our overall wealth.

If only this were the case. People are not machines. They lack the computational power and the strength of will needed to manage their finances on a consolidated balance sheet. It would be intellectually difficult, and emotionally taxing, to calculate the cost of every short-term transaction (buying a new song, for instance, or going to a movie) against the size of every long-term goal or need (planning for retirement or saving for college). So to cope with this daunting organizational task, people separate their money into mental accounts, necessarily treating a dollar in one account differently from a dollar in another, since each account has a different significance. A vacation allowance, for instance, is presumably treated with less gravitas than the same amount of money socked away in an Individual Retirement Account.

But what's wrong with that? The average person, maybe more self-aware than the average economist, knows that he or she is not as smart or as iron-willed as economists maintain. And that's why people set up mental accounts in the first place. So rather than being illogical or irrational, the ability to corral money into different mental accounts often has beneficial effects. Most important, perhaps, it allows you to save effectively for future goals. After all, "house money" for many Americans is not casino winnings, but the money they manage to squirrel away for a down payment on their dream home. Even out-of-control spenders often manage to avoid tapping into these savings, often for no other reason than that they've placed it in a sacred mental vault.

To be sure, mental accounting is not always effective, given the problems human beings have with self-control. That's one reason tax-deferred retirement accounts such as IRAs, 401(k)s, and SEPs penalize early withdrawals, and it is why they enjoy such popular support. And that is why, when attempting to balance and evaluate their investment portfolio, people often err by failing to knock down mental walls among accounts. As a result, their true portfolio mix—the combination of stocks, bonds, real estate, insurance policies, mutual funds, and the like—is often not what they think, and their investment performance often suffers.

Yes, the often useful habit of treating one dollar differently from another has a dark side, too, with consequences far more significant than increasing your willingness to make crazy bets at roulette tables. By assigning relative values to different moneys that in reality have the same buying power, you run the risk of being too quick to spend, too slow to save, or too conservative when you invest—all of which can cost you. Just think about the way people value earned income as opposed to gift income. That is, we'll spend $50 from Mom (or $50 we find in the street) with less thought than $50 we've earned on the job. In fact, studies suggest that we'll spend $50 we're given as a bonus at work more easily than $50 we've been told was owed to us in salary but mistakenly withheld. Think about that: same money ($50), same source (an employer), but you're more likely to spend one check than the other. Don't quite believe it? Consider an experiment conducted by Nick Epley, a psychologist at the University of Chicago, along with Harvard's Dennis Mak and Lorraine Chen Idson. Two dozen Harvard students were told they were receiving a $25 windfall as part of a research project and could spend as much of it as they wanted at a "lab store," which carried stuff students are used to seeing at campus bookstores or co-ops: school mugs, snack foods, pens, etc. Any unspent money, the students were told, would be sent to them by check. All the students had been told that the research lab was partially funded by tuition dollars, but—and here's the interesting part—for half the participants the $25 was described as a "rebate" and for the other half it was described as a "bonus." That small difference, though, was all that was necessary to dramatically affect how the students handled their windfall: 84 percent of those whose $25 was framed as a "bonus" spent some or all of it, but only 21 percent of students who had their $25 described as a "rebate" opened their wallets. Mental accounting is a powerful driver of our actions even if the accounts aren't meaningfully different—all the students, after all, were told that the lab was partially funded by tuition dollars. The framing of the $25 should have been immaterial, but it wasn't, by a long shot.

This has obvious implications for economic policy. Twice in recent years, the government has tried to stimulate economic activity by giving people tax rebates. There is considerable evidence that the programs did not work as well as intended on either occasion, and calling the checks "rebates" may have been part of the problem. As Epley describes it, "Reimbursements send people on trips to the bank. Bonuses send people on trips to the Bahamas."

Note, though, that the rules of mental accounting are flexible—people are complicated. Sometimes they will categorize tax refunds, especially when they are small, as found money—and spend it accordingly. They do so even though a refund is nothing more than a deferred payment of salary. Forced savings, if you will. If, on the other hand, those same people had taken that money out of their paycheck during the course of the previous year and deposited it into a bank account or money market mutual fund, they would most likely think long and hard before spending it on a new suit or iPhone. However, because Uncle Sam runs the bank account in which those funds have been sitting, taxpayers' mental accounting systems attach a different value to those dollars.

A DOLLAR HERE, A DOLLAR THERE—PRETTY SOON WE'RE TALKING ABOUT REAL MONEY

As the example of tax refunds makes clear, one way that mental accounting can cause trouble is the resultant tendency to treat dollars differently depending on the size of the particular mental account in which they are stashed, the size of the particular transaction in which they are spent, or simply the amount of money in question. Here's an illustration of what we mean:

> *Imagine that you go to a store to buy a lamp, which sells for $100. At the store you discover that the same lamp is on sale for $75 at a branch of the store five blocks away. Do you go to the other branch to get the lower price?*

> *Now imagine that you go to the same store to buy a dining-room set, which sells for $1,775. At the store you discover that you can buy the same table and chairs for $1,750 at a branch of the store five blocks away. Do you go to the other branch to get the lower price?*

Once again, studies tell us that more people will go to the other branch to save on the lamp than would travel the same distance to save on the dining-room set, even though both scenarios offer the same essential choice: Would you walk five blocks to save $25? You probably don't need to think long to come up with instances in which this tendency can become quite costly. We certainly don't. As a struggling college student in the early 1980s, Gary decided against replacing his car radio with a new cassette deck, for the simple reason that he couldn't justify the $300 to $400 it would cost to buy the new equipment. In his last year of college, though, Gary finally bought a new car (with a hefty loan). The cost: $12,000—plus another $550 for a cassette deck to replace the optional AM/FM radio. Three months earlier, before his car broke down, Gary had shopped for cassette decks and deemed $300 too extravagant. Yet a car salesman had little trouble convincing him to spend almost twice that amount for the same product, even though Gary's finances were presumably more precarious now that he had to make $180 monthly payments for the next four years.

The main culprit, of course, was mental accounting— $550 seemed to have less value next to $12,000. But also contributing to Gary's decision was the subconscious preference, shared by most people, to "integrate losses." Translation: When we incur a loss or expense, we prefer to hide it from ourselves within a bigger loss or ex-

MYSTERY SOLVED

Mental accounting helps to explain one of the great puzzles of personal finance—why people who don't see themselves as reckless spenders can't seem to save enough. The devil, as they say, is in the details. Although many people are cost-conscious when making large financial decisions—such as buying a house, car, or appliance—mental accounting makes them relax their discipline when making small purchases. The cost of such purchases gets lost among larger expenses, such as the week's grocery bill, or charged against a lightly monitored "slush fund" account. The problem, of course, is that while you might purchase a car or refrigerator every few years, you buy groceries and clothes and movie refreshments every week or every day. Being cost-conscious when making little purchases is where you can often rack up big savings.

pense. So, for Gary, the pain of spending $550 for a cassette deck was "eased" by the greater pain of spending twelve grand.

Businesses, by the way, understand this tendency very well. That's why consumer electronics stores sell extended warranties or service contracts. Would anyone buy an insurance policy for a sound system or flat-screen TV at any other time? And it's why insurance agents sell exotic "riders" at the same time they push broader policies. Would any rational person buy life insurance for, say, their kids if the policy was offered to them separately?

The principles of mental accounting are governed not only by the size of a purchase or investment, but also by the size of a payment received, be it a bonus, rebate, refund, or gift. So a payment that might otherwise be placed in a "splurge-on-myself" mental account—a bonus from work, say, or a tax refund—will be deposited in a more serious, long-term account if it is big enough (and vice versa). That's curious, when you think about it. If you get a small refund or bonus—say, $250—chances are you're far more likely to buy a $250 pair of shoes with it than if you get a $2,500 bonus or refund, even though you can presumably afford it more in the second instance. Somehow, a bigger chunk of found money makes it more sacred and serious and harder to spend, actually lowering your "spending rate," or what economists call your "marginal propensity to consume." It's a clunky term, but understanding this concept will help you see why it may be tough for you to hold on to money and why a bonus or a gift may actually do you more harm than good. Your spending rate is simply the percentage of an incremental dollar that you spend rather than save. So if you receive a $100 tax refund and spend $80, your spending rate is .80 (or 80 percent). You might think, then, that the highest spending rate you can have is 1—that is, for every incremental dollar you receive, the most you could spend is a dollar. If only wishing made it so. Let us explain.

About thirty years ago, an economist at the Bank of Israel named Michael Landsberger undertook a study of a group of Israelis who were receiving regular restitution payments from the West German government after World War II. Although these payments could fairly be described as blood money—inasmuch as they were intended to make up for Nazi atrocities—they could also be described as found money. Because of this, and because the payments varied significantly in size from one individual or family to another, Landsberger could gauge the effect of the size of these windfalls on each recipient's spending rate. What he discovered was amazing. People who received the larger payments (equal to roughly two-thirds of their annual income) had a spending rate of about 0.23. In other words, for every dollar they received, their marginal spending increased by 23 percent; the rest was saved. Conversely, the group that received the smallest windfall payments (equal to 7 percent of annual income) had a spending rate of 2. That's correct: For every dollar of found money, they spent two. Or, more accurately, for every dollar of found money, they spent $1 of found money and another $1 from "savings" (what they actually saved or what they might have saved).

Obviously we can't explain this curious phenomenon with certainty. Perhaps restitution payments were made in proportion to a family's earlier earnings in Europe. If so, maybe folks who earned a lot before the war were also earning a lot in Israel and therefore had less pent-up "need" to spend their restitution checks. In Israel, like everywhere else, the wealthy save a higher proportion of their income than the poor. But this cannot explain why the spending rate of those receiving the smallest restitution payments was a whopping 200 percent. The poor don't help themselves by spending twice as much as they receive. A clearer understanding may be had from the experience of a friend of Gary's. This friend, let's call him Gideon, worked overseas for a small U.S. company. While on vacation in New York, he stopped by corporate headquarters to say hello and, to his surprise, received a $400 bonus. Lucky, eh? Well, maybe not. By the end of his trip, Gideon realized he had spent that $400 about five times over. It seems that every time he went into a store or restaurant, Gideon and his wife used that $400 bonus to justify all manner of purchases. Not only was the bonus mentally accounted for as found money suitable for discretionary spending, it also sucked in $1,600 of the couple's money that had been accounted for otherwise.

If Gideon's story sounds familiar, it's probably because his thinking was similar to another mental accounting mindbender, quite possibly the most common and costly of all. This arises when we justify spending in one area because of the money we've "saved" in another. So your thinking might go something like this: "I was thinking of buying a Lexus but got a Camry instead. I think it's okay to spend some of the $10,000 I saved by staying at the Ritz-Carlton instead of the Radisson." Or: "That companion ticket deal saved us $800 on flights. I think we can afford to buy that new video camera now." Mind you, there's nothing inherently wrong with this reasoning, but we pity the car shopper who fantasizes about getting á Rolls-Royce then decides he has $360,000 in "savings" to spend when he buys a MINI Cooper!

FUNNY MONEY

*Americanesia Expressaphobia, n 1. Financial afflic-
tion, first diagnosed in late twentieth century, where
the sufferer forgets the amount charged on a credit
card but is terribly afraid that it's way too much.
Closely related to Visago, n, where a high level of
debt prompts feelings of nausea and dizziness.*

There's one more thing we ought to tell you about Gideon's
vacation saga, not least because we don't want to discourage
bosses who might be reading this book from handing out
bonuses, large or small. Much of Gideon's shopping spree
was abetted by credit cards, one of the scariest exhibits in
the Museum of Mental Accounting. In fact, credit cards and
other types of revolving loans are almost by definition mental accounts, and dangerous ones at that. Credit-card dollars are cheapened because there is seemingly no loss at the
moment of purchase, at least on a visceral level. Think of it
this way: If you have $200 cash in your pocket and you pay
$100 for a belt, you experience the purchase as cutting your
pocket money in half. If you charge that belt, though, you
don't experience the same loss of buying power that empty-
ing your wallet of $100 brings. In fact, the money we charge
on plastic is devalued because it seems as if we're not actually
spending anything when we use the cards. Sort of like Mo-
nopoly or Sims money. The irony, of course, is that the dollar we charge on plastic is actually more dear, inasmuch as it
costs an additional fifteen cents to spend it—15 percent or so
being the typical interest rate for such borrowing.

Irony aside, we're not likely to surprise many readers by
pointing out that credit cards play directly into the tendency
to treat dollars differently. Because they seem to devalue dol-

lars, credit cards cause you to spend money that you might not ordinarily spend. So common is credit-card use and abuse today—at this writing, the average U.S. household that has credit cards owes more than $8,000 on them—that you've probably suffered a bout or two of Americanesia Expressaphobia yourself. No revelation there. But you may be surprised to learn that by using credit cards, you not only increase your chances of spending to begin with, you also increase the likelihood that you will pay *more* when you spend than you would if you were paying cash (or paying by check).

Want proof? Consider this landmark experiment, conducted in the 1990s by marketing professors Drazen Prelec and Duncan Simester. They organized a real-life, sealed-bid auction for tickets to a Boston Celtics game. Half the auction participants were informed that the highest bidder would have to pay for the tickets in cash (with a day to come up with the funds). The other half was told that the winning bidder would have to pay by credit card. Prelec and Simester then averaged the bids of those who thought they'd have to pay in cash and those who thought they could pay with a credit card. Incredibly, the average credit-card bid was roughly twice as large as the average cash bid. Simply because they were dealing with plastic—with money that was devalued in some way—the students became spendthrifts. Put another way, credit cards turn us into big spenders in more ways than one. We become poorer because we're more likely to spend, and more likely to spend poorly.

IT'S NOT GRANDMA'S MONEY

One final thought about mental accounting (for now). We've noted that the tendency to categorize, segregate, or label money differently can have the side effect of causing people to be more reckless with their finances. Dollars assigned to some mental accounts are devalued, which leads us to spend more easily and more foolishly, particularly when dealing with small (though not inconsequential) amounts of money. But there's a flip side to this coin that can have the opposite effect—the tendency to mentally account for money as so sacred or special that we actually become too conservative with it.

The best way to demonstrate this is with a story about a woman in her thirties named Sara. Sara is actually a fairly sophisticated investor, with a well-diversified portfolio of stocks and stock mutual funds. Good for her, considering that stocks have offered the best average annual return of all the major savings and investment categories over the past eighty years—about 9 percent a year on average—yes, even after the market gyrations of recent years—vs. 5.5 percent a year for bonds and 3.7 percent for cash in the bank. Some years ago, though, Sara inherited about $17,000 from her grandmother. Although she didn't need the money for any particular short-term or long-term goal, Sara parked her grandmother's inheritance in a bank account paying about 3 percent a year in interest. Her grandmother, whom Sara adored, had worked and saved all her life to scrape together the money that she eventually left to Sara and her four siblings. As a result, Sara was hesitant to put her grandmother's money at risk in the stock market, not least because Sara was raised by parents whose memory of the Great Depression and the stock market crash of 1929 made them and their daughter overly fearful about the risks of stocks. In any event, it didn't seem right to Sara, who would have been far more crushed if she lost "Grandma's money" than if she lost her own.

Her hesitation was costly. If Sara had simply invested that money as she does her other savings—in mutual funds that roughly approximate the overall performance of the stock market—she would now have more than $42,000. Instead, earning a meager 3 percent, she has just $26,000. Now, it would be one thing if Sara had decided that she needed her grandmother's money for a specific short-term goal such as a down payment on a house, which would justify avoiding the stock market for fear of needing the money at just the time when stock prices were experiencing one of their inevitable dips. But Sara had no such constraint. Although other factors may cause people to be overly conservative with their investments, Sara's mistake was to mentally account for the $17,000 as "Grandma's money," or at least as money that was more sacred than her own savings and thus money that shouldn't be risked. In reality, of course, the money was hers, and the cost of her mental accounting was about $16,000.

Sara's mistake, we should add, is replicated by millions of Americans who choose the most conservative investment options in their 401(k), 403(b), and 457 plans at work because they mentally account for those funds as too sacred. That's especially true now, given the recent tumult in global stock markets. But stock markets have always dipped and dived over periods of months or years even as they have steadily climbed over decades. Later in the book, we'll address the role that stocks should play in the average investor's long- and short-term planning, but now seems like a good time to tell a story that Gary uses whenever he lectures to general audiences about behavioral economics. One of the core principles of the field is a heuristic called "availability," whereby people make decisions based on the information that comes most quickly to mind—often the most recent or remarkable information around. (To use our jungle analogy from the introduction, we're all descended from people who were more afraid of being murdered by a rival tribesman than of drowning, in part because the gruesomeness of the average murder makes it stand out more than the average drowning.) But availability can be misleading. When Gary was a young financial reporter in New York in the late 1980s, he came under the tutelage of a veteran money manager. Let's call him Bill. Two days after Black Monday—when stock markets around the world crashed and the Dow Jones Industrial Average dropped 22 percent—Gary called Bill, who liked to teach young journalists lessons, and the two of them had the following conversation (some details have been changed for privacy's sake).

> *Bill:* Guess how many clients I have.
>
> *Gary:* I don't know, fifty?
>
> *Bill:* Wrong. One hundred and eighty. Guess how many have called me over the past two days.
>
> *Gary:* I don't know, a hundred?
>
> *Bill:* Wrong, one hundred and fifty-eight. Guess how many of them told me to sell some or all of their stocks.
>
> *Gary:* I don't know, half?
>
> *Bill:* Wrong, one hundred and fifty-six. Guess how old the other two are.
>
> *Gary:* Huh? How am I supposed to know?
>
> *Bill:* You're not, but don't forget this. Both those clients are older than eighty. Both called to tell me to buy. You know why?
>
> *Gary:* No, why?
>
> *Bill:* Because they've seen this before.

Lesson learned. What Bill's octogenarian clients saw in October 1987 was an availability problem being acted out on a large scale: millions of people reacting to the most recent and most remarkable data while ignoring equally significant information, such as the fact that stocks, although volatile, were still the average person's best bet for long-term capital appreciation. More on that in a few pages, but Sara's kind of thinking—"I have to be careful with my retirement money"—is absolutely correct in theory but also exposes many people to a far more dangerous risk than the short-term ups and downs of the stock market: They run the risk that they won't have saved enough when retirement finally rolls around.

HOW TO THINK AND WHAT TO DO

Warning Signs

You may be prone to mental accounting if . . .

- you don't think you're a reckless spender, but you have trouble saving.
- you have savings in the bank *and* revolving balances on your credit cards.
- you're more likely to splurge with a tax refund than with savings.
- you seem to spend more when you use credit cards than when you use cash.
- most of your retirement savings are in fixed-income or other conservative investments.

How's this for practical advice about mental accounting: Stop it! If you charge too much on credit cards, cut 'em up. If you blow tax refunds at the track, cut it out.

If only it were that easy. The difficulty with trying to remedy your tendency toward mental accounting is that you don't want to throw out the baby with the binge borrowing. For people who generally can't seem to control spending, mental accounts can often be the most effective way to ensure that the mortgage gets paid, the kids' colleges get funded, or there is enough money to live comfortably in retirement. And, of course, for every Sara who is too conservative with windfall money, there is someone else who would mentally account for an inheritance as gift money and blow it impulsively on a new car. In fact, those two people may be one and the same—Sara may put inheritance money in one mental account, while stashing a tax refund or gambling winnings in another.

So in order to begin to eliminate the harmful elements of mental accounting, while preserving its benefits, you have to audit your own internal accounting system. We'll give you two ways to begin this process, one that's fun and one that's a bit more serious. First the fun stuff, in the form of another set of scenarios.

Imagine that you're at the racetrack for a day of gambling or at your favorite store shopping for a suit. Yesterday you won $1,000 from your state's instant lottery game. Will you bet more tonight than you would otherwise, or will you buy a more expensive suit?

Now imagine that you're once again at the racetrack for a day of gambling or at your favorite store shopping for a suit. Yesterday you realized that you had $1,000 in a savings account that you had forgotten about. Will you bet more tonight than you would otherwise, or will you buy a more expensive suit?

If you would bet more in the first instance and buy a pricier suit in the second—as most people would—you're prone to mental accounting, which means you're prone to wasting money because you wrongly put different values on the same dollars. No doubt skeptics will say that it is perfectly logical to be more reckless with lottery winnings than rediscovered savings, so what is Belsky and Gilovich's problem? Our problem is that while it may not make a difference if you blow a Powerball payoff, this habit can cost you in ways you might not consider. Our second test should help doubters see the light.

> All you need to do is review your finances and answer two questions: (1) Do you have emergency or other nonretirement savings?; and (2) Do you carry balances on your credit cards from month to month?

If the answer is yes to both, you're a victim of mental accounting. Why? Because you've placed too high a value on your savings dollars and too low a value on your borrowed dollars. As a result, you're at best earning 2 to 4 percent a year on your emergency savings while paying 15 percent a year in credit-card interest. For every $1,000 on your credit card, that's a yearly loss of roughly $110 to $130. If you do nothing else after reading this but pay off $1,000 in credit-card balances with short-term savings, then you've earned the price of this book about ten times over. And for those who say that emergency money should be left just for emergencies, our response is that if you pay off your credit-card balances with short-term savings, you could always fill up those same credit cards in the event that you or your spouse is laid off or laid up. Believe us when we tell you that your credit-card company won't cut or eliminate your access to their high-rate loans if you pay off your balances. More than likely they'll raise your credit limit, so that you'll be that much more prepared for emergencies. And all the while you'll be saving the difference between the money you would have been paying in interest and the money you would have earned from a money market account.

Imagine a world without plastic. We're not suggesting you deep-six your Visa or Sears card. We're just recommending that you start asking yourself how much you would pay for a prospective purchase if you were paying with cash out of your pocket. You might answer that you would pay a lot less than you're willing to charge or even that you wouldn't make the purchase at all. Gary thought a lot about this a few years back when the Internal Revenue Service started allowing people to pay their tax bill via credit card. We're all for e-filing, but we suspect that the average taxpayer might be a little less vigilant about every deduction if she knows that she's going to charge what she owes. Good news for governments, maybe not so good news for people who want to be as aggressive as possible when claiming deductions. (Within legal limits, of course.)

See the trees for the forest. That's another way of saying that when you make a big purchase or investment—such as a car or a house—break every deal into its component part. Would you, say, pay $3,000 to put a skylight into the den of your current house? If not, then don't tack on that extra when contracting for a new home—$3,000 may not seem like a lot when you're buying a $150,000 home, but it buys just as much as $3,000 in your checking account (more, actually, when you count the interest you'll pay over the course of your loan).

Hurry up and wait. To the extent that you fall prey to the tendency to view windfall money—tax refunds, gifts, inheritances, or bonuses—as found money that can be spent relatively care-lessly, our advice is to train yourself to wait awhile before making any spending decisions. In other words, tell your-self that you can do whatever you want with that cash, but in three or six months. In the meantime, park it in a bank or money market account. Make that the rule. At the least you'll have a few extra dollars for your trouble. More than likely, by the time your deadline rolls around, you'll view this money as savings—hard earned and not to be wasted.

Imagine that all income is earned income... This idea for dealing with money that you didn't earn—or even money for which you did work—may be the best way to train yourself to view all your money equally. Basically, the trick is to ask yourself how long it would take you to earn that amount of money af-ter taxes. Quite often the answer will clear up your account-ing problems faster than you can say "marginal tax rate."

...And trick your kids (and citizens) into believing it, too. Parents who want their kids to save birthday gifts or other forms of financial largesse—as well as governments that want citizens to spend stimulus checks—should heed Nick Epley and Co.'s "bonus" and "rebate" experiments. Telling your kids that a check is for all the good work they've done over the past year is more likely to make them save it; telling citizens that they're re-ceiving a "rebate" check makes them less likely to spend it. Sometimes it's all in the way you put it.

Divide and conquer. This might be especially useful advice for peo-ple who have a hard time believing they can afford to save. It arises from research conducted a few years ago by market-ing professor Dilip Soman. He was working with Chinese and Indian workers who were paid every five days, and who said they wanted to save money but found it hard to control their spending. So Soman arranged for their pay to be given to them in six envelopes, one for each day they worked and a sixth not tied to any day. Although earning the same amount for their efforts, the workers were able to increase their savings fourfold within three months because they viewed the sixth envelope as extra money, and were thus more likely to save it. Try that trick if you're having trouble making ends meet and finding money to put away. Determine what you take home over, say, a year, then divide that amount by 13 months, rather than 12. Then divide *that* amount by the number of pay periods at your company and try deducting that "extra month's pay" from your check. You'll be surprised how quickly you'll adjust and how much you'll soon be saving. Which brings us to our last piece of advice.

Use mental accounting to your advantage. This kernel of counsel is essentially an endorsement for payroll deduction plans. Folks who have difficulty holding on to small amounts of money often have difficulty saving, for the obvious reason that small amounts are what are left over from our paychecks after we have paid the bills. That's where labeling tricks can help. By funneling money into a mutual fund or savings account directly from your paycheck, the $50 that you might have accounted for as bowling money and spent easily is mentally (and literally) accounted for as savings—and thus less likely to be wasted and more likely to be around when you need it.

There is another reason that payroll deduction plans are a good idea, one that involves an important psychological principle we discuss in the next chapter. Psychologically it's much easier to part with your money—to set it aside—this way than by writing a check to your savings account. We'll explain why in the next chapter.

2

WHEN SIX OF ONE ISN'T HALF A DOZEN OF THE OTHER

Imagine that you're the head of the Centers for Disease Control, facing a dangerous virus outbreak in a small, isolated town. Your staff says there's a strong chance that all six hundred residents will die unless you administer one of two experimental drugs. If you choose drug A, two hundred people will be saved. If you choose drug B, there's a one-third chance that all six hundred people will be saved and a two-thirds chance that none will. Which drug should you choose?

If you ever have occasion to read the thousands of scholarly books and articles written about behavioral economics— and, further straining belief, if you read the bibliography at the end of each—you'll notice one article referenced in these works more than any other, by far. Written by Daniel

Kahneman and Amos Tversky and published in the March 1979 issue of the journal *Econometrica*, the article is actually the second most cited article in *all* of economics publishing since 1970. Its title is "Prospect Theory: An Analysis of Decision Under Risk." And if Richard Thaler's concept of mental accounting is one of two pillars upon which the whole of behavioral economics rests, prospect theory is the other. Like mental accounting, prospect theory deals with the way we frame decisions, the different ways we label—or code—outcomes, and how they affect our attitude toward taking risks. As we'll see, the same outcome can often be described either in the vocabulary of gains or in the vocabulary of losses, and such unconscious and inconsistent coding has far-reaching effects. Indeed, we might just as easily have constructed this book as one long essay explaining prospect theory and all of the ideas that flow from it—that's how important the ideas discussed in the paper are.

Instead we've divided the ramifications of prospect theory—and the inconsistent way people treat losses and gains—into a pair of basic concepts. The first, which we'll discuss in this chapter, is the way that our feelings about loss (called "loss aversion" in behavioral economics lingo) and our inability to forget money that's already been spent (the "sunk cost fallacy") make us too ready to throw good money after bad. In the next chapter, we'll explore the second concept: how a preference for keeping things the way they are (the "status quo bias") combines with a tendency to fall in love with what we own (the "endowment effect") to make us resist change. A deeper understanding of both concepts should lead you to better investment and spending decisions.

RISKY BUSINESS

*Imagine that you're once again the head of the CDC,
battling a mysterious virus in a small, isolated town.
This time, your staff tells you that if you choose drug
A, four hundred people will die. If you choose drug
B, there's a one-third chance that no one will die and
a two-thirds chance that all six hundred will perish.
Which drug should you choose?*

Take another look at the scenario laid out at the beginning of
this chapter. Each hypothetical is, on the surface, subtly but
significantly different from the other. Indeed, research first
conducted by Kahneman and Tversky suggests that more
than likely you chose the first drug in the first scenario (two
hundred people saved) but the second drug in the second (a
one-third chance that no one will be killed). What's curious about this is that yes, the final outcome in both versions,
for both the first and second options, *is exactly the same.*
With drug A—the sure saving of two hundred lives in the
first version, the sure loss of four hundred in the second—
you end up with two hundred at-risk people alive and four
hundred dead in either case. With drug B, you'd have a one-
third chance that all six hundred at-risk people will be alive
and a two-thirds chance that none of them will—in both
cases.

But by picking drug A in the first case and drug B in the
second, people demonstrate how different their decisions
can be depending on how they frame a problem (or how it is
framed for them). When the problem is seen as a matter of
how many lives might be saved, the tendency is to be cautious, to save as many as possible. But when viewed in terms
of lives lost, the tendency is to be more adventurous, to gam-

ble in the hopes of saving everybody rather than accepting the death of four hundred people.

In financial matters this phenomenon results in a willingness to take more risk if it means avoiding a sure loss and to be more conservative when given the chance to lock in a sure gain. Read these next two scenarios to get a clearer idea of what we mean.

> *Imagine that you have just been given $1,000 and have been asked to choose between two options. With option A, you are guaranteed to win an additional $500. With option B, you are given the chance to flip a coin. If it's heads, you receive another $1,000; tails, you get nothing more. Which option would you choose?*
>
> *Now imagine that you have just been given $2,000 and are required to choose between two options. With option A, you are guaranteed to lose $500. With option B, you are given the chance to flip a coin. If it's heads, you lose $1,000; tails, you lose nothing. Now which option would you choose?*

Once again, research tells us that you'd choose option A in the first scenario (the sure gain of $500) but option B in the second (an even chance between losing $1,000 or nothing at all). And, again, the final outcome in both versions, for A and B, is the same. With option A—sure gain in the first version, sure loss in the second—you finish with $1,500 in either case. With option B, you have an even chance of ending up with $1,000 or $2,000 in both scenarios. But by choosing option A in the first case and option B in the second, you again show a willingness to take more risk if it means avoiding losses and to be more conservative if you can lock in sure profits. This outlook, by the way, is one reason gamblers often up their bets when luck isn't going their way; they're willing to take a bigger risk to avoid losing money. It's also a likely reason—as Mebane Faber, a portfolio manager at Cambria Investment Management, has shown—why stock prices bounce up and down more drastically during falling markets than during rising ones: If you're a stock trader who's lost a lot, the temptation to gamble big in the hopes of recouping money is very powerful.

The reason for this difference in outlook can be found in a psychological principle known as Weber's law, named after the nineteenth-century German physiologist Ernst Weber. Loosely speaking, Weber's law says the impact of a change in the intensity of a stimulus is proportional to the absolute level of the original stimulus. In conversational English, it means you're likely to notice if someone goes to a tanning booth in January, but not in July. In financial terms, the difference between earning $10 or $20 for a job well done has a bigger effect on how happy you are than the difference between earning $110 or $120.

Weber's law implies that people will be cautious when dealing with potential gains. The difference between nothing and $500 is greater psychologically than the difference between $500 and $1,000, so most people want to lock in the sure $500. The same process, though, implies a greater tolerance for risk when dealing with potential losses. Again, the difference between losing $500 and losing nothing is greater psychologically than that between losing $500 and losing $1,000. Why not expose yourself, then, to the risk of losing that last (relatively unimportant) $500 in exchange for the possibility of losing nothing?

Prospect theory, at its essence, is an attempt to incorporate Weber's law and many other psychological principles to explain why people choose the way they do. Our mission, at *its* essence, is to explain how the ways people code gains and losses can lead to poor investing and spending decisions. Traditional economics suggests that your inclination to choose option A should be no stronger in either of the two situations just described because your final position in either case is identical: You have $1,500 more than you had before behavioral economists started handing out free money. The only choice that matters, then, should be whether you prefer the certain $1,500 or the gamble that offers you an even chance of having either one grand or two. That's what traditional economic theory suggests, anyway.

Prospect theory offers an alternative approach. It says that people generally do not assign values to options based on the options' expected effect on their overall level of wealth: The typical head of an American family, with a net worth of $300,000 or so, doesn't see a $500 loss or gain as one-sixth of 1 percent of her overall financial position. She sees it as $500 that she did or didn't have five minutes before she lost or gained it. Prospect theory says we assign values to gains or losses themselves—based on their own merits, if you will, as gains or losses. It is the actual gaining or losing—and our feelings about it—that matters more to us, rather than how those gains or losses leave us overall.

People's reactions to gains and losses highlight a key feature of human judgment—namely, that judgments are constructed "on the spot" in response to specific tasks and are therefore very sensitive to how the problems arise or the way in which they are framed. Tom oversaw a public opinion survey a few years ago in which half of the respondents were asked whether they thought they could save 20 per-

YOU'VE BEEN FRAMED

Framing is an especially interesting phenomenon because we may not even be aware that we are experiencing its effects. A great example of this turned up when researchers were examining the 2000 Arizona general election. After ensuring that no other obvious force (say, income or political affiliation) had been influencing voters, the researchers found that people were noticeably more likely (63.6 percent vs. 56.3 percent) to say yes to a school tax increase if their polling location were located . . . in a school! Simply being in a school when voting, which presumably reminded some voters of education's importance, was enough to frame the choice in a different light for a big chunk of them.

cent of their income. Only half of these respondents said yes. But when the other half were asked whether they thought they could live on 80 percent of their income, nearly 80 percent said yes. To save 20 percent of your income is to live on 80 percent of it, so this pattern of responses makes no logical sense. But it does obey the psycho-logic of prospect theory. To save 20 percent is to lose that amount from your disposal income. But to live on 80 percent of your income is to do without what you would gain from that last 20 percent.

As another demonstration of the power of framing, you might think that if someone prefers, for example, a cell phone to extra coverage on a car insurance policy, then he'd be willing to pay more for the phone. Not so, or at least not always so. Choosing and pricing call upon different psychological processes, so there are times when a person will choose the phone but would have been willing to pay more for the policy. Likewise, you might think that the similarity between, say, *a mother and her daughter* would be the same as that between the very same *daughter and her mother*. Not so. People assess similarity differently depending on the direction from which they start. For instance, people typically report that North Korea seems more similar to China than China seems to North Korea. Finally, you might think that if one pair of items is more similar to one another than another pair—oranges and apples vs. shovels and spoons— then they also have to be less *dissimilar*. Wrong. Assessments of similarity use different mental processes than assessments of dissimilarity, so it's possible for one pair to be both more similar and more dissimilar than another pair. Slightly different twists on the same questions can enlist different modes of thought and therefore lead to very distinct responses.

IT DEPENDS ON HOW YOU LOOK AT IT

New York Yankees legend Yogi Berra reportedly was once asked into how many slices he wanted his pizza cut. Berra's alleged reply: "Better make it four; I'm not hungry enough to eat eight."

The importance of how a decision is approached—how it's framed—was nicely illustrated in an experiment conducted by psychologist Eldar Shafir, who presented one group of students with the following question:

Imagine that you are planning a week's vacation in a warm spot over spring break. You currently have two options that are reasonably priced. The travel brochure gives only a limited amount of information about the two options. Given the information available, which vacation spot would you prefer?

Spot A: Average weather	*Spot B:* Lots of sunshine
Average beaches	Gorgeous beaches/coral reef
Medium-quality hotel	Ultramodern hotel
Medium-temperature water	Very cold water
Average nightlife	Very strong winds
	No nightlife

Another group of students Shafir interviewed was offered the same vacation spots but with a slightly different frame of reference for their decision, marked by us in bold.

> *Imagine that you are planning a week's vacation in a warm spot over spring break. You currently have two options that are reasonably priced,* **but you can no longer retain both reservations.** *The travel brochure gives only a limited amount of information about the two options. Given the information available, which* **reservation do you decide to cancel?**

Both sets of students were asked to make the same decision—where to vacation. But one group viewed the problem as one of selection (which spot was preferable), and the other as one of rejection (which to cancel). That difference was significant. Of students who were asked which spot they *preferred*, 67 percent opted for spot B. Conversely, 48 percent chose to *cancel* their reservations for spot B. Spot B, in other words, somehow has more appeal when choosing than when rejecting.

What happens, as Shafir explained, is that when people view a decision as one of preference, they focus on the positive qualities of the options. Spot B had more negatives than spot A, but it also had more obvious positive attributes. In contrast, when asked to cancel a reservation, people focus more on negatives. So students who might have otherwise preferred spot B because of its more compelling weather, scenery, and accommodations were thinking more about what they didn't like. As a result, more students chose to cancel their reservation to spot B.

According to prospect theory, people feel more strongly about the pain that comes with loss than they do about the pleasure that comes with an equal gain. About twice as strongly, according to Kahneman and Tversky, meaning that you feel the misery of losing $100 (or $1,000 or $1 million) about twice as keenly as you feel the pleasure of gaining that amount. That's why you're likely to choose the sure gain of $500 in the first scenario but reject the sure loss of $500 in the second, even though both would leave you with $1,500. The idea of losing $500—for certain—is so painful you're willing risk winding up with $1,000 simply to avoid that discomfort. Similarly, in a sort of mirror-image effect, the idea of letting that $500 gain in the first scenario slip away, for the chance of maybe winding up with a $1,000 gain, is discomfiting enough to cause you to opt for the sure thing.

KNOW WHEN TO HOLD 'EM; KNOW WHEN TO FOLD 'EM

At this point, some readers may object to the implication that loss aversion is bad. They might point out that the tendency to weight losses more heavily than gains is in many respects a net positive. They might especially be prone to pointing that out in the wake of the kind of stock market turmoil that became the norm in the first decade of the twenty-first century. After all, beings who care too much about possible gains and too little about potential losses run too great a risk of experiencing the kinds of losses that threaten their survival. Better to care more about falling too far when climbing a tree in search of plumper fruit than about climbing so high. One can leave you better fed; the other can leave you dead.

True enough. Loss aversion can be helpful and conservative (in the nonpolitical sense). But oversensitivity to loss can also have negative consequences.

Take investing, for example. In the short term, being especially sensitive to losses contributes to the panic selling that accompanies stock market crashes (we'll discuss other causes later). The Dow Jones Industrial Average tumbles (along with stock prices and mutual fund shares in general), and the pain of these losses makes many investors overreact: The injured want to stop the bleeding. The problem, of course, is that pulling your money out of the market on such a willy-nilly basis leaves you vulnerable to a different sort of pain—the pangs you'll feel when stock prices rise while you're licking your wounds.

And don't be fooled into thinking you can make amends for your low pain threshold by jumping back into the market once you regain your senses. Although stocks seem to rise steadily over time, they actually do so in major fits and starts—a few big gains on a small number of days sprinkled throughout the year. Indeed, the stock market is much like that common description of war: long periods of boredom interrupted by episodes of pure terror. By pulling your money out in reaction to short-term drops, you run the risk of missing those productive days. And it's a serious risk. According to finance professor H. Nejat Seyhun, if you had missed the ninety best-performing days of the stock market from 1963 to 2004, your average annual return would have dropped from almost 11 percent, assuming you had stayed fully invested, to slightly more than 3 percent. And there were 10,573 trading days over that period, so we're talking about missing only 0.85 percent of the action. On a $1,000 investment, those different rates of return translate into the difference between having $74,000 after four decades or having about $3,200.

In any event, being overly sensitive to the pain of losing money can sometimes make us too quick to abandon investments. What's tricky about this concept, though, is that loss aversion can often lead us in the opposite direction—to *hold on* to losing investments for longer than we should. Ask yourself if you've ever sold a stock not because you thought it was finished rising, but because you wanted to "lock in profits." And ask yourself how many times you've held on to a losing investment (or home or piece of art) because you were sure it would "come back."

Even if your own answer to these questions is no, it's a fact that individuals tend to sell winning investments too quickly and keep losing ones too long. It was verified in 1997 by two researchers, Terrance Odean and Brad Barber. They

HOME ECONOMICS

Loss aversion affects more than stock investors. A woman Gary knows bought a condo in Boston for $110,000, just before the real estate market there collapsed. A year later, when her job forced her to move to another city, the highest offer she received for her place was $100,000. She passed, unable to face taking a $10,000 loss. Instead she leased an apartment in Los Angeles while renting out her Boston home. Eventually, though, she had to sell her condo when she decided to buy a home in L.A. Her selling price: $92,000. No need to wonder why an overdeveloped fear of losses can lead you to make financial decisions that aren't in you best interest.

analyzed the trading records of ten thousand accounts at a large national discount brokerage firm over a seven-year period beginning in 1987 and ending in 1993. Among other findings, their gargantuan research effort highlighted a pair of remarkable facts. First, investors *were* in fact more likely to sell stocks that had risen in price rather than those that had fallen.

Think about this in nautical terms: Your investments are the flotilla you hope will carry you to the shores of a secure retirement over the choppy seas of life. But rather than sticking with boats that have proven their seaworthiness, you routinely abandon ship in favor of dinghies that already have leaks. This may strike you as logical, particularly if you're a person who sells winners more often than losers. The argument for such reasoning would be that the winners have already had their run, while losing stocks have yet to make their move. It's a version of regression theory, discussed in the introduction to this book: The seaworthy boats (which had their tailwind of good fortune) are due to spring some leaks, while it's about time the leaky boats become more secure; better to sell the good boats now before they sink.

Obviously no sailor in his right mind would behave in this fashion, yet many investors do so routinely.

And the Odean data show the folly of this behavior: Stocks that investors *sold* outperformed stocks they kept by 3.4 percentage points over the ensuing twelve months. In other words, investors sold shares they should have kept and kept shares they should have sold. And remember, this isn't an occasional result; it's a pattern among thousands of investors studied. What makes their research even more extraordinary is that when you sell an investment at a loss, the Internal Revenue Service often allows you to reduce your taxable income by at least some amount of the loss. So Uncle Sam stands

SAVING GRACE

Loss aversion is especially tricky and harmful because we may feel the pain of a loss that's not really a loss. Exhibit A: the trouble some people have trying to save. Many of us experience the lessening of *current* buying power (which saving for the future entails) as a loss. No matter that the money we save is ours to spend later; a sense of loss, and our aversion to it, makes it tough to sock money away. But Richard Thaler, along with fellow behavioral economist Shlomo Benartzi, devised a clever plan a few years ago to overcome that problem, at least at the workplace. It's called SMarT (Save More Tomorrow) and here's how it works: Rather than expecting employees to pull money from their paychecks and direct it toward retirement accounts—which seems impractical or just plain unpleasant for many workers trying to make ends meet—SMarT asks workers to commit a portion of *future* raises to retirement savings, thus eliminating the feeling of loss from current spending. Sounds simple, but when put into practice, SMarT has had dramatic results, in some cases helping employees more than quadruple their savings rate, from around 3 percent to nearly 14 percent. SMarT indeed.

ready, whenever you're willing to take a hit, to subsidize it for you. Yet people still refuse to "book the loss."

Now, we could spend a lot of time considering all the reasons that might cause investors to make this expensive mistake over and over again. Odean and Barber, in fact, raised many: "Alternative explanations have been proposed for why investors might realize [gains on] their profitable investments while retaining their losing investments. Investors may rationally, or irrationally, believe that their current losers will outperform their current winners. They may sell winners to rebalance their portfolios. Or they may refrain from selling losers due to the higher transaction costs of trading at lower prices. I find, however, that when the data are controlled for rebalancing and share price, the disposition effect is still observed."

The "disposition effect" referred to is the name that finance professors Hersh M. Shefrin and Meir Statman gave to the tendency to hold losers too long and sell winners too soon. It is, in effect, an extension of prospect theory and loss aversion. Most people are much more willing to lock in the sure gain that comes with selling a winning stock or fund than they are willing to lock in the sure loss of selling a losing investment, even though it generally makes more sense to sell losers and keep winners. The prospect of selling a losing investment (and the pain associated with making the loss final) makes them more willing to dig in their heels and take risks—the risk, of course, being that if they hold on to the losers, the investment will continue to drop in price. After all, until you actually sell a losing investment, the drop in price is only a "paper loss"—it's not official. Once you sell it, though, it's real. This, of course, is creative mental accounting at its worst: Unrealized losses are segregated or compartmentalized in a separate account precisely *because* they're unrealized. Thus you can ignore them (or treat them as a potential future gain) and they don't disprove your investing "prowess."

Losing investments, then, represent a variation of the choice presented in the second scenario earlier in this chapter: option A, sell and guarantee a loss; or option B, hold on and risk losing more for the opportunity to get your money back. Winning investments, on the other hand, represent a variation of the choice presented in the first scenario: option A, sell and guarantee a gain; or option B, hold on and risk losing your profit for the opportunity to earn more. Loss aversion tells us it's less painful—and more common—to sell winners and keep losers. The Odean research says it's a lot smarter to do the opposite.

Two final thoughts about loss aversion: Kahneman and Tversky noted that being overly sensitive to loss leads people to opt for a certain gain over one that offers a high possibility of a larger gain. In real life, that usually translates into a preference for fixed-income investments over stocks. A guaranteed 4 to 6 percent annual return from T-bills or corporate bonds may seem a lot more appealing than the "chance" to earn 9 percent or more a year in stocks. But as we'll see later on, the dangers of the stock market may not be as important as the ravages of inflation. So to the extent that you opt for "safe" investments—bonds, annuities, and other fixed-income or life insurance products—over riskier but generally higher-paying ones, your loss aversion may be costing you money.

The other thing about loss aversion to remember is that it varies among people to a surprising degree. The more education you have, for instance, the less likely you are to be afflicted. But the richer you are and the older you are, the more likely it is that you will react strongly to the prospect of loss. This may make sense on some level—as you get older your prospects for recouping losses grow dimmer—but a sixty-five-year-old retiree may easily live for another two or three decades, and too conservative an approach to investing could leave her woefully underfinanced when her (noninvesting) prospects for earning more are truly limited.

GOOD MONEY AFTER BAD

Imagine that you've been given courtside tickets to a Cleveland Cavaliers basketball game or a classical music performance. You're dying to go because you've always wanted to see LeBron James or Yo-Yo Ma. Before you leave your house, you learn that James is injured and won't play, or that Ma won't perform. Plus, a sudden snowstorm makes the trip to the game or ballet unpleasant and somewhat dangerous. Do you go?

Now imagine the same game or concert, except in this instance you paid a small fortune for the ticket yourself and there's no chance of selling it to someone else. Do you go?

A particular form of loss aversion to which we are all prone is what Richard Thaler described in 1980 as the "sunk cost fallacy." This psychological trap is the primary reason most people would choose to risk traveling in a dangerous snowstorm if they had paid for a ticket to an important game or concert, while passing on the trip if they had been given the ticket for free. The distinction makes no sense, of course: The money for the ticket is spent—or sunk—in either case; you won't get it back whether you go to the event or watch it on television. As a matter of fact, going to the game or concert means incurring an extra cost: the chance you might die or be seriously injured. Therefore the danger posed by the snowstorm should carry equal significance for people who receive the ticket for free or pay for it. That it doesn't—that there is more significance because we have sunk money into the deal, regardless of whether or not that money can be retrieved—is an example of the sunk cost fallacy. And this isn't just hypothetical theorizing.

For a seminal 1985 research paper entitled "The Psychology of Sunk Cost," published in the journal *Organizational Behavior and Human Decision Processes*, psychologists Hal

R. Arkes and Catherine Blumer conducted an interesting
real-life experiment. They randomly distributed discounts to
buyers of subscriptions to Ohio University Theater's 1982–
1983 season. One group of buyers paid the normal ticket
price of $15; a second group received a $2 discount per ticket;
and a third received $7 off each ticket. Members of the last
two groups were told that the discount was being given as
part of a promotion by the theater department. The result?
People who paid more for their tickets attended the performances more often than those who had received discounts.

Logically there shouldn't have been any difference in attendance. Not only did all the groups presumably have similar inclinations to attend when they bought their tickets, they
all were prepared to pay the same price and all had the same
tickets, on average, as the season progressed. Although this
phenomenon tended to lessen—predictably—as the theater
season progressed (farther away from the date of purchase),
the experiment's conclusion is unavoidable: The more people
spent on their tickets, the greater their sunk costs, and the
more seriously they took attendance at the plays.

Arkes and Blumer tried to explain why sunk costs have
such a powerful effect on people, beyond the obvious, if irrational, notion of loss aversion: If people didn't go to a performance, they likely equated the unused ticket with a loss.
Therefore the higher their ticket price, the greater the loss to
be averted and the greater the likelihood that they'd expend
effort to see the performances. No matter that the money
was already spent whether they went to the play or stayed
home and lazed on the couch. One of the more interesting
suggestions the researchers made—which we're inclined to
agree with—is that people fall prey to the sunk cost fallacy
because they don't want to appear wasteful. Not necessarily to other people, mind you; most people act as their own

judge and jury when it comes to their own finances. In any case, Arkes and Blumer buttressed their point with the results from the following scenario, which was posed to eighty-nine survey participants:

> *On your way home you buy a TV dinner on sale for $3 at the local grocery store. A few hours later you decide it is time for dinner, so you get ready to put the TV dinner in the oven. Then you get an idea. You call up your friend to ask if he would like to come over for a quick TV dinner and then watch a good movie on TV. Your friend says sure. You go out to buy a second TV dinner. However, all the on-sale TV dinners are gone. You therefore have to spend $5 (the regular price) for the TV dinner identical to the one you just bought for $3. You go home and put both dinners in the oven. When the two dinners are fully cooked, you get a phone call. Your friend is ill and cannot come. You are not hungry enough to eat both dinners. You cannot freeze one. You must eat one and discard the other. Which one do you eat?*

Not surprisingly, most survey participants had no preference, since the costs and benefits of choosing either dinner are the same: You've spent eight bucks, and no matter which dinner you eat, one of the meals will go to waste. Amazingly, though, around one quarter said they would eat the $5 dinner, a choice that Arkes and Blumer suggested could only be the result of those folks having the impression that throwing away a $5 meal would be more wasteful than throwing away a $3 meal. (As for the two people who said they would eat the $3 meal, your guess is as good as ours.)

Whatever the causes of the sunk cost fallacy, the importance of ignoring money already spent and focusing on future costs and benefits should be obvious. If it's not, ask yourself how many times you've opted to repair a car or furnace, or to spend money on some other endeavor, based largely on the fact that you've already invested so much. Here's a personal example from our files: When Gary was in college and learning to play hockey, he bought a pair of goaltender leg pads for $350. Truth be told, Gary discovered quickly that he had little potential as a goalie. But when the time came to buy more equipment, he opted to purchase skates, sticks, gloves, and shoulder pads that were designed especially for goaltenders. Why? Because he had already spent such a large amount on the leg pads, and because facing up to his weakness in goal was difficult. You won't be surprised to hear the conclusion to this tale: Eventually Gary figured out that his future lay elsewhere on the ice. The used leg pads, along with $650 spent on the other equipment, were eventually resold for a grand total of $400. His initial sunk cost: $350; his final loss: $600.

It turns out that the sunk cost fallacy affects your pocketbook in more ways than you might first imagine, including your taxes. Arkes and Blumer observed that government spending decisions are often based on how much has already been spent. They noted that in late 1981, funding for the very expensive Tennessee-Tombigbee Waterway Project was scheduled for congressional review. In defending the project, Tennessee senator James Sasser remarked: "Completing Tennessee-Tombigbee is not a waste of taxpayer dollars. Terminating the project at this late stage of development would, however, represent a serious waste of funds already invested." In other words, good project or not, we have to finish it because we've already spent so much money on it. No matter that the money is already gone. Arkes and Blumer wisely pointed out that canny folks who are aware of the sunk cost fallacy can use it to their advantage. They cited a 1981 article in *Mother Jones* in which a nuclear power industry executive is quoted as saying: "When it comes down to it, no one with any sense would abort a $2.5 billion construction project. And, by extension, no administration would abort a $200 billion national investment in nuclear energy. So the trick for the industry is to get more new plants under construction without the (antinuclear) movement knowing about it. By the time they get around to demonstrating and challenging the license, we'll have a million tons of steel and concrete in the ground, and no one in their right minds will stop us." Thus a common gambit in government is to get as much money as possible spent on a favorite project so that it is protected by the sunk cost fallacy by the time more sober minds and more rational analysis point out its flaws.

HOW TO THINK AND WHAT TO DO
Warning Signs

You might be a victim of loss aversion or the sunk cost fallacy if . . .

- you make important spending decisions based on how much you've already spent.
- you generally prefer bonds over stocks.
- you tend to sell winning investments more readily than losing ones.
- you're seriously tempted to take money out of the stock market when prices fall.

Throughout this book we'll gradually build an argument that many individuals should consider an automatic approach to investing by relying primarily on mutual funds—specifically index mutual funds, which try to do nothing more than mimic the performance of the stock and bond markets in general. That said, many of you might not want to scale back your active involvement in your portfolio. After all, it's fun. But loss aversion and the sunk cost fallacy have pronounced effects beyond the decision to buy or sell a stock or bond. So here are several suggestions that should help you make wiser decisions no matter what the issue.

Limit the damage you can do. Investing in individual stocks is not only fun, it can be profitable and educational. But we know too many amateur investors who lost too much money because they risked too much of their savings on their own stock-picking skills. Our advice? Put no more than 10 percent of your nest egg into stocks of individual corporations. The rest should be spread out over other kinds of investments.

Test your threshold for loss. Broadly, the best advice we can give you regarding loss aversion is to assume you're more sensitive to losing money than you think. That way, you're more likely to avoid making decisions that will leave you with the belated knowledge that you exposed yourself to more risk than you were willing or able to handle. Still, most people aren't keen to admit they're prone to any of the psychological traps we discuss in this book, particularly those who pride themselves on their skill as investors. You may be the smartest, most rational investor in the world, or you may just think you are.

That's why it's important to assess your loss aversion, which is another way of saying test your risk tolerance. As mentioned earlier, loss aversion can have two very different effects, so you need to ask two very different questions. The first aims to let you know if you're likely to be quick to abandon ship, if your aversion to loss is so great that you'll panic at the first sign of real trouble. That's a very relevant question given today's uncertainty in the global economy in general and the stock market in particular. So ask yourself: "If the stock market drops 25 percent tomorrow, would I be tempted to pull all or some of my money out?" If the answer is yes, you're probably unprepared for the ups and downs of the stock market.

The second question should help you see if your brand of loss aversion will lead you to dig in your heels on bad investments. Consider the following query and, again, answer as realistically as you can: Say you have $10,000 of Wal-Mart stock that you bought for $5,000, and $10,000 of Sears stock that you bought for $20,000. Your child's first-semester tuition bill of $10,000 is due. Which shares would you sell? If your answer is the Wal-Mart, you're mortal like the rest of us. And your aversion to loss is likely to leave you poorer than you need to be. (The best strategy, perhaps, might be to sell $5,000 worth of each company's stock, thus avoiding the need to pay any taxes!)

Diversify. The best way to avoid the pain of losing money, of course, is to avoid losing money. We haven't figured that one out yet, but there are ways to minimize investment losses. One of the best is *diversification:* doling out your investments among stocks (or stock mutual funds), bonds (or bond mutual funds), money market funds, even real estate (if you don't own a house, then ideally through real estate investment trusts). We'll omit portfolio allocation theory and other types of investment advice for now, but the behavioral economics idea behind diversification is that a loss in one portion of your nest egg will likely be offset by gains in another. So you'll be less likely to react emotionally and do something drastic if at the same time that you take a hit you are experiencing gains in another part of your portfolio.

There's another reason we preach diversification. You needn't be a psychic to deduce that we think equities— stocks or stock mutual funds—are still the best way for most Americans to build wealth. This view is based on the historical performance of stocks over hundreds of years. That said, we'd be negligent if we didn't throw up a warning flare. As mentioned, we're writing this during one of the most tumultuous periods in stock market history. But one reason why many investors have become so disenchanted with stocks is that over the years they came to believe that stocks can only go in one direction: up. There are a lot of people to blame for this mass self-delusion, but we're not among them. To quote from this section in our previous edition of the book: "As mentioned, we're writing this during one of the greatest bull markets in history. It is, quite frankly, an environment in which share prices seem headed for a fall, if for no other reason than history *also* teaches us that stocks tend to underperform for a while after they outperform. Of course, we can't know for certain when or if that drop will happen. No one can, which is basically the point of this brief intermission. What we want to do is explain why you can't count on stocks to perform as well in the future as they have in the past, and then explain why you nonetheless have little choice but to rely on stocks as the driving engine of your investment portfolio."

That last sentence applies today, although we'd insert the words *long term* just before *investment portfolio*. The point we're trying to hammer home is that there are no guarantees that any asset will thrive in the future as it has in the past. That leaves you with two options: (1) keep your money under a mattress and hope you save enough during your career to last in retirement; or (2) take some risk and invest your money in assets that have a reasonable chance to increase in value over time. For most people (1) isn't really an option, if only because most people can't save enough after living expenses to support themselves in retirement, especially during eras (like the current one) when inflation exists and erodes the buying power of money.

That leaves (2), and since you have to do *something* with your money, the challenge is picking the assets with which to cast your lot. And that brings us full circle. Although there are many sound reasons to invest in stocks—the most important being that stocks are most likely to increase in value faster than inflation decreases the buying power of money— the philosophical rationale for making stocks the largest slice of your investment pie boils down to this: If you think about it, the best way to guarantee that you'll *have* money in the future is to *make* money in the future. That is, forget about trying to predict which assets will increase in value and focus instead on owning a business that profitably sells products or services for substantially less than it costs to provide them. Of course, most people don't have the inclination or the money or the skill to start their own business, so the next best way to share in the profits is through the stock market. Stocks, remember, represent ownership interest in businesses. This is how Warren Buffett views his company's stock investments—as pieces of businesses. And, quite literally, when you invest in the stock market you become a partial owner of concerns that (hopefully) will make money regardless of economic conditions in the future. You're betting on the collective growth potential of businesses. Logic dictates that the owners of such firms will eventually be rewarded, either because share prices will rise or because profits will be distributed as dividends.

To be sure, it's unlikely that you'll be able consistently to identify the specific companies that will thrive, but we explain how to deal with that challenge elsewhere. What's important to focus on now is that stock prices, over time, reflect the ability of companies to make and distribute profits. Consider that stocks on average have returned almost 6 percent a year over the past seven decades, adjusted for inflation. That figure didn't materialize by virtue of magic or voodoo. During the period in question, corporate profits rose an inflation-adjusted average of about 3 percent annually, while the average stock yielded roughly 3 percent a year in dividends. From these numbers does the 6 percent figure arise. Of course, in the short run stock prices may rise for reasons having little to do with dividends or profitability. But, again, over long periods of time it has been proven that share prices rise in relation to companies' earnings and distribution of profits to shareholders.

None of the above, by the way, is meant to imply that stocks should be your *only* investment. It's wise to spread your wealth among a variety of asset classes, including stocks, bonds, real estate, cash, and maybe even gold.

Follow the Law of Five Years. This is a crucial bit of advice that we included in our last edition of the book, albeit with less force. Stock prices, as most investors now know personally, can bounce up and down violently, sometimes staying down for years at a time. That's why any money you'll need within the next five years should be removed from stocks and put into cash or cash equivalents like government bonds. And we're not just talking down payment money. When a parent or guardian decides to start saving for a child's college account, the time horizon for junior's freshman year tuition is not eighteen years from birth, but rather thirteen. That's when that first year's money has to be taken out of the stock market and put into a CD or some such. Otherwise you risk having a fat tuition nest egg chopped in half by a market swoon. The same goes for retirement. Money that you'll need when you're, say, sixty-five, needs to be safeguarded from market dips when you're sixty. It takes discipline to pull that cash out in the middle of a bull market, but the alternative is just too risky.

Heed the Rule of 100. But if you don't plan to start tapping your long-term savings for at least five years, stocks should represent a significant chunk of your portfolio, depending on your ability to tolerate the ups and downs of the stock market. Even folks who draw current income from their investments—retirees, for example—should probably have a portion of their savings in stocks so that their money will grow faster than inflation. We like the "100 minus your age rule": if you're, say, eighty-four years old, about 16 percent of your long-term nest egg (100 − 84 = 16) should be in stocks (preferably through an index mutual fund or two).

Focus on the big picture. For diversification to work as a salve for the pains of loss, you must avoid looking at losses or gains in isolation. You must train yourself to view individual investments as parts of a broader whole. This takes discipline. It's not easy for anyone to say, "Hey, my U.S. stock mutual fund dropped 10 percent, but at least my European bonds went up 8 percent." That's why it's often helpful to invest in a spreadsheet computer program such as Excel, a software package like Quicken, or any number of Internet sites, that can display and total all your investments.

Use your pen. It's also important, however distasteful the task may be, to spend time developing an investment strategy and to put it down on paper. For example, determine the portion of your portfolio that should be invested in stocks, bonds, real estate, and cash. Then write it down, with a notation as to when that allocation should be reexamined (perhaps as you approach your goal). You might also write down the investing rationale for each of your investments. That will serve as a reminder to hang tight if the price drops ("Coke is still the most popular brand name in the world") or to sell if need be ("Asia's economies might not be as strong as I thought when I invested in the Thai Fund").

Writing things down, research suggests, raises the "ante" and increases your commitment. In fact, it's a way of using the sunk cost fallacy to your advantage, because by increasing your investment in taking a broader view of your wealth (by investing time and effort in the task), you'll increase the likelihood that you'll stick to your plans. In any event, if you take such an approach—identifying your goals and justifying all your investments in the context of achieving those goals—you'll be less likely to react impulsively to the inevitable ups and downs of the markets.

Forget the past. Very often our decisions about the future are weighed down by our actions of the past. People stay in unsatisfying careers because of the time and money they invested in school, not because they enjoy the work or expect to in the future; we finish a bad book because we've already gotten so far, not because we're anxious to see how the characters live; we sit through a boring movie because we bought the ticket, not because it's a good flick. The same motivations affect our decisions about money: We spend more money on car repairs because we've already spent so much on the car; we keep spending money on tennis lessons because we've already spent so much. We hold on to bad investments because we can't get over how much we paid for them and can't bear to make that bad investment "final."

Well, get over it.

No, we're not trying to be harsh. If we could, we'd send you a pill that erases the memory of every dollar you ever spent (except, perhaps, when filling out expense reports and tax returns). That's because once spent, it's gone. It has no relevance (except maybe for refunds). To the extent that you can incorporate that notion into your financial decisions, you'll be that much better off for trying. If you're debating the sale of an investment (or a home), for example, remember that your goal is to maximize your wealth and your enjoyment. *The goal is not to justify your decision to buy the investment at whatever price you originally paid for it.* Who cares? What counts, in terms of getting where you want to be tomorrow, is what that investment is worth today. That's why you must evaluate all investments (and expenses) based on their *current* potential for future loss and future gain.

Press rewind. How does one go about forgetting the past? One trick we like is a method of reframing decisions to remove emotional investments. We call it pressing the rewind button. Assume you can reverse history and start anew. Imagine that you've got a ten-year-old minivan that needs a new transmission. The sunk cost fallacy suggests you're more likely to buy the new transmission if you've recently sunk money on repairs. So ask yourself: If someone gave you the minivan as a gift yesterday, would you spend the money today to get it running? If the answer is no—because that large an investment is not worth it on its merit—it's time to think about buying a new car. Similarly, it is relevant only to your ego that your Amalgamated Thingamabobs stock, for which you paid $100 a share, is now selling for $25 a share. If you believe that the lower price is a bargain, hold on and maybe even buy more shares. But if it is not—if, given the chance, you would pass on the opportunity to buy the same shares at any price today—then it is time to sell. So ask yourself when evaluating investments: "Would I buy this today, at this price?" If not, you may not want to own it any longer.

Turn losses into gains. Sometimes investments fall in price; if the economy is weak, only lucky investors avoid temporary declines in their portfolio. So each investment must be evaluated individually with an eye on your financial situation. Once you've identified assets that need to be dumped, you might still find it difficult to make the loss real and final. One way to hop this hurdle is to turn the loss into a gain, and the easiest way to do that is to remember that selling investments at a loss creates a tax-deductible event: Losses on investments that you've held for less than twelve months can be written off against capital gains; losses on investments held longer than twelve months can be deducted from ordinary income. By viewing your potential loss as a gain—the lower taxes you'll owe—you master your own mental tendencies. Need an example? Say you bought one hundred shares of Amalgamated Thingamabobs three years ago for $100 a share, or $10,000. If you sell today at $70 a share—for a loss of $3,000—and you're in the 28 percent federal tax bracket, your loss is worth $840 to you. If that isn't a kind of gain, we don't know what is!

Use Weber's law to your advantage. Adding five pounds to a fifteen-pound dumbbell matters a lot, but adding five pounds to a two-hundred-pound barbell is hardly noticed. What this means is that to stretch your enjoyment from the good things in life, you should "segregate gains" whenever possible. Spread them out. You would not want to receive both your state and federal tax refunds on the same day, for example, because you would doubtless combine them mentally into one overall windfall and thus diminish your enjoyment. The pleasure you experience from receiving, say, $1,000 on one day would be less than what you would derive from getting $700 one week and $300 the next.

Of course, you cannot determine exactly when your tax refunds will arrive. But you can time many of life's windfalls, and when you can, spread them out. The same logic, of course, implies that you will be better off if you "integrate losses." If you have a number of cavities to be filled, get them all taken care of in one trip to the dentist. Don't subject yourself to multiple traumas by having a few filled on one visit and the rest on another. Weber's law implies that the pain of two moderately bad experiences will typically exceed the pain of experiencing both at one time. If you *owe* the government money, then pay your state and federal taxes at the same time.

Finally, pay less attention to your investments. Numerous surveys indicate that anywhere from a third to half of investors check on their portfolios once a week, if not more frequently. And that's too often. The more frequently you check, the more you'll notice—and feel the urge to react to—the ups and downs that are an inevitable part of the stock and bond markets. That's a bad idea. Stock movements in the short term are about emotions and rumors. In the long run, they're about facts and profits. As the legendary investor and finance professor Benjamin Graham once said about the stock market: "In the short run it's a voting machine, but in the long run it's a weighing machine." So don't vote, weigh. That means that for most investors who don't trade professionally, a yearly portfolio review is frequent enough to make necessary adjustments in your allocation of assets. Counterintuitively, *that's even more true in very volatile markets,* when the fall in your assets is largely due to forces that are affecting everyone, and therefore leaves you as well off, relatively, as you were before the drop. True, you might miss a market dip or rise when the chairman of the Federal Reserve sneezes or smiles. Which means that you might miss an opportunity to let your psyche get in the way of your financial peace of mind.

3

THE DEVIL THAT YOU KNOW

I went down to the crossroads. Fell down on my knees.
—from "Crossroads," by legendary bluesman Robert Johnson

If you choose not to decide, you still have made a choice.
—from "Freewill," by the 1970s rock group Rush

In personal finance—all finance, really—there are sins of omission as common as those of commission. In fact, some of the more costly financial mistakes people make result from inaction. (A lot of nonfinancial mistakes, too, for that matter.) It's not always what you do that hurts your pocketbook, but what you choose not to do. To explain why people decide not to decide—or, more accurately, why people resist change—we return once again to the spadework of behavioral economics pioneers Daniel Kahneman and Amos Tversky. Prospect theory, as we saw earlier, helps explain how loss aversion and an inability to ignore sunk costs lead people to act in ways that are not in their best interest. The sting of losing money, for example, often leads investors to pull out of the stock market unwisely when prices dip. Similarly, it leads car owners to pay for expensive repairs because of money already spent on previous fixes.

Both examples show how loss aversion and the sunk cost fallacy often lead us to *take* action—to actually *do* something. But prospect theory also explains how those same tendencies can lead us to avoid or delay action. Indeed, loss aversion and several other factors—particularly the fear of regret and a preference for the familiar—contribute to a phenomenon we call "decision paralysis," which makes the idea of many proactive decisions daunting and uncomfortable. So let's examine the way people reach decisions—how choices are made generally and why you might decide not to decide. Once you're familiar with all of the forces at work, you'll better understand why choice and change can be intimidating. It's a phenomenon that hampers people in all walks of life, from renting a car to buying a house to selecting a mate. Not surprisingly, the higher the stakes, the more conflict we feel. And for most of us, the stakes are never higher than when the choices involve money.

EENY, MEENY, MINY, MO...

Imagine you're considering the purchase of a TV, but as yet you haven't decided which brand or model you want, or even how much you want to spend. Walking past an electronics store one day, you notice a sign in the window advertising a popular Sony TV on sale for $299. You know this price to be well below retail. Would you:

1. buy the Sony?

2. wait to learn more about other models?

Now imagine the same situation, except that the store is also advertising a high-quality Aiwa TV for $359. As with the Sony, you know the price for the Aiwa to be a bargain. Would you:

1. *buy the Aiwa?*
2. *buy the Sony?*
3. *wait to learn more about other models?*

A funny thing happened when Tversky and Princeton University psychologist Eldar Shafir presented two similar hypotheticals to two different groups of students at Stanford and Princeton—in those cases, the electronics of choice were CD players. The majority of one group, which was presented with only the first scenario, said they'd buy the Sony, while roughly a third said they'd wait and shop some more. The decision to buy makes sense, given that the price on the Sony was obviously a good deal and the presumption that the students were on the prowl for a CD player. Meanwhile, when the other group of students was presented with the second situation, roughly one in four said they'd buy the Sony, while a like amount said they would buy the Aiwa. *This time, though, nearly half the students said they wouldn't do anything;* they'd wait to see what else was out there. Note the irony: Adding a second good deal from which to choose makes people less likely to take advantage of either opportunity.

At one level, the conclusion to be reached from this and similar experiments is not surprising: The more choices people face, the more likely they are to simply do nothing. But Tversky and Shafir also found that diversity of choice alone was not the determining factor in the students' decision to put off buying a CD player once the number of choices increased. They showed that was *not* the case in another experiment, in which a group of students was presented with a scenario similar to our second one, except that the Aiwa was replaced by a less appealing brand of CD player. In this instance, only one in four students said they'd wait to buy.

What Tversky and Shafir realized in formulating their theory of "choice under conflict" is that a decision to delay an action, or take no action at all, becomes more likely when there are many attractive options from which to choose. Consider this landmark study by psychologists Sheena Iyengar and Mark Lepper, conducted at an upscale grocery store in Menlo Park, California. In catering to the refined tastes of its clientele, the store offers patrons 250 flavors of mustard, 75 different olive oils, and more than 300 types of jam. The store also offered Iyengar and Lepper the chance to conduct their clever field experiment by allowing them to set up a tasting booth in the store on two consecutive Saturdays. Every hour the two psychologists rotated the available goods at the booth—one hour it was a selection of twenty-four different jams, and during the alternating hour, it was a more limited selection of six. The two sets of jams were chosen carefully so that they were rated, on average, by an independent sample of tasters to be equally delicious. Anyone who approached the booth during the course of the study was given a coupon good for $1 off any jam in the store. A bar code on each coupon contained information specifying whether the customer had visited the booth when it displayed six or twenty-four jams.

The two psychologists wanted to see if customers who were exposed to a set of twenty-four jams would be so befuddled by all the options that they wouldn't be able to decide which to buy—and thus be less likely to make a purchase than those exposed to fewer jams. And, in fact, customers who'd seen fewer jams did buy more. Although roughly 40 percent more people visited the booth when it contained twenty-four jams, they were far less likely to buy. In fact, 30 percent of those exposed to six jams subsequently made a purchase, whereas only 3 percent of those exposed to twenty-four did so. The more choice, in other words, the harder the choice.

The ramifications of these findings throughout modern society reverberate wide and deep. Indeed, we suspect that choice conflict is one of the reasons "progress"—defined in early twenty-first-century America as the freedom to choose from an ever-expanding selection of products, services, and opportunities—seems to engender as much angst as it does excitement. We may think we want nearly unlimited selections of televisions, of vacations, of jobs. But in some immeasurable way, this exploding freedom of choice raises its own discomfort and difficulties, particularly when the choices are good and getting better.

How much discomfort it raises for you depends, to some extent, on whether you are a "maximizer" or "satisficer." These crucial distinctions—which arise from work done in the 1950s by the great polymath Herbert Simon (Google him and be amazed)—represent the two primary ways most of us make decisions. Maximizers are folks who want to know everything about a choice. They spend a lot of time, effort, and emotion researching options in hopes of making the best choice possible. Satisficers, on the other hand, are looking for "good enough," and they generally make choices through a combination of the best available information, gut instinct, and the advice from what we like to call "trusted screeners" (more on that in the advice part of this chapter). Of course, some people have more maximizing or satisficing tendencies than others, but nearly all of us act like maximizers in some circumstances and like satisficers in others. Studies suggest that maximizing is a positive trait because it can leave people more confident about their choices. But we'd suggest that, for many people, maximizing may net out with more negative feelings than positive ones. One reason to think so was highlighted in a 2001 paper called "Doing Better but Feeling Worse." In it, Iyengar (along with Columbia University colleague Rachael Wells and Swarthmore psychology professor Barry Schwartz) detailed the results of an experiment that tracked college seniors through a year of job hunting and actual work. As you might have guessed, students who scored high on a maximizer scale that the researchers administered landed jobs that paid 20 percent more, on average, than students who leaned toward satisficing. But satisficers were much happier with their choices, and stayed so throughout their early job experiences.

Why might that have been so? Why were satisficers doing worse but feeling better? Part of it may just be a function of personality type, although there's not a lot of research suggesting that satisficers are generally happier than maximiz-

BIG EYES

Options are con artists. They seduce with a promise of joy, but often leave us confused and wanting. Consider this experiment conducted a few years ago by marketing professors Debora Viana Thompson, Rebecca Hamilton, and Roland Rust. When they offered consumers a choice of different digital devices (video players, PDAs, and the like) some six in ten picked the option with the most features. Also, when given the chance to customize their device, the average person chose twenty features out of a possible twenty-five. But when actually using their new gizmos, most consumers quickly fell prey to what the researchers call "feature fatigue"; that is, they quickly tired of using all those extras (if they even figured out how to). In their paper, the researchers discuss our tendency, when buying, to value capability over usability. We might just say that humans have "big eyes," which is relatively harmless when loading up at a salad bar but costly when spending more for features and options you'll likely never use.

ers. But in this area, as in most others in life, there really may
be such a thing as TMI—too much information. Maximizing, after all, very often leaves deciders with more good options from which to choose. And we know that too much
choice is a cause of anxiety and paralysis. But even if you're
able to pick from a wider set of choices—even if, like many
maximizers, you are highly motivated—Iyengar and Lepper's research suggests that you'll be less happy with your
choice. In another shopping experiment, the researchers set
up a chocolate-tasting booth that alternated between a set
of six options and a set of thirty. In either case, after making their choice shoppers were asked to rate their satisfaction
level on a scale of one to ten. And guess what? Chocolate lov-
ers who picked from a limited selection of treats were nearly
15 percent happier with their choice. It makes sense, if you
think about it: With six choices, you can only imagine a few
different ways that your decision to pick one chocolate over
the others might not have been wisest. But with thirty options, you're left with the thought that however much you
like the chocolate you chose, there are twenty-nine possible
ways you might have chosen better.

TOO MUCH OF A GOOD THING

One important result of decision paralysis in financial choice
is that by deferring buying decisions, you may miss a sale entirely or run the risk that prices will rise. How many tales
have you heard—or lived through—in which Jane and John
Homebuyer couldn't pull the trigger on their dream house
only to see the price go up when another bidder entered the
game? Of greater concern, though, is the conflict sparked by
the glut of investment options available today.

It's ironic that one of the most significant developments

in the democratization of wealth in this country—the explosive growth of mutual funds and the increasing prevalence of defined contribution retirement plans—is also a cause of tremendous anguish. Today there are roughly eight thousand publicly traded stock and bond funds, and for many folks, the prospect of choosing among them is paralyzing.

This paralysis is inflicted in several ways, both obvious and subtle. First and most obvious, decision paralysis is one culprit responsible for the trillions of dollars that Americans have stashed in passbook savings accounts, certificates of deposit, money market accounts, and other bank products. Yes, some of that money needs to be highly liquid, and yes, federally insured bank deposits are about the safest investment around today, which matters a lot to people when financial markets are choppy. But liquidity and surety cannot be the only reason for such a high level of bank deposits. After all, money market mutual funds typically offer yields that are higher than those paid by banks, and with nearly as much safety. For example, a money market fund that invests only in U.S. Treasury securities is about as safe—and accessible—a place to stash money as a bank that is insured by the Federal Deposit Insurance Corporation. But picking a money market fund in which to invest among the hundreds of available options means choosing among a number of seemingly equal and excellent choices (along with a lot of bad ones, too). And for many people, that is a very intimidating task.

Similarly, decision paralysis helps explain why so many people fail to make timely and appropriate investment decisions in employee-directed retirement plans, such as 401(k), 403(b), and 457 accounts. Faced with a choice between, say, several international and domestic stock funds and several high-yielding fixed-income products, many people choose the equivalent of a wait-and-see default option: They allocate all their money to the most conservative investment available on the theory that at some point they'll get around to figuring out what they should do. Or, having chosen among a few options when they first joined a retirement plan, many employees balk at changing their initial selections even when new and potentially better options are introduced. In fact, in 2001, Iyengar and two other colleagues from Columbia (Gur Huberman and Wei Jiang) looked at participation rates of workers in 647 employer-sponsored plans. They found that every ten investment choices added to a plan decreased employee participation rates by 2 percent!

Such intransigence is a mistake on two counts. First, tax-deferred retirement accounts are the portfolios for which the risks of investing in stocks are most mitigated: Who cares if the short-term value of your 401(k) account goes up and down with the stock market? By the time you'll need

THINK SOCKS, NOT STOCKS

The title of this digression is a cliché that bears repeating, given that many investors panic when share prices drop although they should celebrate. Unless they need their cash right now—as discussed, *money needed within five years should not be in stocks*—investors should be pleased when stock prices fall. That means they're getting the same shares they might have bought yesterday at a lower price today. We think a lot of people who might have stopped investing in stocks because of recent market turmoil—but didn't because of regular and automatic purchases made on their behalf in 401(k) and other retirement plans—will be glad for their "decision" to stay in the game. If you were buying socks for next winter, you'd be thrilled to get them on sale. The same goes when buying stocks for your retirement.

the money—presuming you have at least ten years until retirement—chances are that the roller-coaster nature of equities will be a memory. What you'll have left is a large pot of money, assuming you take advantage of the historically high returns that stocks have posted in comparison with bonds and other types of investments. So the longer you let decision paralysis contribute to procrastination—the longer you defer choice—the greater the chance you'll miss the heady returns that stocks can offer.

More important, the longer you defer making a decision, the less likely you are to ever get over your hesitation. To illustrate this point, Tversky and Shafir once offered students a $5 reward for answering and returning a long survey. One group was given five days to complete the survey, another twenty-one days, and a third group was given no deadline at all. Result: 66 percent of the first group (five-day deadline) turned in the survey and collected the reward, 40 percent of the second group (twenty-one days) finished on time, and 25 percent of the third group (no deadline) had turned in their questionnaire by the time the researchers stopped calculating. Now, maybe students in that last group are still planning to collect their $5, but we doubt it. The reality is that the more time you have to do a task—any task—the less pressure you feel to get with it, and the frequent result is you never get to it at all. Such delays, needless to say, can be costly.

THE CHOICE IS YOURS (SORT OF)

Indecision is typically overcome when people feel they have sound reasons for choosing one option over another. What could be more sensible? It turns out, though, that the search for decisive reasons can make people vulnerable to psychological tendencies of which they are unaware. Tversky and marketing professor Itamar Simonson demonstrated the impact of several of these tendencies in a key 1992 paper published in the *Journal of Marketing Research.*

In one experiment, people were given pictures and descriptions of five microwave ovens taken from a popular catalog. After studying the offerings carefully—which you might want to do, too, since it's a bit confusing—half the participants were asked to pick between two of these products: a 0.5-cubic-foot Emerson microwave, on sale for 35 percent off its $109.99 retail price; and a 0.8-cubic-foot Panasonic I oven, selling for 35 percent off its $179.99 price. As it happened, 57 percent chose the Emerson, *while 43 percent favored the Panasonic I.* Meanwhile another group of participants was given three ovens from which to choose— the two already mentioned and a 1.1-cubic-foot Panasonic II, selling for 10 percent off its $199.99 price. Interestingly, the inclusion of the second Panasonic, not nearly as good a bargain as the other two, boosted the number of people who favored the Panasonic I. *Some 60 percent chose the Panasonic I,* while 27 percent chose the Emerson and 13 percent chose the Panasonic II.

Tversky and Simonson explain this as an example of "trade-off contrast," whereby choices are enhanced or hindered by the trade-offs between options—even options we wouldn't choose anyway. In other words, when the Panasonic I was compared with the Emerson alone, few people had a decisive reason to choose one over the other; it was a trade-off between size (Panasonic) and price (Emerson). However, when the Panasonic II was introduced into the mix, the Panasonic I now had a couple of things going for it: Its size was adequate, and it could be had for a good price (35 percent off, as opposed to the 10 percent savings on the Panasonic II). The Panasonic I thus became a better deal—not only versus its pricier cousin, but also in comparison with the Emerson. Consider it this way: If A (Emerson) is better than B (Panasonic I), people will generally choose A. But if B happens to be better than C (the Panasonic II) in ways that are not applicable to A, many people will now choose B if for no other reason than B's appeal has been enhanced by comparison with C.

In his bestselling book *Predictably Irrational,* the behavioral economist Dan Ariely recounts a telling episode from Williams-Sonoma's history, when the retailer first introduced a bread-making machine to its stores. Priced at $275, the machines didn't sell very well. Then Williams-Sonoma added a second bread maker to its selection, one quite a bit larger and more expensive. And wouldn't you know it, the chain started selling more bread machines. Not the larger and pricier model, but the $275 option, which in comparison suddenly looked more appealing. Trade-off contrast at work!

Another intriguing phenomenon was revealed in a related experiment from Tversky and Simonson, in which they offered one group of participants a choice between two 35mm cameras—a Minolta X-370 priced at $169.99 and a Minolta Maxxum 3000i selling for $239.99. The preferred choice? An even split—50 percent chose each model. Meanwhile a second group of participants was offered a choice of the same two cameras as well as a Minolta Maxxum 7000i selling for $469.99. You might expect that however many opted for the new model, the remaining people would split their choices evenly between the two cheaper models. Instead, the medium-priced camera was now preferred over the cheaper model by more than a two-to-one margin. Tversky and Simonson call this phenomenon "extremeness aversion."

Stated simply, people are more likely to choose an option if it is an intermediate choice within a group, rather than at one extreme end. The X-370, for example, was the choice of half the subjects when it was one of two options, but the choice of little more than a fifth when it was at one end of the spectrum.

Evidence of trade-off contrast and extremeness aversion abound in real life, but one of the most costly examples occurs when people are at their most vulnerable—when buying coffins, which range in cost from less than $500 to $70,000 or more. It's common practice within the funeral industry to show bereaved relatives a selection of caskets designed specifically to highlight the enhancements of more expensive caskets in comparison with cheaper ones in the showroom (and to make sure low-cost versions aren't as cheap as they might be). To illustrate this point, we quote from a 1996 *Time* magazine story about a Vancouver, Canada, "death care" company, the Loewen Group: "Loewen also institutes its 'Third Unit Target Merchandising' system in the casket showroom, which capitalizes on the propensity of survivors to avoid the cheapest two caskets and choose the next one up in price. 'It's no different from any other business operating a showroom,' says Lawrence Millers, president of Loewen's cemetery division. But often, two former officials agree, this means banishing a newly acquired home's usual lowest-price offerings and replacing them with more expensive substitutes, so that when the customer picks that third-unit target, he ends up choosing a casket that yields a much better profit."

KNOWN QUANTITIES

A close cousin to decision paralysis is resistance to change. That is, people are naturally disposed to favor the familiar and keep things much as they have been. Behavioral economists call this the "status quo bias," and it has been demonstrated numerous times. Among the most compelling demonstrations was a series of landmark studies by economists William Samuelson and Richard Zeckhauser. In one, people with a working knowledge of finance were presented with a problem much like the following:

> *You are a serious reader of the financial pages, but until recently you have had little money to invest. Now a great-uncle has bequeathed to you a large sum of money. In considering how to invest these funds, you have narrowed down your choices to the following four investment options:*
>
> 1. *Shares of XYZ Inc., a stock of moderate risk with a 50 percent chance that over the next year its price will increase by 30 percent, a 20 percent chance that it will stay the same, and a 30 percent chance that it will decline 20 percent.*
> 2. *Shares of ABC Inc., a more risky stock with a 40 percent chance that over the next year its price will double, a 30 percent chance that it will stay the same, and a 30 percent chance that it will decline 40 percent.*
> 3. *U.S. Treasury bills, with an almost certain return of 9 percent over the next year.*
> 4. *Municipal bonds, with an almost certain return over the next year of 6 percent, tax-free.*
>
> *Which option would you choose?*

As you might expect, students in this study selected one or another of the investment options depending on their willingness to take risk. And it pretty much broke down in a bell curve, with extreme risk tolerance or intolerance on both sides and the bulk of people clustered around the middle. So 32 percent opted for the moderately risky stock investment, 32 percent opted for the moderately conservative municipal bond option, 18 percent chose the risky stock investment, and another 18 percent opted for ultrasafe T-bills. Those results, though, were not important on their own. The good stuff came when Samuelson and Zeckhauser offered other students a similar problem, except that for each of these other groups a status quo was established. That is, each one of the groups was told that an investment decision had already been made, and they were now being asked if they wanted to stay where they were or if they wanted to switch to another option. For example, one such alternative scenario went something like this:

> *You are a serious reader of the financial pages, but until recently you have had little money to invest. A while back, however, a great-uncle bequeathed to you a large sum of money, a significant portion of which is now invested in the shares of XYZ Inc. Now you must decide whether to leave the portfolio as is or change it by investing it elsewhere. You have no concern about the tax and brokerage commissions. Which option would you choose?*
>
> 1. *Retain the shares of XYZ Inc., a stock of moderate risk with a 50 percent chance that over the next year its price will increase by 30 percent, a 20 percent chance that it will stay the same, and a 30 percent chance that it will decline 20 percent.*

2. *Invest in shares of ABC Inc., a more risky stock
with a 40 percent chance that over the next year
its price will double, a 30 percent chance that it
will stay the same, and a 30 percent chance that
it will decline 40 percent.*
3. *Invest in U.S. Treasury bills, with an almost certain return of 9 percent over the next year.*
4. *Invest in municipal bonds, with an almost certain return over the next year of 6 percent, tax-
free.*

The results? No matter which investment option was presented as the status quo, it was the favorite choice of subjects
in each group. Ponder this for a moment: When all things
were equal, only three in ten people chose munis as their preferred investment. Yet once they were told that they already
owned these securities—even though they had not chosen
that investment themselves—nearly half the people decided
that munis were the way to go.

This is a classic example of the status quo bias. But the
question begging for an answer, of course, is "Why?" Why
are people so resistant to change, so intent on not rocking
the boat? More to the point: Is there something so intrinsi-
cally attractive about the status quo? Or is there something
inherently frightening about the prospect of change? The answer to both questions, as you will understand in a moment,
is a definitive yes.

WHAT'S MINE IS MINE, AND
WHAT'S YOURS ISN'T WORTH AS MUCH

*Imagine that you recently found a ticket to the most
prestigious inaugural ball of the recently elected U.S.*

president. You very much want to attend. Now a stranger offers to buy your precious ticket. What is the smallest amount for which you would sell?

Now imagine that you don't have a ticket to the ball, but you really want one. How much would you pay that same stranger for his?

If you think about it, the status quo bias is in part a measure of satisfaction. By forgoing change in favor of the familiar, you are to some extent demonstrating a level of happiness with your present situation. True, the decision to invest or not, to spend or not, or to marry or not may be influenced by fear, confusion, or doubt. Nonetheless, keeping things as they are is a vote of confidence for current circumstances, however weakly that vote may be cast. In fact, the preference for holding on to what you have is a lot stronger than most people think. People tend to overvalue what belongs to them relative to the value they would place on the same possession or circumstance if it belonged to someone else.

Behavioral economists call this the "endowment effect," and it helps to explain why most people would demand at least twice as much to *sell* the aforementioned ticket to the inaugural ball as they would to *buy* it. Richard Thaler demonstrated the endowment effect in a series of experiments several years ago. In one, half the students in a Cornell econ class were given a mug emblazoned with the school's logo. The mugs, which sold at the campus bookstore for $6, were examined by all the students—those who'd just received them as a gift and those who hadn't. Given that the mugs were handed out randomly, it's unlikely that those who received the free mugs loved coffee (or Cornell) more than the students who did not. Thaler then conducted an auction of sorts to see how much money mug owners would require to part with their ceramic cups and how much students who didn't have mugs would pay to own one.

You can probably guess what happened: The median price below which mug owners were *unwilling to sell* was $5.25. That is, they wouldn't give up their newfound possession for less than that amount. Conversely, the median price above which mug buyers were *unwilling* to pay was about $2.75. That is, they wouldn't pay more than that amount to buy a mug. The only way to explain this discrepancy is with the endowment effect. The mere fact of ownership was enough to make mug owners value a pretty basic campus commodity almost twice as much as did students who didn't own the mugs. And remember, there was no sunk cost effect at work here; no money had been spent on these mugs.

Because people place an inordinately high value on what they have, decisions to change become all the more difficult. To be sure, people manage to overcome this tendency all the time. If they didn't, folks wouldn't sell their homes, divorce their spouses, or trade used cars for new ones. But to the extent that the endowment effect makes it hard to properly value what is—and isn't—already yours, you may fail to pursue options that are in your best interest. In essence, the endowment effect is really just another manifestation of loss aversion: People place too much emphasis on their out-of-pocket expenses (what they have to pay now) and too little value on opportunity costs (what they miss by not taking an action).

One of the most costly and regrettable examples of how the endowment effect leads people to ignore opportunity costs occurs in connection with retirement savings plans at work. First, a little background. Tens of millions of U.S. workers are eligible to participate in 401(k), 403(b), or other

---

A FOOT IN THE DOOR

Marketers of all kinds exploit the endowment effect. That's why so many offer trial periods and money-back guarantees. Persian rug dealers are noted for the former, but it's common in many industries. Retailers know that once you take a product home, there's a good chance the endowment effect will kick in. Whatever value you might have placed on, say, a stereo at a store will likely increase once it sits in your den. Likewise, clever eBay sellers typically start bidding at a much lower price than they expect items to fetch. This increases the number of bidders, making the item look popular. And it boosts the number of people who will at some point be the high bidder, and thus for a while feel like an item is theirs—which will make them bid longer. Remember this when you next consider bidding on something for the heck of it, or try out a product because you can always return it. Maybe you can, maybe you can't.

---

so-called defined benefit retirement plans, which are tax-deferred savings vehicles funded mostly by workers themselves. But the typical employer matches fifty cents to each dollar contributed by plan participants, up to 6 percent of the employee's salary. In other words, someone who makes $50,000 a year and contributes $3,000 will receive an extra $1,500 from his or her boss. That's right: $1,500 *free of charge*. But tens of millions of people who are eligible for this free money choose not to accept it, either because they don't contribute to their 401(k) plan at all or because they don't contribute enough to qualify for a full employer match.

Certainly some people fail to contribute because they don't know how the plans work or because they cannot spare a dime from their salary. Mostly, though, this mistake can be blamed on loss aversion and the endowment effect. Parting with money today is experienced as a loss, or out-of-pocket cost, and is therefore hard to do. At the same time, future benefits from doing so are experienced as foregone gains and therefore relatively easy to ignore. Stated differently, people overvalue what they have (today's salary) and fail to properly value what they could have (employee matches and the benefits of tax-deferred savings).

ANYTHING BUT SORRY

Suppose Fred owns $1,000 worth of stock in Toyota. A trusted friend suggests that Fred sell it and buy $1,000 of Ford stock. Fred does not sell, and over the next year Toyota's share price drops 30 percent, turning his $1,000 holding into a $700 investment.

Now suppose that Wilma owns $1,000 worth of Ford stock. During the same period, a trusted friend of hers suggests that she sell her shares and buy $1,000 worth of Toyota. She does this, and over the next year Toyota's share price drops 30 percent, turning Wilma's $1,000 investment into a $700 investment stake in Toyota.

Who do you think feels worse, Fred or Wilma?

The last piece of the puzzle that we call decision paralysis is a concept that may be the easiest to understand, given its everyday emotional resonance. In many ways, it is a concept that envelops much of prospect theory and its related tendencies—loss aversion, the status quo bias, and the endowment effect. The idea, which behavioral economists call "regret aversion," is as simple as it sounds. Most people want to avoid the pain of regret and the responsibility for negative outcomes. And to the extent that decisions to act—decisions to change the status quo—impart a higher level of responsibility than decisions to do nothing, people are averse to sticking their necks out and setting themselves up for feelings of regret. Or worse. If you think about it, the status quo bias likely had powerful advantages in human evolution. Imagine a long-ago group of our ancestors walking in a field. They're used to eating blueberries, which are tasty and nutritious, but they're also a little bored with them. Suddenly our forefathers and mothers happen up on some unfamiliar red berries, and are faced with a quandary: be the first to eat the berries, which could be delicious, but risk being the first to die, since they could also be poisonous. The prevalence of the status quo bias today suggests that we are all descended from people who ate the new berries—but only after someone else tried them first.

And that's why most people, when evaluating whether Fred or Wilma feels worse about the decline in Toyota's stock price, assume that Wilma would be more unhappy than Fred. After all, Wilma took action that resulted in her losing money, while Fred did nothing—or at least seemed to do nothing. There's no question that both investors probably feel lousy, but the assumption is that Wilma will kick herself harder. She is likely to castigate herself with thoughts of "This need not have happened" or "I brought this on myself." And that feeling of regret is one that people will often go to great lengths to avoid.

They might even pay for it. Richard Thaler, in a 1980 paper published in the *Journal of Economic Behavior and Organization*, offered the following hypothetical to make the point:

Mr. A is waiting in line at a movie theater. When he gets to the ticket window, he is told that as the one-hundred-thousandth customer of the theater, he has just won $100.

Mr. B is waiting in line at a different theater. The man in front of him wins $1,000 for being the one-millionth customer of the theater. Mr. B wins $150.

Who would you rather be, Mr. A or Mr. B?

Incredibly, writes Thaler, many people would actually prefer Mr. A's position (up $100) to that of Mr. B (up $150)! The reason is regret aversion. These souls would feel so bad about missing out on the $1,000 prize that they would effectively pay $50 to avoid regret over having been a step late to the theater.

This isn't surprising. Knowingly or not, you probably pay good money all the time to avoid feelings of regret or to otherwise maintain the status quo. Leaving money in a bank account rather than putting the cash in an investment with a higher return; staying in a relatively low-paying job rather than making a switch to one with a higher salary; failing to sell an investment only to see it drop in price (selling it with the crowd only to see it rise); delaying a purchase only to see the price rise; keeping revolving balances on a high-rate credit card rather than switching to one with lower finance charges: All of these inactions are examples of the ways that regret aversion, decision paralysis, and the status quo bias combine to influence your financial decisions and to cost you money.

One last thought about regret. The claim that people have a particularly acute fear of regrettable action may not feel right to you. Your own biggest regrets, for example, may

CALLING ALL STUDENTS!

Regret aversion is at the root of costly conventional wisdom among test takers: the idea that you shouldn't change a doubted answer because your first instinct is usually correct. That's what 75 percent of students at the University of Illinois at Urbana-Champaign thought a few years back when surveyed by two professors at the school, psychologists Justin Kruger and Derrick Wirtz, and their colleague Dale Miller of Stanford University. But Kruger and colleagues examined test results of those students and found that when they changed an answer, it was more often than not the smart move: Half the time the first answer was wrong and the second answer was correct, and in only 25 percent of switches did students go from correct to wrong answer. So why do most people think changing is bad? In related experiments, Kruger and colleagues showed that students felt the pain of switching to a wrong answer more than answering incorrectly and staying put. Such "counterfactual thinking"—aka "if only . . ." thinking—is more memorable for most people than a successful answer change, and thus a major contributor to regret aversion. But you heard it here first: When in doubt, change your answer.

involve things you have failed to do. Or you may recall the words of John Greenleaf Whittier, who wrote, "For of all sad words of tongue or pen, the saddest are these: 'It might have been!'" A valid point, to be sure. In fact, Tom has conducted research indicating that most people's biggest regrets in life center around things they have failed to do. Not spending enough time with the kids. Not taking a career more seriously. Not reconciling with a now-departed relative. But note that these regrets take time to develop and are unlike the pain of losing money by switching one stock for another, a pain that descends immediately. Tom's research indicates that people experience more regret over their mistakes of action in the short term, while regrets of inaction are more painful in the long run. The evidence thus reinforces the wisdom of Mark Twain, who said, "Twenty years from now you will be more disappointed by the things you didn't do than by the ones you did do."

HOW TO THINK AND WHAT TO DO

Warning Signs

You might suffer from decision paralysis if . . .

- you have a hard time choosing among investment options.
- you don't contribute to retirement plans at work.
- you tend to beat yourself up when your decisions turn out poorly.
- you frequently buy things that offer "trial periods"—but infrequently take advantage and return them.
- you delay making investment or spending decisions.

We need to be careful in offering advice on how to deal with decision paralysis. After all, caution can be as much a positive force in your life as a negative influence, if it keeps you from making unwise decisions rather than beneficial ones. Only *you* can determine if an inability to pull the trigger on decisions costs or saves you money. But if you perceive choice conflict as a problem for you, here are seven helpful ideas to keep in mind:

Choose fewer choices. So now you know: The more good choices you have, the less likely you are to choose—and the less satisfied you'll be even if you do manage to decide. One way to avoid a lot of this pain is to limit your choice sets. There are a lot of ways to do this, but the one we like is this: Find someone

you trust and who knows or is willing to research the subject of your decision. Then ask your "trusted screener" to offer you three options from which to choose. Gary uses this
strategy with one of his nephews, and invariably he is given
three solid options to choose from and feels confident with
his final pick—at the time and down the road.

Remember: deciding not to decide is a decision. Postponement, delay, procrastination. They may seem like the path of least resistance,
but a passive approach to decision making can be as conse-
quential as any other choice. Every time you decide to maintain the status quo is really a vote of confidence for the way
you've been doing things. Is that confidence warranted?

Don't forget opportunity costs. Gary's former colleague at *Money,* the
financial writer Jason Zweig, likes to remind people that
someone who invested in a lousy stock mutual fund fifteen
years ago—and stuck with it—is probably better off today
than someone who didn't invest in stocks at all. Our point
here is this: Even if a financial decision is not perfect (most
aren't), it may still leave you in a better position than if you'd
done nothing. When mulling money decisions, you're more
than likely to pay too much attention to what you have now
than what you might have down the road. And because of
the status quo bias and regret aversion, you're more likely
to focus on the ways in which your decision to spend or invest can make you feel bad for having undertaken change.
*To combat these tendencies, imagine how you'd feel if a pro-
active step you are considering worked out—but you didn't
take the chance.* Think how you'd feel if that investment rose
in price as you thought it might, or if the price of that stereo
went up 10 percent by the time you realized that you really
do want better sound quality. The imaginary feelings of re-

gret you may conjure up could help you overcome your real-life resistance to change.

Put yourself on autopilot. Instead of having to make an endless series of decisions about whether now is a good time to invest, use dollar cost averaging. This is a strategy that involves investing a set amount of money at regular intervals in a stock or bond or mutual fund—regardless of whether the markets are rising or falling. In this way, you end up buying fewer shares when the price of an investment is high and more when the price is lower. Similarly, people who have trouble controlling their spending can have their mortgage payment—most any payment, really—deducted from their bank account so they'll never have to "choose" between making a loan payment or spending that money on something else.

Make deadlines work for you. Dan Ariely has run some of the most creative experiments in behavioral economics, and one of his better ones—in terms of suggesting practical advice for decision paralysis sufferers—concerns deadlines. In brief, Ariely and his colleagues experimented with different deadline structures for three classes: Students in one class could turn in three required papers at the end of the semester; students in a second class could choose any three deadlines for their papers during the semester but faced grade-lowering penalties for lateness; and students in a third class had three equally spaced deadlines given to them by their teacher. All the papers, by the way, would be graded at the end of semester. So which students did best on all the papers? Those in the class with equally spaced deadlines handed down by the teacher. Our point here is obvious: A good way to overcome decision paralysis is to set deadlines, but an even better way is to give someone you trust the power to pick those deadlines for you. In the penultimate chapter of this book, we'll discuss other ways to motivate yourself toward desired goals, but involving other people in order to limit your ability to get in your own way is a good start. Even if a friend doesn't have the power of a professor over you, the fear of disappointing her or looking bad is a powerful motivator.

Play your own devil's advocate. A simple way to make decisions more easily is to change your frame of reference. One method we have found helpful is to approach decisions from a neutral state. In other words, force yourself to imagine that you're starting from ground zero rather than from a status quo position. For example, in the Ford/Toyota scenario mentioned earlier, Fred probably approached his choice as a decision to stick with or abandon his stock in Toyota. A more helpful way to have evaluated his choice would be to imagine that his money was invested in neither stock. His decision would then be this: In which automobile maker do I want to invest, Ford or Toyota? In most cases such an approach would allow Fred to evaluate the two companies on their merits, rather than weighting the evaluation in favor of Toyota because it occupied the status quo position.

Another way to alter your decision-making frame is to reverse the choice perspective. That is, turn a decision of which option to reject into one of which option to select, and vice versa. This should help you focus on both the positive and negative attributes of your options, rather than give too much weight to one or the other. For example, if you're deciding among investment options and you find yourself unable to choose which one you prefer, ask yourself instead which options you would in no instance choose. Or, assume instead that you already own all the choices. Now your decision becomes which one to sell—which ones you definitely do not want to own. This is pretty simple. The hard part is recognizing that your decision is hampered by the way you're viewing the problem to begin with.

If you're not an expert, ask one. In the main, your authors probably lean toward a satisficing approach to decision making, but the endowment effect can wreak havoc on people who have too little experience. Consider a real-life experiment conducted in 2003 by economist John A. List, who recruited visitors to a sports card fair to learn something about the effects of expertise. In exchange for agreeing to fill out a questionnaire, participants received a moderately valuable sports card. After filling in their answers, they were offered the chance to switch for a card of comparable value. List expected people to switch roughly half the time, since the values were roughly equal. In reality, participants with below-average trading experience switched less than 10 percent of the time, but those with significant trading experience switched 46.7 percent of time, pretty much as List predicted.

The lesson here? When you know a subject cold, you are better situated to properly evaluate the issue at hand and at least in part remove yourself and some of your biases from the equation. But when you are out of your element, that's all the more reason to call on experts you trust for help.

4

NUMBER NUMBNESS

In a memorable episode of *The Simpsons,* Homer's boss, Mr. Burns, wants his plant's softball team to defeat the squad of a rival. To aid in that effort, he hires a sports psychologist, who hypnotizes Homer's team in a bid to extract maximum performance.

> *Psychologist:* You are all very good players.
> *Team (in trancelike tones):* We are all very good players.
> *Psychologist:* You will beat Shelbyville.
> *Team:* We will beat Shelbyville.
> *Psychologist:* You will give 110 percent.
> *Team (still in trance):* That's impossible. No one can give more than 100 percent. By definition, that is the most anyone can give.

We trust that the reader is every bit as savvy as Homer and his teammates and is thus annoyed by sportscasters who mention athletes whose efforts exceed 100 percent. Nevertheless, the episode does illustrate an important truism about the human condition—people have trouble with numbers. And although you doubtless did well on this particular example, there are some surprising facts about mathematics that confound almost everyone. Of course, we're hardly the first to reach this conclusion. In his wonderful book *Innumeracy: Mathematical Illiteracy and Its Consequences,* the mathematician John Allen Paulos notes that "some of the blocks to dealing comfortably with numbers and probabilities are due to quite natural psychological responses to uncertainty, to coincidence, or to how a problem is framed. Others can be attributed to anxiety, or to romantic misconceptions about the nature and importance of mathematics." Our task here is to explain how innumeracy—defined by *Webster's* as an "ignorance of mathematics"—has practical and negative consequences for your finances, and to show how you can avoid them. We'll do that by focusing on three issues, although we could probably fill a book about the ways in which ignorance of numbers can affect (and afflict) your life.

The first issue is the tendency to ignore inflation, thanks to a psychological phenomenon known as the "money illusion." Next we'll have some fun with probabilities, and we'll show how failing to understand the role of odds and chance in life can lead you to make unwise investment and spending decisions. Finally we'll tackle what, for lack of a better phrase, we call the "bigness bias," or the way in which indifference to small numbers can cost big bucks, especially over time.

HOME AT LAST

In three successive years, Peter, Paul, and Mary each bought a home that cost $200,000, and each ended up selling their home one year later. During Peter's year of homeownership, the country experienced a period of 25 percent deflation—that is, the average price of all goods and services in the United States fell by 25 percent—and Peter sold his house for $154,000, or 23 percent less than he paid. During the twelve months that Paul owned his home, the situation was reversed: The average cost of goods and services actually rose 25 percent, and Paul eventually sold his home for $246,000, or 23 percent more than he paid. As for Mary, the cost of living during her yearlong stretch of owning a home stayed pretty much the same, but she ended up selling her house for $196,000, or 2 percent less than she paid. Soon after, the three friends met for a drink, but their bonhomie ended in anger when they couldn't agree on the answer to what seemed a simple question: Factoring in the changes in overall consumer prices, which of the three came out the best in their home sales?

Not sure yourself who fared best? Not quite sure you even want to figure it out? Several years ago the psychologist Eldar Shafir conducted a study in which participants were presented with just such a story and then asked to evaluate how each seller fared—relative to each other and keeping in mind the state of the economy in general. Interestingly, most participants thought Paul (who notched a 23 percent gain during a period when the average price of goods rose 25 percent) came out on top and Peter (a 23 percent loss in a period when average prices *fell* 25 percent) fared worst. These majority conclusions are interesting, of course, because they're wrong. In reality, Peter fared much better; he was the only homeowner who made money. When inflation is accounted for, he registered a 2 percent gain in buying power, while both Paul and Mary posted a 2 percent loss. In other words, although Paul received 23 percent more dollars for his home when he sold it than when he bought it, what those dollars could actually buy during his year of ownership declined by 25 percent. Peter, on the other hand, received 23 percent less upon selling than he'd shelled out a year earlier, but the overall decline in prices was actually 25 percent. Although a dollar's worth of goods or services last year could now be purchased for seventy-five cents, Peter received seventy-seven cents for every dollar he had spent on his home a year earlier. So Peter's buying power increased even as the average person's decreased.

By failing to grasp this complicated distinction, participants in Shafir's study fell victim to what behavioral economists call the "money illusion." This involves confusion between "nominal" changes in money (greater or lesser numbers of actual dollars) and "real" changes (greater or lesser buying power) that reflect inflation or, more rarely these days, deflation. It's understandable, for a couple of reasons. First, accounting for inflation requires the application of arithmetic, which is often annoying and downright impossible for many people. Second, inflation today, at least in the United States, is an incremental affair—2 percent to 4 percent, on average, over the past decade and a half. As we've touched on already in our discussion of mental accounting in Chapter 1—and as we'll delve into more deeply later in this chapter—little numbers are easy to discount or ignore. We suspect, though we don't know, that had Shafir conducted his study in certain Latin American or Eastern European countries, where double-digit or even triple-digit inflation has often been the norm, he might have found that participants were not as prone to the money illusion.

But most people *we* know routinely fail to consider the effects of inflation in their financial decisions, a gaffe that has myriad and negative short-term and long-term implications. For now, we'll focus on three. First, the money illusion is dangerous because failing to grasp inflation's effects may lead you to underestimate how much money you'll require to meet future needs such as retirement or college. For example, a person who invests $10,000 today in the stock market will have about $67,000 in twenty years, assuming a 10 percent average annual return, whereas a person who invests $10,000 in U.S. Treasury bonds earning 6 percent a year will have about $32,000. Many people, of course, willingly give up the greater returns—and the ups and downs—of stocks in exchange for the ironclad security of government bonds. After all, $32,000 is still a lot of money—at least, that is, until inflation takes its toll. Consider: Assuming average annual price hikes of 4 percent, the above stock investor would have the equivalent of $32,000 in today's buying power after two decades had passed. The bond investor, though, would have less than $15,000. That's the irony of a so-called conservative investment strategy: It may be more risky to leave yourself vulnerable to the ravages of inflation than it is to subject yourself to the hills and valleys of the stock market.

A related way in which the money illusion plays tricks with finances is by providing a false sense of history, a sort of 20/20 hindsight. Consider residential real estate. For longer than we can remember, a rule of thumb for home buyers has been to buy the biggest home possible—any home, really, even if you have to stretch—on the logic that rising home prices will reward owners later with a tremendous return on their investment. This bedrock belief that home values always appreciate—and that residential real estate is perhaps the best investment an individual can make— crystallized during a relatively short but dramatic period in the late 1970s when home prices skyrocketed. What most people forget or ignore, however, is that inflation during that period was soaring as well. Of course, home prices were rising like soufflés; the price of everything was skyrocketing. As Yale University economics professor Robert J. Shiller has said: "Since people are likely to remember the price they paid for their house from many years ago but remember few other prices from then, they have the mistaken impression that home prices have gone up more than other prices, giving a mistakenly exaggerated impression of the investment potential of houses."

This was driven home in spades by recent events in the housing market in the United States and elsewhere. The housing bubble that, once punctured, sent the world's economies and stock markets into a tizzy was the result of forces having nothing to do with the virtues of home ownership, but rather were a result of banks and other financial institutions making too much money available to borrowers. With so many buyers flush with borrowed cash, the prices of all investment assets reached crazy highs, home prices chief among them. Certainly we're not advising people to sell their house (or avoid buying one) and pour *all* their money into the stock market. But to the extent that people have counted on residential real estate to build wealth . . . well, that's just another example of how the money illusion can cloud your vision and hurt your pocketbook.

Our final example of the deleterious effects of the money

illusion is an example of how inflation, in one form or another, can lead us to foolish or irrational behavior. This is just supposition, but we suspect that many of the wild swings of stock prices in recent years (and the media frenzy that seems to go along with them) are a direct result of the tremendous appreciation of share prices in recent years. Most investors (professional and amateur) have not adjusted their psychology to account for seemingly larger swings in prices. That is, in 1987, a two-hundred-point swing in the Dow Jones Industrial Average was equal to a 10 percent change in value. Today, with the benchmark stock average trading near nine thousand, the same two-hundred-point swing is equivalent to a less significant 2 percent change in price. Yet a form of the money illusion causes people to react to the nominal changes in price as opposed to the more meaningful percentage change. Fueled by a media that also falls prey to this illusion, investors often react irrationally and inappropriately, which causes a cascade of further irrational and inappropriate reactions. We'll talk more about such chain reactions later on, but the money illusion certainly plays a part in the psychology of the markets.

ODDS ARE YOU DON'T KNOW WHAT THE ODDS ARE

Steve, a thirty-year-old American, has been described by a former neighbor as follows: "Steve is very shy and withdrawn, invariably helpful, but with little real interest in people or the social world. A meek and tidy soul, he has a need for order and structure and a passion for detail." Which occupation is Steve currently more likely to have: that of a salesman or that of a librarian?

If you're like most people—at least like most of the people to whom Richard Thaler has put this question over the years—you cast your vote for Librarian Steve. After all, aren't librarians shy and reserved, while salespeople are sociable extroverts? Maybe, maybe not. But without even debating the merits of these stereotypes, there's a more fundamental reason why choosing books over sales as Steve's profession may be wrongheaded. There are more than 16 million salespeople in the United States, but only 197,000 librarians. Sure, a neighbor described Steve in a way that seems to make him ill-suited for a life of sales, but one person's opinion hardly outweighs the fact that, on statistical grounds, Steve is more than eighty times more likely to be a salesman than a librarian. And while most people don't have easy access to Bureau of Labor Statistics data, the notion that salespeople far outnumber librarians is probably obvious to you—as is the idea that among the millions of people in sales, there are probably hundreds of thousands who don't match the conventional image of that profession. Given how little you really know about Steve, the fact that more people tend to be in sales than in stacks should be the major determinant in assessing the odds that Steve is a librarian.

This tendency to disregard or discount overall odds is what Daniel Kahneman and Amos Tversky called "neglecting the base rate." In our example, it's related to the representativeness heuristic discussed earlier in the book, whereby people assume commonality between objects or ideas of similar appearance. As mental shortcuts go, assuming that a shy person who doesn't like people but loves order is a librarian won't get you into too much trouble, even if you don't factor in employment data. But there are lots of ways that neglecting the base rate can be costly. Buying a lottery ticket is a classic example, since the odds are greatly against your picking the right combination of numbers. Still, in falling prey to Powerball fever, you are likely ignoring the base rate *knowingly*—few people really believe they'll win. That's fine; everyone has their vices.

Even with lotteries, though, it is tough to grasp how high the odds against you really are. For example, in a lottery in which six numbers are selected out of fifty, what are the chances that the six numbers will be 1, 2, 3, 4, 5, and 6? Most people would say that such an outcome is never going to happen, which, although an exaggeration, does capture the long odds against such an occurrence. It's important to note, however, that the odds of 1 through 6 being selected are the same as the odds of *any* six numbers being selected. It doesn't seem right, but it is.

Another reason it can be tough to get an accurate picture of the true probabilities is that exceptions to the over-

---

ADVICE FOR LOTTERY LOVERS

We don't think lotteries are a very smart use of your cash, but if you mean to play, we want to make you smart gamblers. And most people aren't. In a 1994 examination of the "gambler's fallacy"—the false notion behind the common belief that, say, three heads in a row means a flipped coin is "due" to come up tails—the economist Dek Terrell found that payouts in New Jersey's pick-three numbers game were about 33 percent higher than average for numbers that had come up one or two weeks prior. Since lotteries are pari-mutuel pools (the fewer people who pick the winning number the higher the individual payouts), that means fewer gamblers chose those numbers because they thought the chances were extra slim that they would win again so soon. That's the gambler's fallacy in action. Just because a set of numbers wins on Tuesday doesn't mean the odds of it winning the following Wednesday are any lower. They are the same as always.

all odds are often more easily called to mind. That's why so many swimmers avoided the beach after the movie *Jaws* came out in 1975. Though fewer than seventy shark attacks had occurred in U.S. waters during the previous decade—and despite the fact that the odds against being attacked by a shark were enormous—Americans were inordinately terrified of toothy predators that summer. That's also why, after the stock market crash of 1987, many investors stopped investing in stock mutual funds for the next eighteen months or so, opting instead for cash or bonds. These folks ignored the base rate—the overwhelming historical evidence that stocks significantly outperform bonds—and focused instead on a memorable event that was more easily called to mind but highly anomalous. The same phenomenon is evident as this book is being written.

Ignoring the base rate, particularly because of a misguided reliance on memorable events or on inconclusive information, contributes in a variety of ways to poor financial decisions. We say "contributes," by the way, because few financial decisions, good or bad, are the result of one and only one behavioral-economic bad habit. For example, thousands of otherwise sane amateur investors throw away good money each year in the commodities markets—you know, soybean futures and the like—because of the confluence of several tendencies. These include a mistaken overconfidence in their own abilities to forecast weather on the Great Plains and a willingness to be led astray by the opinions and recommendations of others. But, knowingly or not, these investors are also guilty of ignoring the base rate. They disregard (or may be unaware of) the evidence that an estimated three out of four investors—both amateur and professional—lose money when they trade commodities.

Insurance is yet another area in which people routinely

ignore the base rate and, thus, spend money needlessly. We're talking here about wedding insurance, flight insurance, dread disease insurance, and the like, interest in which is caused by notable but ultimately insignificant news or media events (a plane crash or a movie about the latest killer virus) that lead us to believe these calamities are more common than they are. We're not saying that the Ebola virus or cancer won't kill you or a loved one; we're simply saying that (unless there's a specific genetic reason to think otherwise) the base rate odds that it will are so long, it makes very little sense to buy a specific policy to cover the eventuality. Insurance is one of those areas where behavioral-economic biases can work most powerfully. Consider a recent series of experiments by Israeli psychologist Orit E. Tykocinski.

RAISE YOUR DEDUCTIBLE, RAISE YOUR SAVINGS

Consumers routinely neglect the base rate when they insist on buying insurance policies—home, health, auto—with very low deductibles because they assume the chances that they will have to file a claim are greater than they are. Consider homeowners' insurance. A higher deductible would reduce premiums on most policies by an average of 10 to 25 percent. But people forgo these savings because they fear having to pay a large chunk of out-of-pocket costs if they have to file a claim. They ignore the low odds they'll ever have to (about one in ten in any given year). Assuming the average insurance consumer raises her homeowners' policy deductible from $250 to $1,000, and assuming her annual premium falls 25 percent from $500 to $375, her total premium savings over the course of ten years would be $1,250 ($125 yearly savings times ten years). Even if she files a claim that requires her to pay the full deductible, her savings during those ten years would be $500: $1,250 in premium savings minus the $750 difference between the $250 and $1,000 deductibles.

In one, participants who were reminded that they were covered by medical insurance believed they were less likely to suffer health problems than people who were not reminded. But in a second study, participants who were prompted to remember that they *didn't* have auto insurance were more likely than insured participants to think that a car accident or other travel-related mishap was in their future. Simply being presented with the possibility that you *could* be insured evokes the kind of powerful counterfactual thinking we discussed in Chapter 3. This "if only" thinking inflates your assessment of the odds of an event for which you are not insured occurring.

The final point we need to make while discussing odds is the role of chance in everyday life. Or, more specifically, the tendency to underestimate the role of chance in everyday life. As is our wont, we'll begin our lesson with a little fantasy.

> *Imagine you're the coach of a basketball team. There are ten seconds left in the game and your team is down by a basket. Your star player, who over the course of his five-year career has made 55 percent of his shots, is only two for ten on the night, missing several wide-open jump shots. Another veteran player on your team has made his previous ten shots, even though his five-year career shooting percentage is just 45 percent. To whom would you give the ball for the last shot of the game?*

We suspect that the majority of sports fans, and nearly everyone else as well, would probably give the ball to the player who has made ten shots in a row. Their thinking—shared by most players, coaches, and announcers—is that this player has what is often called the "hot hand." But this notion, one of the core beliefs in sports, does not hold up to scrutiny. Several years ago, Tom (along with Amos Tversky and then Stanford graduate student Robert Vallone) examined this belief by analyzing the field-goal records of the Philadelphia 76ers and three other professional basketball teams. Without spending too much time on the details of their research, the inescapable conclusion from the evidence was this: Regardless of how many shots a player has made or missed in a row, the odds that he will make or miss his next shot are the same as you would expect from his overall, career-long shooting average. That is, a 55 percent career shooter is more likely to hit any given shot, regardless of his previous short-term history, than is a 45 percent shooter, regardless of his previous short-term performance. This presumes, of course, that no exceptional factors are at work—the 45 percent career shooter would have a better chance of making a layup than the 55 percent shooter would have of making a much harder three-point shot.

When this research was first made public—the *New York Times* sports page devoted a great deal of space to the matter—it was greeted with heated opposition within the sports world. People were, and still are, unwilling to believe that the hot hand is a myth. One way to understand it is to think of a series of coin flips. The odds that a coin will come up heads on any given flip are 50 percent; there's a one-in-two chance. Most people know this. Yet if you flip a coin twenty times in a row—try this at home; it's safe—there is an 80 percent chance that you will get three heads or three tails in a row during the series. There is also a 50 percent chance of getting four in a row and a 25 percent chance of a streak of five. But at any given point in this series, even after several heads in a row, the odds that the next flip will be heads are exactly the same as they ever were—50 percent.

Similarly, what happens in basketball, and in many other sports, is that in a given series of shots, there are bound to be "three or four heads in a row," or a streak of random hits or misses. Before any given shot, however, the odds that a player will make or miss the basket will roughly conform to his or her overall long-term average.

To some extent, the problems you might have in understanding the myth of the hot hand reflect the difficulty most people have with probability and statistics. Indeed, some of the greatest mathematical minds in the world can be tripped up by paradoxes of probability, as was made clear a while back by, of all people, Monty Hall, host of the classic television show *Let's Make a Deal*. Here's what happened: In September 1990, *Parade* magazine columnist Marilyn vos Savant—listed in the *Guinness Book of World Records* as having the world's highest IQ—published the following question from one of her readers:

> *Suppose you're on a game show, and you're given the choice of three doors. Behind one door is a car; behind the others, goats. You pick a door, say, No. 1, and the host, who knows what's behind the doors, opens another door, say, No. 3, which has a goat. He then says to you, "Do you want to pick door No. 2?" Is it to your advantage to take the switch?*

After vos Savant published her answer—saying that it's wise to switch—she was besieged by thousands of letters. These writers, whose ranks included mathematics professors from numerous universities, contended that the world's smartest person had it all wrong. The choice between Door 1 and Door 2, they said, was a clear case of even odds—a fifty-fifty chance that the contestant had picked correctly or incorrectly. Because the car is not behind Door number three, they reasoned, it is equally likely to be behind Door 1 or 2. One professor remarked, "As a professional mathematician, I'm very concerned with the general public's lack of mathematical skills. Please help by confessing your error and, in the future, being more careful." Another reported, "Our math department had a good self-righteous laugh at your expense." A third suggested, "There is enough mathematical illiteracy in this country, and we don't need the world's highest IQ propagating more."

But it was they who were propagating misinformation. Ms. vos Savant was correct. When the contestant chose Door 1 initially, the odds that it shielded the car were one in three—there were three doors, and behind only one of them was a car. Those odds do not change after Monty Hall reveals a goat behind Door 3. After all, Monty would never open a door to reveal the car—that would ruin the drama—and at least one of the doors not chosen by the contestant is hiding a goat. Put another way, chances are that when the contestant made his or her original choice, that pick was a goat. *That fact doesn't change when there are only two doors from which to choose,* since the original choice was among three doors (two of which shielded a goat). So, assuming the contestant picked a goat (since there was a two-in-three chance that he in fact did), what Monty does by revealing the other goat is to let the contestant know where, in all likelihood, the car is stashed: behind Door 2.

Here's one more way of thinking about it. Imagine three playing cards laying facedown on the table, two black (representing the goats) and one red (the car). Now imagine that you pick one of the cards. At that moment, would you bet that you had picked a black or red card? Assuming you answered black, since the odds are two to one that you picked the darker color, you must now assume that of the two remaining cards, one is black and one is red. If you are then shown a black card (by someone who knows the color of each), the only logical conclusion, based on the probability that you picked the other black card to begin with, is that the remaining card is red. In fact, sixty-seven times out of one hundred you would be wiser to switch when offered the chance—unless, of course, you prefer goats over cars.

Whether you understand the *Let's Make a Deal* conundrum or not, it is our belief that most folks don't understand the role of chance in everyday life. Tom proves this point to his students in the following way. He asks each member of the class to write down a mock series of twenty random coin flips and to represent that series on a piece of paper using Xs and Os for heads and tails, respectively. One student, however, is told to actually flip a coin twenty times and write down his or her results. The challenge for Tom, who leaves the classroom during this exercise, is to examine the evidence upon his return and determine which among the many pieces of paper contained the results of the real-life coin flips. Invariably, Tom manages to identify the real-life coin flips. How? The real series of flips nearly always contains the longest streak of either heads or tails, perhaps looking something like this actual series of flips: OXXXXXOXOOXOOXOOXOOX. The *imagined* series of flips, meanwhile, often look like this: XXOXOOOXOOXOXXOOXXOO. The students, like most everyone else, underestimate the likelihood that chance will result in long strings of heads or tails, so they don't write down any such streaks. But while it is true that in the long run the number of heads and tails will even out—as is the case in the first sequence listed above (go ahead and check)—it is also true that there will be random instances of bunching. More important, this is also true in a variety of circumstances in life in which chance plays a surprisingly significant role.

One especially relevant example is investment performance, or more specifically the performance of mutual funds. It's true that some mutual funds outperform their peers and the market in general over time because the funds' managers have superior investment skills. But it is also true that no formula has been found to identify those brilliant managers (who are a rare breed indeed: Over periods of a decade or more, roughly three-fourths of all stock funds will underperform the market). More important, it's also true that past performance, at least in the short run, cannot be counted on as an indication that the mutual fund is being run by an above-average manager. Even bad fund managers will, by dint of chance, "come up heads" several years in a row— that is, they'll enjoy a prolonged series of investment successes that are just as much a function of luck as skill. In fact, University of Wisconsin finance professor Werner De Bondt estimated that more than 10 percent of stock mutual funds are likely to beat the average performance of the average equity fund three years in a row, *just as a matter of chance*.

In some parts of the country, folks would explain this by using an aphorism: Even a blind squirrel finds an acorn or two once in a while. Even a lousy mutual fund manager will make a few smart investments every now and then. For investors, though, the implications should be startling. It means that even a solid record of above-average performance could simply reflect a string of two or three years of especially superior results that may have been the product not of investment acumen, but of random luck. Would you bet your retirement savings on that possibility? Most people do just that. A study by Columbia University business professor Noel Capon and two colleagues found that the single most common criterion people use to select mutual funds is past performance. That's the case even though many studies have shown that, at least in the world of mutual funds, past performance offers little in the way of reliable guidance about future results.

THE BIGNESS BIAS

Meet Jill and John, twenty-one-year-old twins who just graduated from college. Jill, immediately upon entering the workforce, began contributing $50 a month to a stock mutual fund and continued to do so for the next eight years, until she got married and found more pressing uses for her money. John, who married his college sweetheart immediately upon graduating and soon after started a family, didn't start investing until he was twenty-nine. Then he, too, contributed $50 a month to the same stock fund, and he continued doing so for thirty-seven years until he retired at age sixty-five. All told, John invested $22,200, while Jill contributed just $4,800. At age sixty-five, which of the two siblings had the most money assuming they earned an average of 10 percent a year?

By now, no doubt, you've got the hang of the little italicized scenarios that we present to you: The seemingly obvious answer is almost always wrong. In this instance, that means Jill is the sibling who ends up with the most money upon retirement—$256,650, vs. $217,830 for John. The reason, of course, is that John could never make up for the extra eight years that Jill's money was growing while he tended to other matters. Gary has offered this problem to hundreds of people over the years, and folks usually get the answer wrong. They assume incorrectly for a number of reasons, including a failure to understand the benefits of compound earnings over time (sort of a happy mirror image of the deleterious effects of inflation over time). But we think another contributing factor is the tendency to pay more attention to big numbers and to give less weight to smaller figures. So Jill's eight years of contributions pale against John's thirty-seven years, while John's $22,200 in annual total contributions dwarf Jill's $4,800.

If this notion—that people tend to discount the importance of small numbers—strikes you as being related to the concept of mental accounting, we couldn't be happier: You're starting to think like a behavioral economist. What makes the story of Jill and John especially meaningful, however, is that it drives home the point that failing to take small numbers seriously can have profound effects when stretched out over time. It's one thing to tack on a $500 stereo when buying a new car; such things happen infrequently enough. But it's another thing to incur small expenses or small losses repeatedly over a long period; such things add up. In everyday life, you can call this the Starbucks effect: People are routinely surprised to realize, when they do the math, that they're spending more than $1,000 a year for their morning cup of coffee. In personal finance, this mistake shows up most often and (most obviously) in the surprisingly poor performance of individual investors who trade stocks or bonds frequently: Too often their gross profits are eroded by the commissions or transaction costs they incur with each trade. Although seemingly small, these trading costs eat away profits.

A similar phenomenon is seen in mutual funds, where the research costs, salaries, and other management expenses of a fund are represented as something called an expense ratio (fund operators are required by law to make this information public). Expense ratios from stock mutual funds range from as low as a fifth of 1 percent (of fund assets) to more than 3 percent, depending on the kinds of securities the fund buys (foreign stocks, for example, are more expensive to trade than U.S. shares) and the greediness of the fund operator. The expense ratio tells you how much the fund operator will subtract from your account every year. For example, a 2.50 percent expense ratio means the fund operator will rake off $2.50 from every $100 you have in the fund.

Given these seemingly small numbers, many if not most investors disregard a fund's expense ratio when choosing among the thousands of options available today. Big mistake, particularly over time. Consider: At this writing, the average expense ratio for all diversified U.S. stock mutual funds is around 1.5 percent. Assuming a 10 percent gross average annual return and applying various levels of expenses, we can highlight the effects of such costs over time. On a $10,000 starting investment, for example, an expense ratio of 0.5 percent will cost an investor $181 over three years, while a 1 percent ratio will double that figure to $360 and a 1.5 percent expense tab will cost you upward of $538. And these differences grow more dramatic as the years go by. Over fifteen years, for example, a low-expense fund will eat up less than 7 percent of your potential investment return, while a high-expense fund will devour almost 20 percent!

$10,000 invested in . . .	After three years	After five years	After fifteen years
High-cost mutual fund	$12,772	$15,036	$33,997
Low-cost fund	$13,129	$15,742	$39,013

Assuming a 10 percent average annual return.

HOW TO THINK AND WHAT TO DO
Warning Signs

Number numbness may be leading you to money mistakes if . . .

- you invest in last year's hot mutual funds.
- you have very low insurance deductibles.
- you don't really understand the relationship between inflation and buying power.
- you invest without much concern about commission costs and management fees.
- you ignore the implications of compound interest and let your credit-card balances carry over.
- you don't really understand compound interest.

There's no easy way to turn you into an expert on probability theory or an Ivy League mathematician. But there are some hard-and-fast rules you can live by that will help you overcome the problems that number numbness may present.

Don't be impressed by short-term success. There are many reasons not to chase after last year's hot investment, be it a mutual fund, variable annuity, or the stock-picking success of a particular brokerage firm. But the most important reason is that there is no earthly way of discerning if one year's performance is meaningful at all. It may simply be a matter of luck. Indeed, even a ten-year record of above-average performance may reflect nothing more than one or two years of random success amid otherwise lackluster results. So when you are evaluating investments such as mutual funds or annuities, don't be swayed by one or two years of strong results. Even when you look at long-term performance, pay careful attention to year-by-year results. We're at least somewhat willing to be-lieve that ten years of leading the pack is less a matter of luck than skill. But watch out: The people responsible for the ten years of success may no longer be managing the fund.

Because chance plays a far greater role than you think in investment performance, you should play the averages. You might well ask how exactly we would have you pick investments—particularly mutual funds—if you can't use past performance as a guide. This ques-tion might be particularly vexing given that we view mutual funds as perhaps the best thing to have happened to inves-tors and savers since banks started giving away free toasters. The advantages of pooling your money with others to invest in a basket of diversified securities are myriad: a cheap way to spread out your risk (it would be prohibitively expensive for most investors to own shares in 180 different companies, which is what the typical U.S. stock mutual fund owns), pro-fessional management (the folks who run funds spend all day evaluating investments), and liquidity (you can generally get your money anytime you want).

That said, many people overestimate the likelihood that an individual fund manager will outperform his or her peers or the stock market in general. It's not so much that such brilliant stock pickers or bond mavens don't exist. Rather, the odds that you'll be able to identify them are small. We hope that's more obvious to you now that you understand why the performance numbers often used to promote and evaluate funds are much more the result of chance than you might have thought. Lucky for you if you manage to find an above-average fund manager. If not, you would probably have been better off just investing in the stock market in gen-eral. Which, as it turns out, is exactly what we're suggesting you do, through a kind of mutual fund that's become hugely popular in recent years—index funds. Index funds (forgive us if you know this) are essentially mutual funds that mirror the benchmark stock averages in different categories. The archetype is the S&P 500 index fund. This sort of vehicle simply invests proportionately in the shares of the five hundred stocks that make up this average, which is generally considered the best proxy for the U.S. stock market (unlike the Dow Jones Industrial Average, which represents only the shares of thirty large U.S. companies).

The idea behind index funds is that if you can't beat 'em, join 'em. If you can't guarantee that you'll find a mutual fund manager who will outperform the average fund manager or the average stock or bond index, then it's better to guarantee that you will at least keep up with the market as a whole by investing in an index fund. Today, by the way, all manner of index funds are available. In addition to ones that mirror the general performance of large U.S. companies (as represented by the S&P 500), there are index funds that mirror the performance of the international stock market, the U.S. bond market, the U.S. small-company stock market, and so on. Better still, because index funds don't require a lot of buying and selling—since the stocks in the indexes they attempt to mirror don't change that often—their expense ratios (and tax bills) are generally the lowest in the fund world. That's the icing on the cake—you virtually guarantee yourself better performance and more profits from the get-go because you've eliminated the high commission and management costs that other, more actively managed mutual funds can't help charging you.

Know when time is on your side and when it isn't. This is just our way of reminding you that it's too easy to overlook the deleterious effects that time, in the form of inflation, can have on buying power and to remind you that stocks have proven to be the best way to maintain buying power, given their long history of far outpacing the general rise in consumer prices. It's also a gentle reminder that it's smarter to start saving *as early as possible* for long-term goals, inasmuch as the longer your money has to earn interest and capital gains, the more you will have down the road. This works for borrowers, too. Imagine a consumer with an $8,000 credit-card balance who is being charged 16 percent annual interest and is making the minimum monthly payment ($200 to start). By paying $50 more than the minimum each month, this fellow will pay off his debt in three and a half years instead of nearly five and will save more than $1,000 in interest. It works the same for mortgage payments, too: If you tacked on an extra $50 to your regular monthly payments—assuming you pay $599 a month on a $100,000 thirty-year fixed-rate loan at 6 percent—you'd save around $24,000 in total interest and shorten your loan by more than five years.

Embrace the base rate. Recall our earlier discussion of how people neglect base rates much too readily. There are times, certainly, when it is okay to do so—base rates represent general odds, not certainties. There are occasional warm, sunny days in Minnesota during February, but good luck trying to predict them much in advance. If unusual meteorological indicators point to a stretch of warm weather, then fine, you might go ahead and send your winter coat to the dry cleaners. In the absence of such signs, though, it's best to keep the coat nearby. What this means is that your predictions or your bets—your investments—should follow the base rate unless you have a very good reason for them not to. This allows us to repeat the advice we've just given (pardon us, but the redundancy is worthwhile). Because of the historical superiority of stocks over alternative investment options, you should have a significant share (see the Rule of 100 in Chapter 2) of your investment portfolio in the stock market unless there is a compelling rationale for a different allocation of your resources. Also, because of the time-tested advantages of stock market index funds, you should be heavily invested in such funds unless you have a very compelling rationale . . . you get the idea.

Read the fine print. If you invest in mutual funds, pay close attention to their fee structures, which are clearly outlined in the prospectus that fund operators are bound by law to send you before they take your dough. As a rule, steer clear of funds that charge more than 1 percent or so in annual expenses. A half a percentage point or more may not seem like a big difference, but over time it will cost you thousands of dollars. And if you invest in shares of individual companies—something we discourage—remember that those transaction fees add up over time and cut into your profits. If your nest egg isn't growing as fast as your seemingly smart investing record would suggest, higher-than-expected trading costs may be one of the reasons. But only one. As you'll see in the next few chapters, you may not be as clever a stock picker as you think.

5

DROPPING ANCHOR

Which of the following guidebook descriptions for two restaurants sounds more appealing?

> *Restaurant A is one of the crème de la crème in the area. Dinner is served in a candlelit, romantic dining room with carved wooden ceilings, marble fireplaces, and tapestries on the wall. The menu includes veal marsala, beef tournedos, and scampi. The service is superb.*

> *Restaurant B, according to the guide, is one of the few in the area with a national reputation. It offers all the elements for a fine dining experience. The restaurant has a tastefully appointed dining room and a menu that focuses on seafood and veal but also features some delicious beef and poultry dishes. Entrées*

include lobster Newburg, veal Madeira, and beef Wellington.

We've already explained that how you view a decision—as a matter of selection or rejection—can profoundly influence your ultimate choice. So a person deciding among several laptops might choose differently if she viewed her task as deciding which *not* to buy—causing her to focus on the negative qualities of each—than she would if she viewed her mission as deciding which one to purchase, leading her to focus on the positives. Now we're set to explain a related set of behavioral economic tendencies that can also greatly affect your decisions. Although subtly varied, these habits or inclinations share a common result: They lead people to make financial decisions based on inaccurate or incomplete information.

One is "anchoring," or the clinging to a fact or figure or idea that may or may not have any real relevance to your judgments or decisions. Meanwhile, a second force known as the "confirmation bias" often compounds the difficulties that result from anchoring. This bias consists of a tendency to search for, treat kindly, and be overly impressed by information that confirms your initial impressions or preferences. Coming at this from the other direction, this bias could also be called the "disconfirmation disinclination," because it is paired with a tendency, once an idea is in your head, to avoid asking questions that may challenge your preconceptions. As with most behavioral-economic principles, these tendencies are interesting and surprising on their own merits, with sweeping implications for one of the most basic and important aspects of life: the way we process and evaluate information. But they're especially important if you want to know how you make decisions to spend, save, borrow, and invest.

NAME YOUR PREFERENCE

If the descriptions of the two restaurants at the beginning of this chapter sound too similar for you to choose between them, you're not alone. When the psychologist J. Edward Russo, along with colleagues Margaret Meloy and Victoria Medvec, offered similar profiles to a group of students, the would-be diners found no real qualitative differences between the two establishments. They pretty much said it was six of one or half a dozen of the other, the outcome Russo and colleagues had expected. In fact, they had constructed the reviews with that end result in mind.

But a different outcome emerged when Russo and colleagues presented the choice to another group of students, with a twist. Rather than letting these students evaluate full descriptions of both places at once, they revealed equivalent features one pair at a time—say, Restaurant A's beef tournedos with Restaurant B's beef Wellington. The students were then asked to give a tentative preference as each pair of information was given. Finally, when the students had received all the relevant information for both eateries, they were asked to choose which restaurant they preferred. This time the students saw definite distinctions and had no difficulty choosing between the two places.

It doesn't matter which eatery each student preferred. What matters is that they were decisive in favoring one over another, *based on whichever restaurant they had liked after hearing the first pair of attributes*. In fact, 84 percent of the students who favored the attribute of Restaurant A or Restaurant B in the first pairing selected that same restaurant when all the pairings were given.

So why did one set of students find little or no difference between the two restaurants while another could identify distinctions aplenty? The culprit is the confirmation bias, or as Russo and colleagues dubbed it, the "preferential bias." Whatever the name, it means that once people develop preferences—even small ones—they tend to view new information in such a way that it supports those preferences. Or, barring that, they tend to discount any new information that doesn't fit their preconceived opinions and feelings. So once a student decided that he preferred beef Wellington to beef tournedos, he felt that every attribute that came after it supported his choice of Restaurant B. And any comparisons that might not have favored Restaurant B probably became less important, with reasoning that might have gone something like this: "Okay, I'd prefer a romantic dining room to a tastefully appointed dining room, but I'm going there to eat, not to make love."

The psychology behind the confirmation bias results in a very common reaction to a particular type of sound decision making. People who study choice often advise individuals who must pick between two options—say, which of two job offers to accept or which of two houses to buy—to divide a sheet of paper into sections and use them to write out the pros and cons of each option. But many find the exercise unhelpful. They frequently stop midway and exclaim, "This isn't coming out right. It's not favoring the one I want!" A preference they didn't know they had suddenly asserts itself and does away with a procedure that would lead to the "wrong" decision.

The confirmation bias can affect almost any decision you make. Once you develop a feeling about a subject—no matter how unconscious that preference might be—it becomes hard to overcome your bias. Such a bias, by the way, can work in favor of or against a particular person, product, or investment. You can get it into your head that you don't like something based on an initial reaction and subsequently be unable to view its positive attributes as significant enough to make a difference. Think about the last date you might have had, your view of a political candidate, or the first meeting with your boss. Chances are that once you developed a feeling about him or her, you viewed each new bit of information in such a way that it fit your original judgment.

The old wisdom about first impressions—that they're so important because you never get a second chance to make one—is even truer than most of us realize. Once an idea sets in your head, it often sets in concrete; you can break it, but you may need a sledgehammer. In fact, we'd guess that confirmation bias might have a lot to do with the commonly held retailing wisdom that shoppers usually end up buying the first item they look at when they are out shopping. We don't know for certain if that's actually true, but if it is, there's a good chance that it's because an initial attraction to, say, a particular pair of pants results in a subsequent dismissal of other pants as you walk through the aisles. Perhaps the next pair you examine, though it has the same color, doesn't seem to have as attractive a cut. Whatever the reasoning, you find yourself unable to find another pair that matches up well enough.

All of this is fine, though, unless it distorts your decisions so that you end up spending more money than you might have if you were able to view choices objectively, from the start to the finish of your decision-making process. In fact, that your judgment can be tuned in this fashion—that you can be "programmed" to favor a product or service based on your initial impression—is one of the basic principles of marketing and sales. It may sound obvious and simplistic, but that doesn't make it any less powerful.

Consider a related tendency called the "mere-measurement effect," whereby simply asking someone if they're planning to do something increases the likelihood they will do it! And not by just a little: If you ask people if they plan to vote the next day, they're about 25 percent more likely to go to the polls than people who weren't asked. And in a large national survey conducted a few years back, consumers who were asked if they intended to buy a car over the coming year were more likely to do so than survey respondents who weren't asked.

Once, at a party, a friend of Gary's joined a conversation in midstream, just at the moment that one of the other guests was explaining why the high management expenses of a particular mutual fund were actually worth paying (like doctors, financial journalists find themselves in the oddest party conversations). But Gary's friend, let's call him Hank, would brook no excuse for paying such high fees. "I don't care how well the fund has done," Hank intoned. "You can find another one with lower fees that does just as well." Although Gary agreed with that statement, he also knew for a fact that Hank owned shares in another mutual fund with similarly high expenses. Gary didn't mention this point—discretion being the better part of friendship—but he couldn't help thinking that this was an example of the confirmation bias in action. Hank had invested in *his* fund based on a recommendation—from another friend—that focused on the portfolio's excellent record and renowned manager. By the time Hank got around to learning what the fund's fees were, he had discounted their significance enough to overcome any hesitations he might have had: He had developed a bias toward the fund and was subsequently unable to view new information objectively because of that bias. But at the party, when the first fact he heard about the other fund was its high fees, Hank couldn't see his way past that information. His bias was set, and everything else—*that* fund's performance record and *that* fund's respected manager—didn't seem to matter as much.

Marketers count on this. That's why they spend billions of dollars on advertising; merely getting a product or brand anchored in your head may boost the odds that you'll purchase it, and once you're a customer, the confirmation bias might keep you loyal for a while. No matter if it's mutual funds or mattresses, cornflakes or cars, the hope is that you'll be lured into developing a positive bias for that product and thus view subsequent information in a positive light. And, often enough, that's just what happens. But brand loyalty—a stepchild of the confirmation bias—may cost you thousands of dollars. Here's why: Once you've developed a bias for, say, Hondas, you're more likely to view information about Hondas in a favorable light and to view any data about Nissans less favorably. One especially relevant piece of information is price, and the findings of a study by marketing professor Dick R. Wittink and his colleague Rahul Guah suggest that people who replace cars with newer models of the same make pay more than what other consumers pay. A lot more. Analyzing data from a survey of three thousand new car buyers, for example, Wittink and Guah found that loyal Buick customers paid $1,051 more on average than customers who switched from another make to Buick. Mercedes "loyalists" paid an average of $7,410 more for their new cars than did buyers who switched to Mercedes from another make.

Although Wittink and Guah were not investigating the confirmation bias, it's hard to miss the connection. Biased toward Buick from the start—in some manner because of the endowment effect, no doubt—Buick owners were likely to view other aspects of that carmaker's product with less skepticism, such as the dealer's asking price. On the other hand, people who weren't loyal to Buick were more likely to bargain and negotiate when they switched to that brand. This conclusion is reinforced by another finding of the study, which showed that the earlier people replaced their cars, the more likely they were to remain loyal to their make. Because repairs become more likely the longer a car is owned, those who turn in a car early are less likely to have experienced the types of problems that challenge brand loyalty. The confirmation bias notwithstanding, it's hard to view a blown gasket in a positive light. So the longer people own a car, the more data they accumulate that can help to overcome the confirmation bias.

ANCHORS: A WAY (TO THINK)

With Genghis Khan in charge, the Mongols ruled most of central Asia before their leader led them on an ill-fated campaign into what is now Hungary, where he died. Please answer these two questions:

    1. *Did these events happen before or after A.D. 151? [Note: The number 151 was chosen arbitrarily by adding 123 to the last three digits of a New York City zip code.]*

    2. *In what year did Genghis Khan die?*

Like most behavioral economic principles—which by their very nature are woven together like a tapestry—the confirmation bias is both a cause and a consequence of other mental tendencies. One of them, anchoring, is among the toughest to overcome. Anchoring is really just a metaphoric term to explain the tendency we all have of latching onto an idea or fact and using it as a reference point for future decisions. Anchoring can be particularly powerful because you often have no idea that such a phenomenon is affecting you. To give you an idea of what we're talking about, let's return to our little history puzzler. Take another look at it and answer both our questions as best you can.

The first question, as you might have guessed, is nothing more than a straw man, a siren song, if you will. It's there to put a date into your head, that date being A.D. 151. Chances are that A.D. 151 did not seem quite right to you. Too early. Still, when trying to come up with a more accurate date, the 151 sticks in the mind and weighs down your estimate. The net result, in this case, is that your best guess is too low—too close to A.D. 151. (Genghis Khan actually died in A.D. 1227.)

How do we know this? A few years ago, Russo put a similar problem before five hundred MBA candidates, although Attila the Hun was the pillager *du jour* and the second question asked participants to speculate on the year he was defeated, not the year of his death. Russo asked the students to generate the first number themselves (the benchmark date in Question 1) by adding 400 to the last three digits of their own phone numbers. Interestingly, when that number happened to range between 400 and 599, the students' average guess was that Attila had been defeated in A.D. 629. But when the number they concocted was between 1,200 and 1,399, their average guess was A.D. 988. The students knew the benchmark number they had arrived at was meaningless, but it still affected their guess in a meaningful way. The more recent the date, the more recent their estimated year of Attila's defeat (which actually occurred in A.D. 451).

Clever readers, of course, might ask whether the students thought the trick of adding 400 to the last three digits of their phone number was somehow geared toward providing them with a relatively accurate benchmark date. Hard to imagine, since the last three digits of a phone number could range from 000 to 999. More to the point, numerous other experiments have shown that people tend to glom on to meaningless numbers even when there can be no doubt that the numbers are irrelevant. Amos Tversky and Daniel Kahneman, for example, asked participants in one study to estimate the percentage of African nations in the United Nations. First, a wheel of fortune was spun in the presence of the participants, who were subsequently asked whether their answer was higher or lower than the number that had just been spun on the wheel and then to estimate the actual number of African countries in the U.N. Amazingly, given that the number was obviously a matter of chance, participant answers were strongly influenced by the wheel's location. "For example," wrote Kahneman and Tversky, "the median estimates of the percentages

HOME AFFRONTS

An interesting example of anchoring, which could have beneficial or detrimental effects on consumers, was demonstrated a few years back by behavioral economists Uri Simonsohn and George Loewenstein. In their study, the two men found that people could not shake the anchor of prices in their previous real estate market when they moved to a new one: Newcomers from more expensive cities rented pricier apartments than those arriving from less-costly cities, a phenomenon that held true regardless of individual wealth, taxes, or other such reasons. So people who left expensive cities for cheaper ones tended to buy more house than they seemed to need (or could afford) in their old town, while people who left cheaper areas for pricier ones tended not to increase their idea of what a home should cost, ending up in a smaller one. The way to beat this anchor? When moving to a new city, rent for a year before buying. That'll help you lose your old anchor and adjust to your new surroundings.

of African countries in the United Nations were 25 and 45 for groups that received 10 and 65, respectively, as starting points."

Certainly the participants in Kahneman and Tversky's experiment would have been surprised to learn that their answers were so heavily dependent on their starting point— that they unconsciously anchored on whatever number had been spun on the wheel and used it, meaningless as they knew it was, to reach a conclusion about an unrelated matter. Their surprise, though, would probably be no greater than yours if you discovered how often you anchor on some benchmark number or idea and subsequently make serious financial decisions using that as a reference point.

Have you ever been married or engaged or considered either? How much do you think a diamond engagement ring should cost? For many of you, the answer is "two months' salary." That's the rule of thumb most people use for answering that question, a rule promoted by the diamond industry in ad campaigns and informational material. It's a completely ridiculous figure—a ring should cost no more than you can afford! But it has become a standard reference point for engagement ring purchases. Diamond merchants, you see, understand that by leading people to start with a dollar figure equal to two months' salary, they almost certainly guarantee more money for their industry. Why? Because anyone who might have spent less for a ring will have been programmed to think that two months' pay is the point below which he's being a cheapskate (and what man wants his fiancée to think that?). They'll anchor on the equivalent dollar figure if they don't know that this is happening—or even if they do. Meanwhile people who would likely spend more than two months' salary will do so anyway—they'll assume the benchmark is for people who don't have as much money as they do or don't love their fiancées as much.

Note that there are really two different points here, or two types of anchoring, and both of them can be dangerous. Most people are particularly vulnerable to the effects of anchoring when they know precious little about the commodity in question. Most people, for example, have limited knowledge about how much diamonds are "really" worth and are that much more likely to cling to any accepted value because of their uncertainty. The anchor is not actively resisted because one doesn't know any better. But there are other times when you know the stated value is designed to mislead, but, like those respondents whose estimates were influenced by the random outcome of the wheel of fortune, you are sucked in anyway. You know the merchant in the foreign market has stated an outlandish asking price, but what's a fair amount? Chances are that the phenomenon of anchoring will lead you to adjust insufficiently from the merchant's price—even when you know you're being targeted—and thus cause you to pay too much. In one study, by marketing professors Brian Wansink, Robert J. Kent, and Stephen J. Hoch, "end of the aisle" products were listed on sale either as "50¢ each" or "4 cans for $2" in order to anchor people's thoughts about how many they should buy. Sure enough, customers bought 36 percent more cans when the products were advertised as four for $2. In another study, a sign in the candy section read either "Snickers Bars—buy them for your freezer" or "Snickers Bars—buy 18 for your freezer." Anchored on 18, those who confronted the latter sign bought 38 percent more.

If you've ever bought or sold a house, you probably know what sort of powerful drags anchors can be for buyers and sellers. Two stories illustrate this point. The first involves a woman, let's call her Molly, who was shopping for a condominium in New York City not long ago. Molly had her eye on a perfectly nice two-bedroom condo with a view of Central Park. The seller's asking price was $1.1 million, in line with prices for comparable apartments at that time (this was New York, remember). Molly, though, had a friend who recently paid $950,000 for a similar apartment.

Because she had anchored on that figure, Molly had determined that the seller was asking too much—even though her friend's purchase had occurred before real estate prices had begun to take off. Molly loved the apartment and could afford the price, but she hemmed and hawed about it for a week, asking her agent to feel out the seller's willingness to go a bit lower. By that time, another buyer appeared who quite willingly put in a bid equal to the asking price. Don't worry, though; Molly eventually got the apartment. The bad news: She ended up paying $1.25 million, $150,000 more than she could have paid just a week before.

Such things happen in hot real estate markets, and in weak real estate markets the danger from anchoring can shift to the seller. Case in point: Frank and Louise, who put their house up for sale in suburban St. Louis a few years ago when Frank accepted a job in Dallas. Their real estate agent suggested that the couple list their house at $265,000. Although that was about $10,000 below what similar houses in the neighborhood had sold for in recent months, the agent's reasoning was that (1) the couple needed to sell quickly so they could buy a house in Dallas; and (2) their house was a little smaller than most of the homes in the neighborhood.

But Frank and Louise—who paid $200,000 for the house—knew what other homes in the area were selling for, and they insisted that theirs list for $275,000. Indeed, they turned down one offer for $260,000 and a second for $265,000, convinced that their house was as good as any of the others and worth every penny of the list price. Then they waited. And waited. And waited. Alas, two months after they left town—and five months after they first listed their house—a large aerospace company in St. Louis had let go several thousand workers, including many white-collar managers who lived in their neighborhood. That resulted in a flood of houses on the market, many of them bigger and in better condition than Frank and Louise's, which had been sitting empty for months. By the time their real estate broker finally found a buyer, seven months had passed. The final selling price: $230,000, or $35,000 less than they had been offered when they'd first listed the house.

THE POWER OF SUGGESTION

That's an awfully expensive anchor, to be sure, but before you chalk up these two anecdotes to unusual stubbornness or stupidity, remember that people can be susceptible to anchoring even when they are especially knowledgeable about the subject at hand—and therefore presumably less likely to be influenced by facts that might sway those with less experience. Consider the results of a 1987 study by business professors Gregory Northcraft and Margaret Neale. Working with professional real estate agents in Tucson, the professors took one randomly selected group of brokers to a home in town and asked them to appraise its value. In addition to a guided tour, the agents received a ten-page packet of information about the house, including its $65,900 list price. Their average appraisal: $67,811. Fair enough, right? The agents applied their knowledge of the market to come up with an appraisal based on their experience (seven years, on average) and an assessment of all the relevant data.

But wait. Northcraft and Neale brought a second group

of real estate pros to the house, giving them the same tour and the same packet of information, with one exception: The listing price was $83,900. This time the average appraisal came in at $75,190—$7,000 higher than the first group's. Same house, same data. The only thing that changed was the anchor (the listing price). But that was enough to change the "starting point" for these professionals and therefore dramatically influence the way they valued the house. Equally astonishing, by the way, was their complete ignorance of the power of the anchor they had received. When the agents were asked to explain their decisions, fewer than 25 percent mentioned the listing price as one of the factors they considered.

As we mentioned earlier, anchoring can influence almost any financial decision you make, even when you have some expertise about the issue at hand and even when you know the anchor value was chosen to take advantage of you. That said, we can't stress enough that you are particularly prone to anchoring on a particular dollar figure when you're swimming in unfamiliar waters. The less experience you have in that ocean, the more likely it is that you'll cling to any life raft.

When making money decisions in areas in which you have little expertise, anchoring can trip you up on either side of a transaction. If you're on the "buy side"—purchasing life insurance, say—you'll be susceptible to suggestions about normal levels of coverage and premiums. All an agent need tell you is that most people your age have, say, $2 million worth of coverage that costs $4,000 a year—and that will likely become your starting point for negotiations. You might think you're being prudent (or reckless) by lowering your coverage to $1 million and shrinking your premium to $2,000 when in fact both figures may exceed the appropriate range for someone of your age and physical condition.

WHEN IS A DISCOUNT REALLY A DISCOUNT?

When Gary was working in Hong Kong a while back, a colleague, Marge, returned from a day of antiques shopping with several purchases. One of them—a very old vase—seemed expensive at a price in U.S. dollars of about $500. Marge explained that the shop owner had been asking $1,000 for the vase, but after considerable bargaining, she had persuaded him to halve the price. Marge, therefore, felt secure in the knowledge that she had bought the vase at a significant discount. This, of course, is a classic example of anchoring: Marge knew the asking price was artificial and unrealistic, but by starting the bidding at $1,000, the shop owner had anchored that figure as the reference point for the vase's value. This doesn't mean that Marge was ripped off; she was happy. It's just a reminder that a discount is only a discount if you would have been willing to pay a higher price for the item in question. If Marge wouldn't have paid any more than $500 for the vase—or if she could have found it for less elsewhere—then the real discounting should have started at that figure.

On the "sell side," anchoring can cause you to fix on a figure—say, your original purchase price—and cling to it irrationally. This is another factor behind the phenomenon we discussed earlier, whereby many people tend to hold on to losing investments longer than winning ones. If you buy a stock for $50 a share, that amount becomes your anchor when evaluating the worth of the stock down the road. In fact, it's not even necessary for you to have bought the stock to anchor on a price. In 2007, the stock of Garmin, which makes navigation devices, peaked at just under $78 a share. Subsequently, when the share price fell to below $66 in 2008, many investors thought the stock "looked cheap" compared with its all-time high, and they rushed to invest.

They had anchored on that $78 price. Unfortunately the

stock dropped to $15 later that year and at this writing is still priced at less than one-third of its all-time high (a performance much worse than the overall market). Mind you, it's hard not to sympathize with those investors who anchored on the stock's zenith. Even if the current finances or future prospects of a company in question have changed so that its shares have justifiably dropped in value, it's difficult to erase the original purchase price (or highest price) from memory. Pulling up anchor is harder than you might think.

One other thought about anchoring and how easily it can be triggered. Tom and one of his graduate students, Clayton Critcher, recently performed a series of experiments in which they examined whether numbers embedded in a product's name might influence judgments people make about it. In one study, they gave participants information about a "P97" or "P17" smart phone and asked them to estimate the percentage of the phone's sales that would come from Europe. Those asked about the P97 gave significantly higher estimates. In another study, participants were asked how much they would be willing to spend on a meal at restaurant "Studio 97" or "Studio 17." We're sure you can guess the results. On average, participants were willing to pay one-third more for a meal at Studio 97. Buyer beware, indeed.

WHAT YOU DON'T KNOW...

Imagine that sitting before you are four index cards. Each has a letter printed on one side and a number on the other. The sides facing up show the following—A, B, 2, and 3. Your mission is to assess the validity of the following statement by turning over the fewest cards: "All cards with a vowel on one side have an even number on the other." Which cards would you turn over to determine whether that statement is true or false?

In the introduction to this book we expressed our conviction that knowledge was the key to overcoming many of the behavioral economic obstacles we would introduce to you. By recognizing that you're prone to a way of thinking, or a pattern of behavior, you're on your way to correcting it. While that's true, certain tendencies—particularly those discussed in this chapter—are very tough to alter. We've already seen how people find it difficult to ignore certain anchors even when they know the value presented to them is designed specifically to mislead. You might know what a fair price is *not,* but that doesn't necessarily tell you what a fair price is or how much to adjust from that initial unfair value.

The confirmation bias we discussed earlier is also hard to overcome because most people do not find it natural to do what is necessary to overcome it—which is to deliberately seek answers that contradict their beliefs or preferences. This can be seen in the way people approach the card problem given here. Most people choose Cards A and 2, or Card A alone, apparently in an effort to prove the statement true. They look at a vowel card to see if there is an even number on the flip side and look at an even number card to see if there is a vowel on the other side of that. The problem, though, is that even if both cards turn out to support the rule, that's not enough. Why? Because there could be a vowel on the other side of Card 3, which would mean that not *all* cards with a vowel on one side have an even number on the other. That's why the correct response would be Card A (to make sure there's not an odd number on the other side) and Card 3 (to make sure there's not a vowel there).

The irony, of course, is that our explanation may be hard

to understand because of the very issue we're trying to explain. Because people's natural bias is to confirm what they already "know" or think they know, they reflexively try to prove a rule by looking for facts that would support it rather than looking for information that might contradict it. That's why a lot of people say that ignoring Card 2 is wrong, because you could flip it over and discover a consonant on the other side of Card 2. But even if that turns out to be true, so what? All that proves is that a card with a consonant on one side may have an even number on the other; it doesn't prove or disprove the statement that all vowel cards have even numbers on the opposite side.

Still a little confused? Don't worry. What's important about all of this is that the failure to actively seek out disconfirming information—the only reason to pick Card 3, remember, is to prove the statement was *false*—makes it that much harder to overcome the effects of preferential bias and anchoring. That's an important point to keep in mind as you try to incorporate the following advice into your financial decision-making process.

HOW TO THINK AND WHAT TO DO
WARNING SIGNS

You may be prone to the confirmation bias or anchoring if . . .

- you're especially confident about your ability to negotiate and bargain.
- you make spending and investment decisions without much research.
- you're especially loyal to certain brands for mindless reasons.
- you find it hard to sell investments for less than you paid.
- you rely on sellers to set a price rather than assessing the value yourself.

If you think about it, the most insidious problems that stem from the confirmation bias can be summed up with a simple statement: People often hear what they want to hear. They focus on information that confirms their beliefs and explain away or disregard evidence that doesn't. As a result, many choices we make are based on information that is inaccurate, incomplete, or inane.

In fact, Tom has discovered in his research that when people want to believe something, they scrutinize relevant information with the following question in mind: "Can I believe this?" This is a rather easy criterion to meet, since even many dubious propositions are supported by at least some evidence. When people do *not* want to believe something, in contrast, they ask themselves, "*Must* I believe this?" This is a much higher hurdle to overcome because the tiniest flaw in some body of evidence can be seized upon to condemn the proposition. It's akin to the different standards of guilt in a civil case and criminal case.

Unfortunately, knowing that such a bias exists is one thing; fixing it is another. The difficulty lies in the fact that we don't get to watch ourselves go through life from an objective point above the action: If Tom likes Gary and therefore views some obnoxious behavior on Gary's part as a lovable quirk, Tom doesn't think the confirmation bias is affecting his judgment; he thinks Gary has a lovable quirk. Bias is something that plagues other people's judgments. That's why our first piece of advice is this:

Broaden your personal board of advisers. We can't stress enough the importance of getting a second opinion, of conferring with other people when making large financial decisions. True, they may fall victim to the same bad habits as you. But maybe their mental bugaboos are triggered by other factors than yours, and anyway, it's a lot easier to recognize someone else's problem than your own. Today, the Internet makes it so much easier to overcome anchoring issues (although it accentuates other problems, which we'll discuss in Chapter 7). Message boards and chat rooms in particular are a great way to cut ties to an anchor or overcome the confirmation bias. The anonymity of such places allows people to voice opinions without regard to anything but their sense of the truth, and the sheer volume of opinion and anecdote can usually overcome the biases of a single shopper or parent or homeowner.

When in doubt, check it out. The less knowledge you have about a subject, the more likely you are to pay attention to information that really doesn't matter when making decisions that really do—the more likely you will be to anchor on a dollar value that has little basis in reality. That's why it's important to comparison shop—not so much to find the best price as to find the correct starting point of reference. Learn to disregard meaningless information, such as the price you paid for something originally when you are selling something, or when you are a buyer, disregard what your aunt Clara's neighbor paid. Do your research and be thorough.

To set the right price when selling your house, for example, ask your real estate broker for a comparison market analysis, which will tell you the prices of recently sold homes in your neighborhood. But make sure those homes are actually comparable with yours, and be certain that the market today is comparable to conditions when those homes sold. If economic circumstances have changed, you run the risk of anchoring on a list price that might be unrealistic. If that happens, your home might languish for more than three months, the point (in a healthy market) beyond which potential buyers can start to wonder what's wrong with your place and the bids you receive might be lower than you had expected.

Home buyers, on the other hand, shouldn't be swayed by a listing price, any more than someone at an auction should be moved to value a painting at $10,000 simply because the auction house started the bidding at that level. In fact, we've always been amazed at the number of people who put in bids on homes without hiring an appraiser—or doing the necessary research themselves—to make sure the price is even remotely fair. Paying for a second opinion—or, more important, a more experienced opinion—is often one of the smartest ways to overcome misleading anchor values.

Hiring a fee-only financial planner, for example, might be an alternative way to approach life insurance decisions. Such a professional—who will charge anywhere from $75 to $500 depending on the complexity of your needs—can find you the most suitable coverage for the lowest cost. Similarly, mortgage brokers or car-buying services have the expertise to evaluate prices in those respective areas without falling prey to anchoring or preferential bias. But whatever approach you choose, the greater your awareness that you might pay too much attention to facts and figures that matter too little, the greater the chance you'll avoid costly mistakes.

Get real. We could have offered this advice in any number of chapters in this book, but the idea, briefly, is that too many people have too short a memory when it comes to making financial decisions. This can lead to a bad case of anchoring. A booming stock market puts a lot of unrealistic numbers in people's heads, causing a dangerous escalation of expectations. Likewise, a depressed market leads people to be overly pessimistic about future returns. In reality, over the long run stocks have returned about 9 percent a year, bonds about 5 percent. These are the sort of returns you can expect, along with the traditional risks associated with each class of investment.

Be maximally aware of minimum payments. In hindsight, it's obvious, but a recent study involving credit cards points to some important advice. Neil Stewart, a psychologist at Warwick University in England, was interested in learning whether minimum-payment requirements on credit-card bills affected how much people paid each month. For people whose intention it is to pay their entire balance, the answer is no. But for people inclined to pay only a portion of their bill, the answer is a decided yes: When presented with a minimum-payment requirement, such borrowers in Stewart's study made payments that were on average 43 percent lower than people who didn't receive a minimum-payment requirement. Given that card issuers' favorite customers are borrowers who regularly make smaller payments—and thus rack up interest charges for a long time—our advice here is simple: Be wary of letting the card company's anchor drag your finances down.

Finally, be humble. One of the reasons people think so highly of themselves is that they often don't recognize when they've been wrong. Even when events prove a decision foolish, people frequently explain it away and emerge with their confidence intact. Stockbrokers, in fact, have a joke about this tendency, which goes something like this: "When the price goes up, the client thinks he picked a great stock. When the price drops, the client knows that his broker sold him a lousy one." People have an impressive knack for snatching subjective victory from the jaws of objective defeat. To be sure, faith in one's judgment—believing in your ability to make decisions that are in your best interest—is a crucial element to personal progress. But too much faith and too much confidence can lead you to unwise and unproductive decisions. As you'll read in the next chapter, overconfidence is more common than you might imagine.

6

THE EGO TRAP

Quick! According to Catholic dogma, to whom does the Doctrine of Immaculate Conception refer? Now, how much money would you bet that your answer is correct: $5? $50? $500?

This is probably the trickiest chapter in this book for us to write—not because the subject is complicated, but because the message we want to send might seem to fly in the face of our overriding premise. That premise, of course, is that individuals like you can learn from your mistakes. By identifying and understanding your behavioral-economic shortcomings, you can correct them and enjoy more financial freedom. This chapter, though, is a cautionary tale, like the yellow flag that's waved to warn race-car drivers that conditions are a bit treacherous.

The core idea of this chapter is not particularly uplifting:

You're probably not as smart as you think you are. That's okay; neither are we. Few people are. As a matter of fact, for almost as long as psychologists have been exploring human nature, they have been amassing evidence that people tend to overestimate their own abilities, knowledge, and skills. In a favorable light, this might be called optimism, and it's a propelling force in human achievement. It's also a bracing, cheerful way to go through life. After all, who wants to read their children a bedtime story whose main character is a train that says, "I doubt I can, I doubt I can"?

In a harsher light, though, such optimism might be called overconfidence, and in financial matters the tendency to place too much stock in what you know, or what you think you know, can cost you dearly. In fact, depending on how much you would have wagered that you knew who Catholics believe to have been immaculately conceived, you might already be $500 in the hole. You see, we constructed the proposition at the beginning of this chapter to play on people's tendency toward overconfidence. Because people are certain they know what the Immaculate Conception refers to—the idea that Jesus was conceived without his parents, Mary and Joseph, having consummated their marriage—they are supremely confident they can win the proffered bet. In fact, the Immaculate Conception refers to the dogma that when *Mary* was conceived, she was brought into this world without the stain of Original Sin; her soul was immaculate. (Check the dictionary if you don't trust us.)

No fair? All right, we tricked you (or tried to). Guilty as charged. But our point is no less valid. Overconfidence is pervasive, even among people who presumably have good reason to think highly of themselves. Numerous studies over the years have demonstrated significant overconfidence in the judgments of doctors, lawyers, engineers, psychologists, and securities analysts. For example, 68 percent of lawyers involved in civil cases believe that their side will prevail, but—of course—only 50 percent can. Perhaps more important, even when people know as much as they think they know, it's often not as much as they need to know. In this chapter we'll examine the pervasiveness of overconfidence, its psychological roots, and the ways it can adversely affect financial decisions. We'll also explain why it's one of the most difficult behavioral-economic traits to overcome, and we'll offer suggestions about how you might nonetheless do just that.

CONFIDENCE GAME

Give high and low estimates for the average weight of an empty Boeing 747 aircraft. Choose numbers far enough apart to be 90 percent certain that the true answer lies somewhere in between.

Now give high and low estimates for the diameter of the earth's moon in miles. Again, choose numbers far enough apart to be 90 percent certain that the true answer lies somewhere in between.

There are two other barriers we must overcome if this chapter is to be successful. Even if we sell you on the notion that overconfidence is common and troublesome, there's a good chance that you'll think it's not really a problem for *you*. The very tendency we're writing about could make you overly confident that overconfidence is not one of your issues. First, overconfidence is not always arrogance; even if you already think you're a lousy shopper, you might be worse than you think.

Second, overconfidence often appears as unrealistically high appraisals of our own qualities versus those of others. The classic example of this tendency is seen in a 1981 survey of car drivers in Sweden, in which 90 percent described themselves as above-average drivers. Clearly a lot of respondents were giving themselves the benefit of what should have been a very large doubt.

Now, you might think you are immune to this "Lake Wobegon effect," so named after radio personality Garrison Keillor's fictional community where "all the women are strong, all the men are good-looking, and all the children are above average." But try this one: What is your usual reaction when you meet a person who someone has said looks "just like you"? If you are like most people, your reaction is typically one of alarm, even horror: "You're kidding! Is

---

WHEN WORKING OUT DOESN'T

Overconfidence comes in many flavors, one of them unwarranted optimism. In a revealing study several years ago, economists Stefano Della Vigna and Ulrike Malmendier analyzed records from three U.S. health clubs and discovered that gymgoers would have been better off, financially, had they chosen to pay per workout rather than signing up for monthly or annual memberships. That is, even with the "discount" that came with a long-term commitment, members paid more on average per visit than they would have paid had they bought a single-day or ten-visit pass. It seems the average fitness fanatic didn't go the gym often enough to justify the membership expense. So why did members consistently pay more than necessary? Overconfident about their willpower or commitment to fitness, they overestimated the frequency of their future gym visits; because they went less often to the club than they predicted, they paid more per visit than they intended. Sometimes high hopes are just that.

that what I look like?" What this means, of course, is that the picture we carry around of ourselves in our heads is a bit more favorable than the image others have of us.

Among folks who study such things, the prevalence of overconfidence is hardly in dispute. And if you think about it, signs of overconfidence are rampant in all walks of life, particularly when it comes to money. If people were not overconfident, for example, significantly fewer people would ever start a new business: Most entrepreneurs know the odds of success are against them, yet they try anyway. That their optimism is misplaced—that they're overconfident— is evidenced by the fact that half of all small businesses fail within five years of inception. Put another way, the majority of small-business owners believe that they have what it takes to overcome the obstacles to success, but most of them are wrong.

At this juncture we should probably clarify what we mean by overconfidence. We're not talking specifically about conscious arrogance, although overconfidence might certainly manifest itself in such out-and-out hubris. It's not so much that some folks think they are especially gifted and some folks do not, although that is certainly true. Rather, what research psychologists have discovered about overconfidence is that most people—those with healthy egos and those in the basement of self-esteem—consistently overrate their abilities, knowledge, and skill, at whatever level they might place them. If you asked Gary and Kobe Bryant to predict how many free throws they will make out of a hundred tries, Gary might honestly predict thirty-five and Kobe might answer ninety. Both would likely be suffering from overconfidence. Over the years, researchers have demonstrated the pervasiveness of this phenomenon in myriad ways. One of the more famous efforts was a series of studies in the 1970s. Participants were first required to answer a few simple factual questions (for example, "Is Quito the capital of Ecuador?") and then to estimate the probability that their answers were correct (for instance, "I'm 60 percent sure that Quito is Ecuador's capital"). Consistently, participants overestimated the true probability. Even for questions in which they were 100 percent certain that their answer was correct, they were right only 80 percent of the time.

Of course, you might resist the significance of these findings on the grounds that they involve only people's responses to trivia questions. You might be thinking, "Who can get too worked up about one's knowledge of foreign capitals? I bet it would be different if people were asked things they care about and had more opportunities to learn." In fact, researchers have done just that, by asking people questions about the one topic they care more about and know more about than anything—themselves! A while back, psychologists Lee Ross, Robert Vallone, Dale Griffin, and Sabrina Lin asked Stanford undergraduates at the beginning of the year whether they thought they would drop a course, join a fraternity or sorority, become homesick, and so on. On average, the students expressed 84 percent confidence in their answers. But follow-up information obtained later in the year revealed that they were right only 70 percent of the time. Indeed, even when they were 100 percent certain of their predictions, their predictions were confirmed only 85 percent of the time.

No one is immune to this phenomenon, even experts in a given field. Psychologist Phil Tetlock spent years collecting more than twenty-five thousand forecasts from people whose job it is to anticipate at least something about how the future will unfold—distinguished political scientists, economists, State Department consultants, and, of course, television talking heads. These expert prognosticators made predictions about such things as the success of the antiapartheid movement, secession efforts on the part of French Canadians, and the progress of Gorbechev's glasnost program in the Soviet Union. They did so by specifying which of three future states was most likely—that the status quo would prevail, that an existing trend would intensify, or that an existing trend would reverse. They also indicated how confident they were in their predictions. As you probably have guessed by now, these experts were notably overconfident. When they were 80 percent sure they were right, they were actually right less than 60 percent of the time. When they were 100 percent certain of their predictions, they were right less than 80 percent of the time.

A helpful way to understand overconfidence—and how it

HEAR ME NOW, BELIEVE ME LATER

Sometimes the only thing humans like more than self-confidence is confidence in others. That explains the success of some media pundits today—even when such know-it-alls turn out to be wrong. Consider a study by psychologist Don Moore, in which volunteers were given cash for correctly guessing people's weight (from photos). Over eight rounds, guessers could buy "advice" from expert volunteers, who spread their estimates along a wide or narrow range depending on how confident they were about them. As the experiment progressed, experts who proved lousy judges were generally avoided. But when lousy experts stayed confident—when they kept their estimates limited to a narrow range of weights—volunteer guessers kept buying their advice! Lesson: In a gray world we like black-and-white answers, even when we have good reason to believe they're wrong.

can sneak up on you—is to look again at the questions posed at the beginning of this section. Again, make a serious effort to choose pairs of numbers that would give you that 90 percent level of certainty. In other words, come up with answers for which you'd be comfortable betting $9 against the prospect of winning just $1 that the real answers are within your chosen ranges. Go ahead, try.

Okay, we won't keep you in suspense. An empty 747 weighs approximately 390,000 pounds, and the diameter of the moon is roughly 2,160 miles. Chances are these answers don't fall within your high and low estimates for each question. Indeed, when Cornell's J. Edward Russo, along with fellow psychologist Paul Shoemaker of the University of Chicago, offered these and eight other similar questions to more than one thousand U.S. and European business executives, the majority missed four to seven of them. How is this evidence of overconfidence? Because most people who attempt to answer these questions don't recognize how little they really know about the subjects or how difficult it is to bracket high and low estimates so that there's a sufficiently strong chance that the real answer will fall somewhere in between. As a result, most people fail to spread their estimates far enough apart to account for their ignorance.

If you had said to yourself something like this—"I really have no idea how much a 747 weighs, so I better err on the side of shooting too high and too low"—then you might have spread your guesses wide enough apart. Instead, what people typically do is come up with their best estimate of the plane's actual weight and the moon's actual diameter and then move up and down from those figures to arrive at their high and low estimates. Quite frankly, though, unless you work for Boeing or NASA, your initial estimates are likely to be wildly off the mark, so the adjustments up and down need to be much bolder (remember what we discussed earlier about anchoring). Sticking close to an initial, uninformed estimate reeks of overconfidence.

Yet another way to think about overconfidence and its causes is to examine what behavioral economists call the "planning fallacy." Essentially, this is the phenomenon responsible for one of the most common human foibles: the inability to complete tasks on schedule. We probably don't need to prove to you that such a fallacy exists, presuming that your life (like ours) is filled with projects that take much longer to complete than you expected. In one interesting study, a group of psychology students was asked to estimate as accurately as possible how long it would take to complete their honors theses.

The study's authors—psychologists Roger Buehler, Dale Griffin, and Michael Ross—also asked the students to estimate how long it would take to complete the thesis "if everything went as well as it possibly could" and "if everything went as poorly as it possibly could." Here are the results: Their best guess averaged out to 33.9 days; that's how long the typical student thought it would take him or her to finish a thesis. Assuming everything went perfectly, the average estimate for completion was 27.4 days, whereas the average estimate if things went poorly was 48.6 days. As it turned out, the average time it actually took the students to complete their theses was a whopping 55.5 days. Depending on which estimate you use—the best, worst, or most likely case—the students were on average anywhere from 14 percent to 102 percent more confident than they should have been about the time it would take them to complete their theses. Sound familiar?

The planning fallacy, by the way, also explains why so

many public works projects take so long to complete and go disastrously over budget. When government officials in Sydney, Australia, for example, decided in 1957 to build an opera house, they estimated that it would be completed in 1963 at a cost of $7 million. A scaled-back version finally opened in 1973 and cost $102 million. Similarly, when civic leaders in Boston undertook planning for the Central Artery/Tunnel Project—a plan to reroute the city's primary highway into a 3.5-mile tunnel—they expected the $2.8 billion project to be completed by 2000. But when "The Big Dig" was finally finished, in 2007, the total cost at that point was almost $15 billion ($8 billion in 1982 dollars, in case you thought we were succumbing to the money illusion).

SHOW ME THE MONEY

At this point, you might wonder how overconfidence affects financial decisions. Sure, people don't know how little they know about world capitals or plane weights—or how long it will take them to complete a college paper or to build a screened-in porch. And yes, government projects sometimes consume more tax dollars than anyone was able to forecast in advance. Folks underestimate. But what does any of this have to do with personal finances? As it happens, a lot. One consequence is plainly practical. Because people are overconfident, they're likely to think they are in better financial shape than they are. That's less often the case in the near-term aftermath of an economic slowdown or stock market drop, but overconfidence invariably creeps back into force as conditions normalize and improve. Consider the results of a survey of American parents by the International Association of Financial Planning, during the middle of the last bull market. Some 83 percent of respondents with children under the age of eighteen said that they had a financial plan, while three-quarters of them expressed confidence about their long-term financial health. Yet less than half of the respondents said they were saving for their children's education, and less than 10 percent described their financial plan as addressing basic issues such as investments, budgeting, insurance, savings, wills, and estates. Is their confidence justified? Perhaps, but we doubt it.

So that's one major financial consequence of overconfidence: underpreparedness. Another is the willingness with which most people spend large amounts of money for products and services about which they know very little. Oftentimes, certainly, this is the result of nothing more than laziness and resignation: You realize that you know nothing about, say, laptops, but you really don't care. You've heard of Apple, you love those Mac commercials, so an Apple it is. Alas, we can't help you much there (although we love Macs, too). Where we can help is to point out that many people make spending decisions that they think are informed but that are in fact not very informed at all.

One of our favorite stories about this happened a little while back, when a friend of Gary's was shopping for treadmills. A few weeks earlier, Gary had skimmed an article that evaluated more than a dozen brands of treadmills. Gary suggested that his friend read the article. The friend, however, thought that was unnecessary; he believed he had learned all he needed to know about treadmills in discussions with several trainers at his health club. Gary's friend bought Brand X, Brand X fell apart three weeks after the warranty expired, Gary's friend was out $1,100. After that happened, Gary's friend went back and read the treadmill article. Sure enough, Brand X had received a subpar rating, in part because the treadmill testers found that it didn't stand up to prolonged heavy pounding. Bad news for a treadmill, really, but even worse news for Gary's friend.

Our point in telling this story is to show how a little knowledge can lead to a lot of overconfidence. Remember, Gary's friend wasn't arrogant; he didn't assume that he had some innate knowledge about treadmills. He actually spent time researching the subject, shopping at different stores, and buttonholing the trainers at his gym. That's a lot more than many people would do in that situation. No, his problem wasn't hubris—he didn't think he was a treadmill expert—his problem was overconfidence. He thought he knew enough about treadmills to make an informed decision. He overestimated his abilities.

THE FIZZBO FALLACY

Yet another area in which overconfidence seems to thrive is residential real estate, where the acronym FSBO—or "Fizzbo" in industry jargon—stands for "For Sale By Owner." It's the term used to describe the 10 to 15 percent or so of homeowners each year who try to sell their house without aid of a real estate agent, in the hopes of saving the 6 percent broker's commission. But Fizzbo might just as easily stand for "For Sale By Overconfident." That's because most homeowners who try to sell their house on their own underestimate the complexity of the task and overestimate their ability to handle it. Indeed, despite all the optimistic hype you can find at Web sites like homesbyowner.com, more than half of all Fizzbos each year end up being sold through a traditional broker. More important, even those Fizzbos that are successfully completed may not be the money savers people think they are. Many times Fizzbos end up costing their owners large sums of money. It's true they save 6 percent, but because of their lack of experience, the house sells for a lower price, actually costing the owner money. In other words, even though you don't have to pay a commission, you may still end up getting less than you would have had you hired a broker—perhaps as much as 10 percent less (reliable stats are not easily available).

There are several reasons for this. For example, some Fizzbo sellers price their home too low, and miss out on thousands of dollars of potential gain. More likely, many homeowners overestimate the value of their home—an example of the endowment effect we talked about earlier—and as a result their property takes longer to sell. The longer your home stays on the market, the more potential buyers wonder what's wrong with it and the lower the bids you'll get. A good real estate broker, moreover, has the knowledge and skills to market your home in the best possible way, and crucially, he or she is likely to generate a far greater number of interested buyers than you can, which will increase the likelihood that you'll enjoy the luxury of competing and escalating bids. This is because 85 percent of buyers still use a broker to find homes. Finally, buyers these days know what you're up to when you try a Fizzbo: They know you're saving the broker's commission, and they will expect you to share those savings by accepting a below-market bid.

UNFAIR TRADE

To be sure, none of the above necessarily means that you won't save a bundle if you sell your house on your own—or that every real estate broker is worth the commission. It's just a reminder that overconfidence can be your undoing in a variety of ways. Which brings us to the real meat of this chapter, a point that if made successfully will cause us to consider this whole enterprise a success. Our point has to do with investing, and it's bound to be seen by some as the most controversial statement in this book, the one most sure to raise eyebrows among readers. Here it is: Any individual who is not professionally occupied in the financial services industry (and even most who are) and who in any way tries to actively manage an investment portfolio is probably suffering from overconfidence. That is, anyone who has confidence enough in his or her abilities and knowledge to invest in a particular stock or bond (or actively managed mutual fund or real estate investment trust or limited partnership) is most likely fooling himself.

In fact, most such people (probably you) have no business at all trying to pick investments, except perhaps as sport. Such people (again, probably you) should simply divide their money among several index mutual funds, then turn off CNBC and block most financial Web sites. The best that such people (yes, you) should hope for is to match the average performance of the stock and bond markets over their investing life. Such a result ain't too bad.

Okay, now that we've insulted you sufficiently, let's go over our case, which at its essence is that most individual investors have no business thinking they can pick stocks or bonds with any more success than Tom and Gary would have playing doubles at Wimbledon. Consider the following for a moment: As we saw earlier, the typical mutual fund manager—someone who spends every day in pursuit of brilliant investment ideas—will over the course of time be quite lucky if he or she manages simply to match the overall performance of the stock market. In fact, in most years the majority of these *professional* money managers actually perform worse than stocks in general. Indeed, over periods of a decade or more, roughly 75 percent of all stock funds underperform the market. Yes, a few fund managers consistently outperform the market over time, and yes, a small number of investors have become famous over the years for exceptional stock picking. But the operative words here are *few* and *small*. The fact of the matter is that most people have no reason to think they can be more successful identifying worthy investments or timing the ups and downs of the stock and bond markets than they would be if they made their decisions by throwing darts at the financial pages.

That fact was emphasized more than a decade ago in a study by Terrance Odean and Brad Barber. The two researchers, you might recall from earlier in the book, have spent a great deal of time in recent years analyzing the trading records of tens of thousands of individual investors at a large national discount brokerage firm. One of their conclusions, which we discussed earlier, was that individual investors routinely sold winning stocks and held on to losers. In later work, Odean and Barber turned up an equally important find: that individuals who trade stocks most frequently post exceptionally poor investment results. Using account data for tens of thousands of households, Odean and Barber analyzed the common stock investment performance of individual investors from February 1991 through December 1996. During that time, the average household earned an annualized average return of 17.7 percent—a result that itself was hardly better than the relevant benchmark index, which returned an annualized 17.1 percent during the period. More important, the 20 percent of households that traded the most—turning over roughly 10 percent of their portfolio each month, vs. 6.6 percent for all households— earned an average annual return of just 10 percent.

Think about this for a minute. It's no stretch to assume that the people who traded the most did so because they believed their stock-picking skills to be superior to those of the average investor. In fact, a study in 1998 by the German economists Markus Glaser and Martin Weber proved that more confident investors tended to trade more often. But the performance of investors in Odean and Barber's study was actually far inferior to those of the average investor. If that's not a sign of overconfidence, we'd be hard-pressed to explain what it might be. To quote Odean and Barber: "We argue that the well-documented tendency for human beings to be overconfident can best explain the high trading levels and the resulting poor performance of individual investors. Our central message is that trading is hazardous to your wealth."

That's one of our central messages, too, and it further applies to those of you who have sense enough to stay away from individual stock picking but nonetheless believe you have the skill to identify those few mutual fund managers among thousands who can beat the market over time. As far as we know, there has not yet been created a reliable way to predict the performance of individual mutual funds with any greater degree of accuracy than there is for individual stocks or bonds. As you'll soon see, the average individual investor in mutual funds consistently fares worse than the average mutual fund, as hard as that may be to believe. Several traits contribute to this startling fact, but it is our belief that a major reason most individual investors underperform the benchmark investment averages over time is that most individual investors think they know more about investing than they actually do.

The question is why? Not why are people overconfident to begin with, but why do they stay overconfident? You see, the problem with overconfidence is not the innate bias toward optimism that most people seem to possess. That's a good thing; it keeps the world moving forward. The real problem is the inability to temper optimism as a result of prior experience. Frankly, we don't learn well enough from our mistakes. Consider: If overconfidence is as big a problem as we say it is, it should be a short-term problem at worst. The learning process would ideally go something like this: We think highly of ourselves, the world and events show us who is boss, and we become less confident and more realistic about our knowledge and skills. Yet in the main, this doesn't happen. In their analysis of the planning fallacy, Buehler, Griffin, and Ross discussed several reasons why people consistently fall prey to that type of optimism and overconfidence. One reason was a persistent habit of focusing on future plans rather than past experiences. We can always envision specific reasons why *this* project will get done on time. But the best laid plans are typically done in by elements we cannot anticipate. What a focus on the specifics of a particular project does, then, is force us into an "inside" view of the problem that distracts us from thinking about how infrequently we get things done as quickly as we initially expected. In our experiences, a similar phenomenon happens to investors, the result of this and several habits that we suspect you'll find very familiar.

HEADS I WIN, TAILS IT'S CHANCE

The average reader might have a ready explanation for the dogged persistence of overconfidence, an explanation that goes something like this: "People stay overconfident because they conveniently remember their successes but repress or forget their failures." That's not far off: There are powerful psychological forces at work that can indeed make our triumphs more memorable than our defeats. One of them, called "hindsight bias," was first examined in detail nearly forty years ago by the psychologist Baruch Fischhoff. In a series of landmark experiments, Fischhoff asked students at Hebrew University to speculate about the upcoming, historic visit to China by U.S. president Richard Nixon. Essentially, he asked them to lay odds on the likelihood of certain diplomatic and trip-related events taking place. After the trip, Fischhoff periodically asked the students to recall their predictions, as well as the events (or nonevents) in question. Here's what he discovered: Not only did students misremember their predictions, they consistently did so in a way that made them look smarter. With events that they remembered as having taken place, students consistently recalled their predictions as being more optimistic. And with events they remembered as not having occurred, they recalled their predictions as being more pessimistic. Tetlock, the psychologist who collected all that data on "expert" predictions, found a similar tendency among those prognosticators; they systematically distorted the likelihood they assigned to their predictions, "recalling" that they had assigned a higher probability to events that subsequently came to pass and a lower probability to events that had not. They also (again, like everyone) tended to explain away their failed predictions. "The whole revolution *would* have collapsed if Yeltsin hadn't climbed on that tank and addressed the crowd." "They *would* have voted to secede if . . ." These explanations maintain faith in an overall, abstract ability to make accurate predictions in the face of concrete predictive failure. We humans have developed sneaky habits to look back on ourselves in pride.

But wait. Some readers are no doubt scratching their heads, because sometimes it seems as if our *failures* are the most vivid memories of all. And they'd be correct. If you were ever one word away from winning a spelling bee, for instance, it's a lock you'll carry the memory of the word that eliminated you to the grave.

But here's how overconfidence is preserved: Even when you remember your defeats, you may remember them in a way that alters their perceived implications for the future. Psychologist Eileen Langer describes this phenomenon as "heads I win, tails it's chance." The idea is that when things happen that confirm the correctness of your actions or beliefs, you attribute the events to your own high ability. Conversely, when things happen that prove your actions or beliefs to have been mistaken or wrongheaded, you attribute those disconfirming events to some other cause over which you had no control. The result is that you emerge from a checkered history of success and failure with a robust optimism about your prospects for the future. A little better luck, or a little fine-tuning of your analysis, and the outcome will be better the next time.

Case in point: A fellow Gary knows invested in Applied Materials some years ago because the company was the dominant supplier of the machines that computer makers use to make their chips. And he took full credit when the stock raged over the next year. He proudly explained that he understood better than most how ubiquitous computer chips were becoming and how changing technology required manufacturers to constantly update their equipment. His confidence in his ability to pick winners soared. On the other hand, when economic problems in Asia pulverized the share prices of all semiconductor equipment makers, his confidence in his investing acumen was not shaken. After all, how could he know that Asia's woes would hurt Applied Materials' profits? Well, one answer is that he might have known had he bothered to learn that 50 percent of semiconductor equipment purchases at the time originated in Asia. The better answer is that Gary's friend, who is not in the semiconductor business, might not be the best person to evaluate the future of the companies that manufacture chip-making equipment.

But what if Gary's friend worked in the computer industry? What if he did understand the vagaries of the chip-making cycle? Wouldn't that qualify him to invest in high-tech companies? Before you answer, take a look at the next section.

ALL TOO FAMILIAR

The last contributor to investor overconfidence that we want to mention is a hybrid of sorts. In many ways, it's a variation of the endowment effect we explained earlier, whereby people tend to place an inordinately high value on what is theirs, relative to the value they would otherwise place on such things. But this principle applies not only to concrete items, but to ideas as well. Essentially, we place too much value on what we know from our own personal experience simply because it is from our own personal experience. To illustrate, we'll turn to a 1997 study by finance professor Gur Huberman. He was intrigued by the fact that throughout the world, most investors own more stock of companies in their own country than of those in foreign countries.

To some extent, certainly, this reflects the ease of investing domestically; you don't have to worry about another country's laws or currency exchange rates. But Huberman thought that another factor might be at work, a psychological need on the part of investors to feel comfortable about their investments, with that comfort coming from familiarity. This may seem reasonable, but it may also be another example of overconfidence, inasmuch as investors might overestimate their knowledge about companies and stocks simply because they're more familiar with them.

To test his theory, Huberman examined the stock ownership records of (what were then) seven U.S. "Baby Bells," the regional phone companies created by the government breakup of AT&T in the 1980s. His research showed that in all but one state (Montana), more people held more shares of their local phone companies than any other Baby Bell. Again, this may make perfect sense to you: If a person thought regional phone companies were a good investment, why not invest in the one with which they are most familiar? Well, one reason might be that their phone company wasn't the best of the seven Baby Bells. On average, in fact, the odds were six to one against. And since we're pretty sure that most of the investors in question didn't conduct research that showed their Baby Bell to be superior, the only conclusion to be reached is that investors had a "good feeling" about their phone company relative to the others simply because it was their phone company.

This idea—invest in what you know—became increasingly popular in the 1980s and 1990s, associated with such investing legends as Peter Lynch, manager of the highly successful Fidelity Magellan mutual fund for thirteen years, and Warren Buffett, longtime chairman of the even more successful Berkshire Hathaway holding company. Indeed, it is often recounted how Lynch loved the coffee at Dunkin' Donuts and made a fortune investing in the company's stock or how Buffett's addiction to cherry Coke was a key component in his decision to invest in Coca-Cola shares before the company's stock exploded.

Similarly, the invest-in-what-you-know approach is at least partly responsible for the fact that employees typically allocate more than a third of their retirement account assets to the stock of the company for which they work, despite the risks of such a strategy: Your biggest investment—your job—is already tied to the fortunes of your workplace, so by stashing retirement assets in company stock, you're putting too many eggs in one basket. That's why most financial planning pros recommend you keep no more than 10 percent of your 401(k) assets in your own company's shares.

In any event, the problem with all of this is that people overconfidently confuse familiarity with knowledge. For every example of a person who made money on an investment because she used a company's product or understood its strategy, we can give you five instances where such knowledge was insufficient to justify the investment. A classic example is American Express. It's safe to say that many Platinum cardholders were convinced that the company's service, strategy, and customer base were superior to those of its competitors, and as a result, many of them invested in Amex's shares with exceeding confidence. What these investors couldn't foresee

TOO MUCH OF A GOOD THING

There's a reason some investors own too much of their employer's stock: The stock has been a big winner. According to a 2001 study by behavioral economist Shlomo Benartzi, workers at companies whose shares were in the bottom fifth of all stock market performers over the previous decade had roughly 10 percent of their retirement savings allocated to their employer's shares—about what financial pros recommend. But workers at companies whose shares had been in the top fifth of stock market performers over that same period of time had nearly 40 percent of their savings allocated to their employer's shares—which is way too much. If you don't believe us, ask the folks at Enron or GM or Merrill Lynch.

was that Amex was as vulnerable to credit problems as many other financial institutions, and its stock plummeted precipitously when the global economy hit the skids.

HOW TO THINK AND WHAT TO DO

Warning Signs

Overconfidence may cost you money if . . .
- you make large spending decisions without much research.
- you take heart from winning investments but "explain away" poor ones.
- you think you are "beating the market" consistently.
- you make frequent trades, especially with a discount or online brokerage.
- you think selling your home without a broker is smart and easy.
- you favor package deals and annual memberships over à la carte pricing.
- you don't know the rate of return on your investments.
- you believe that investing in what you know is a guarantee of success.

Although you might not have guessed it, it was not our goal in this chapter to beat all remnants of self-confidence out of your system. Some of you may be every bit as smart as you think you are, and far be it from us to keep the next Peter Lynch, George Soros, or Warren Buffett from making his or her mark on the investment world. Our goal, rather, is twofold. First, we'd like to convince most of you to cast the bulk of your investment lot with the overall market by investing almost exclusively in index mutual funds. Because we make the case for this approach elsewhere in the book, we won't belabor the point here. But the plain truth is that most investors miss out on potential profits because they believe they can outthink the market when all evidence says they can't.

Our second goal is based to some extent on the belief that we won't easily achieve our first. Most of you will continue to pick individual stocks, bonds, funds, and the like in part because you think you have the skill and in part because it's fun. That's okay—it *is* fun. What we hope to have accomplished in this chapter is to convince you that you are likely overestimating your abilities and thus need to reevaluate the effort you put into investment decisions (and spending decisions, too). We don't want to abuse you, just humble you, so that you'll be less likely to make mistakes that cause you to lose money or miss out on gains.

Investor, know thyself. Maybe you *are* as good an investor as you think. But experience tells us that many people overestimate their hit-to-miss ratio, either because they conveniently ignore or explain away their failures or because they don't do a full accounting when calculating their performance records (most often both). In other words, your market-beating 15 percent average annual gains might really be a solid 10 percent or an anemic 5 percent if you count the commissions you paid and the taxes you incurred. This is especially true for active traders who buy and sell stocks on a daily, weekly, or monthly basis. We're against such an approach, but if that's your passion, it is essential that you review your investment records carefully, keeping these costs in mind. Because the math required for this effort can often be quite complicated, we suggest you avail yourself of any number of fine computer software programs oriented toward investment record keeping. Or you might simply go to the bookstore and pick up any number of investment books that offer worksheets to figure this out. Be warned, though: What you discover may be a blow to your ego.

If you are a person who's prone to kicking yourself for investment opportunities that you missed, we suggest you undertake the following exercise. For at least a month, write down every investment idea that you have, then tuck that paper away in a drawer somewhere. In about a year, take it out and see how all your picks have done. We suspect that while several will have outperformed the market, an equal or greater number won't. Again, this is a useful and interesting way to avoid succumbing to fond memories.

Take 25 percent off the top, add 25 percent to the bottom. Unfortunately there's no hard-and-fast rule for quantifying how big a problem overconfidence and optimism may be for you or anyone else. Nonetheless, a helpful way to deal with overconfidence is to incorporate an "overconfidence discount" into your projections, both on the upside and on the downside. This notion, as it happens, is already a common rule of thumb in some areas of life. For example, most experts counsel homeowners to add 10 percent to contractors' remodeling estimates, in terms of both cost and completion time. Our experience suggests 25 percent may be a better figure, but you can choose whatever number you're comfortable with. The key is to apply the discount on both sides of the transaction. For example, if you're thinking about investing in a stock, force yourself to come up with a realistic performance appraisal over your intended holding period, as well as the potential downside if things go wrong for the company. Then subtract 25 percent from your optimistic forecast and add 25 percent to your doomsday scenario. If the trade-off between potential risk and reward still seems worth it, go ahead. If not, you might want to walk away. In either case, though, the exercise is almost certain to make you consider aspects of the investment that you had otherwise ignored or forgotten.

Think à la carte. Overconfidence about our willingness or ability to follow through on our commitments and interests often leads us to buy "discount" packages, subscriptions, and memberships that are anything but. Before you sign up for such deals, it's worth experimenting with the product or service in question for a couple of months to determine how much you'll really use it. That "extra" cost might end up saving you a lot more in the long run.

Ask three good questions. Because overconfidence is so powerful, one of the best ways to beat it is to establish rules for decision making now when you're not actually making the decisions. By this we mean a checklist of sorts that you can refer to when important choices come around. And because we know that you're unlikely to do even this—hey, we're realists—we have one simple rule you might be able to follow when making any crucial decision: Ask three good questions before deciding. Which three questions? We don't know, but they usually begin with "Why?" This idea, adapted from the "Five Whys" approach in corporate quality-control philosophies like TQM or Six Sigma, requires you to get in the habit of drilling a little deeper on big decisions, forcing yourself to recognize at the very least that you may not yet have the answers to important questions. So if you're thinking about investing, ask yourself, "Why this particular investment?" And if the answer is because you have a hunch or your friend Jim recommended it, ask yourself, "What is the basis of that good feeling?" Or, "Why does Jim really think this stock will appreciate over time?" And if the answer is that Jim has a good track record in picking investments, ask yourself, "How do I really know?" These generic questions sound silly, but you get the idea. You need a system to help you overcome your own self-confidence.

Get a second opinion. This advice is a great tonic for people who tend to think too highly of their own experiences. But what we're suggesting may not be what you're thinking. Yes, it's always a fine idea to ask your friends and other knowledgeable people what they think about an investment or purchase you're considering. But what if they are as overconfident or uninformed as you are? For example, what good did it do for Gary's friend to have asked his trainers about treadmills? Our idea is slightly different. We're suggesting that when you make important financial decisions, you should ask trusted friends or experts what they think of your decision-making *process*. In other words, don't ask if they agree with your decision, ask if they think the way you went about reaching your decision was wise and thorough. Had Gary's friend asked him that question, Gary might have said he thought it unwise to ignore the opinions of the professionals at the ratings magazine whose job it is to evaluate products. And the thoughts of others need not even be those of pros. Sometimes similarly interested parties can do the trick. We were reminded of this by a 2008 study by Samuel D. Bond of the Georgia Institute of Technology in Atlanta and Kurt A. Carlson and Ralph L. Keeney of Duke University in Durham, North Carolina. When MBA students were asked to generate objectives that most mattered to them in choosing an internship, they came up with an average of seven each. But when the students compared their choices with objectives generated by other students, they identified at least as many new points to ponder that mattered to them as much as the ones they formulated themselves. Sometimes you need a little help, and the best assistance might just come from people in the same boat as you. There are a lot of ways in which the Internet has complicated decision making, but its ability to connect you with folks facing the same choice but asking different questions is a definite plus.

But even as we recommend that you seek counsel from others, we must once again throw up a yellow flag of caution. As you'll learn in the next chapter, people often rely *too* heavily on the opinions and actions of others. You may not be as smart as you think you are, but you may still be smarter than many other folks.

7

HERD IT THROUGH THE GRAPEVINE

*George and Jane recently bought a new Lexus for
$32,000 after carefully researching their decision.
Oddly, over the next few months a flood of strangers began offering the couple smaller and smaller
amounts of money to buy it from them. As far as they
could tell, the vehicle was in fine shape; a few thousand miles and a ding or two, but otherwise the engine was purring. Still, George and Jane seriously
considered selling the Lexus for half what they paid
for it because they worried something might have
been wrong. Should they have sold?*

Before you snicker at the silliness of the above question—
"Why on earth should they sell their car simply because people keep offering them less and less for it?"—ask yourself
what your advice to George and Jane might be if it wasn't a

Lexus they were thinking they should dump, but one thousand shares of Toyota stock they had purchased for $32 a share and that had recently fallen to $16. We're pretty sure many of you would advise the couple to sell their Toyota shares in a hurry. In fact, we're certain of it, since several hundred years of stock market history have shown that all too often that's what many investors do: They buy stock in companies or shares in mutual funds, presumably for sound reasons, but often sell those shares the minute "the market" turns against them. They cut and run as soon as a bunch of complete strangers starts offering them less and less for their investment than what they paid. Conversely, many investors will pay higher and higher prices for stocks (or paintings or real estate or anything else) simply because other people they don't know are willing to pay such prices.

On Wall Street, they call this investing with the herd, and the pervasiveness of this approach to managing money is expressed in another securities industry aphorism, "The trend is your friend." In other words, don't outthink the road signs. "If the bulk of investors think Consolidated Keyboards is a wonderful stock, who am I to disagree?" And if those same investors decide next month that keyboards are a thing of the past, well, they must know what they're talking about. Even people who exhibit the sort of overconfidence we discussed in the previous chapter can fall victim to this lemming-like behavior. That's because their overconfidence allows them to overestimate their ability to identify what the "smart money" thinks about a particular investment or company and to make investment decisions accordingly.

Of course, the idea that people conform to the behavior of others is among the most accepted principles of psychology. It was perhaps most famously demonstrated in the "laboratory" by a renowned social psychologist named Solomon Asch. In several landmark experiments in the 1950s, Asch asked participants to answer a series of judgment questions—which black line among three in one image was the same length as a fourth line in a separate image. The evaluations were meant to be easy, and the vast majority of participants nailed them when answering the questions in private. But when they were put into rooms where other "participants"—who were working for Asch—voiced incorrect answers, the actual participants agreed with them one-third of the time (and three-quarters of them conformed to the obviously mistaken majority during at least one trial).

Conformity often results from uncertainty. We follow others because we don't know what to do. A few years

BUILDING A BETTER BRAINSTORM

A while back, the behavioral economist Dan Ariely conducted a curious experiment: He and a colleague played waiter for a spell at a popular brew house in North Carolina. For half the tables they served, the researchers read out the available beer options before asking each customer to order. For the other half, they read the available options out loud again, but gave each patron an order sheet to fill out. Curiously, when patrons ordered out loud, they chose a wider variety of beers than when they wrote down their orders. This is another example of the concern with public image that led Asch's participants to conform but here with the opposite result. The brew-house patrons likely wanted to be seen by their peers as original thinkers, so they picked brands that hadn't been ordered yet. Privately, though, their true preferences were more likely to emerge. It's a lesson to keep in mind when brainstorming or having other group events where honest exchanges of ideas are crucial. One tip: Have people submit at least some of their ideas before the meeting. That way, they're likely to express what they're really thinking.

back, sociologist Matthew Salganik led a research project that established an artificial music market in which fourteen thousand music fans downloaded unfamiliar songs. When participants were allowed to see songs ranked by how many times they'd already been downloaded, they began herding after those tunes (when the number of downloads were listed but not ranked, the effect was much less pronounced). Experiments with smart-cart technology in supermarkets have demonstrated a similar tendency. When shoppers were informed, as they passed by a product, that many people in the store had chosen that item, they were more likely to grab one for themselves.

No matter what you call it—peer pressure, conforming to the norm, or going along to get along—your life is filled with instances large and small in which the thoughts or actions of a larger group or community influence your individual decisions. Have you ever seen a film simply because "everyone else" seems to be seeing it? Or bought a bestseller for no better reason than because it's a bestseller? Sure you have. Mostly such conformity is a good thing, and it's one of the reasons that societies are able to function: If people in general didn't accept standards of behavior, it would be impossible to drive a car without fear of head-on collisions, let alone hope to establish a system of law and government in which people by and large agree to follow a specific ideology (say, democracy) and a body of rules.

So we're all for conformity in many of its guises. The problem arises when people conform to larger habits or trends that may go against their own interests. In financial matters, that means allowing the judgment of others to steer you into unwise investments, or out of sound ones. You see, our concern is with the manner in which value is determined—or, more precisely, the manner in which you allow other people to determine the value of things for you. To some extent, certainly, what other people think matters a great deal. Beauty may be in the eye of the beholder, but value is often in the eye of the buyer. We might think this book is worth $250 a copy—but if readers don't agree, we're out of luck. Similarly, if George and Jane had *wanted* to sell their Lexus, then it was truly worth only what people were willing to pay for it—but only if George and Jane wanted to sell. If they didn't, then the value of their Lexus was theirs alone to decide. What happens too often, though, is that the Georges and Janes of the world let outside forces tell them when it's time to sell and to buy. They allow popular opinion and behavior to define value for them—sometimes for the good, but often not.

In this chapter, we're going to explore the way herds get rounded up and the ways that people are surprisingly prone to joining them. We're going to focus on investing, because it's the most obvious way to explore the phenomenon, but the principles can apply to almost any financial decision in which you tend to follow the leader. It's a complicated issue, because typically the opinions of others—a friend, a financial adviser, a loved one, or the general public—should count for something. That's why knowing when to go along and when to buck the trend can have a sizable impact on your finances. As you will see, people who rely on the madding crowd for investment advice often end up the poorer for their trouble.

WORSE THAN AVERAGE

Fact 1: From 1988 through 2008, the average stock mutual fund posted a yearly return of 8.4 percent, while the average bond mutual fund returned 7.4 percent a year.

*Fact 2: From 1988 through 2008, the average inves-
tor in a stock mutual fund earned 1.9 percent, while
the average investor in a bond mutual fund earned
less than 1 percent.*

Question: What's wrong with this picture?

The two statements you just read, both of which are true,
should strike you as extraordinarily strange—the equivalent of being told that the average commercial jetliner flies
at an altitude of thirty-five thousand feet, while the average
passenger in a commercial jetliner flies at fifteen thousand
feet. How can this be? How can mutual funds, generally described as the best thing to happen in personal finance since
dividends were invented, often be such a disappointing deal
for their investors? How can funds earn more than the people
who own them? Here's how: Rather than regularly investing
in a few well-researched mutual (ideally index) funds, then
holding on to them for a very long time through thick and
thin—the classic buy-and-hold strategy—most people flit in
and out of a whole passel of funds in an effort to maximize
their returns.

That tendency has become ever more common in recent
years, as the number of mutual funds has exploded and the
information about them has increased in availability. Today
the typical fund shareholder—there are about 90 million of
them in the United States alone—hangs on to a fund for less
than four years, compared with an average holding period of
more than sixteen years in 1970. And that's only an average:
Millions of investors find that bouncing in and out of funds
is as easy as dialing a toll-free telephone number or going
online—which, alas, it is.

None of this would matter, though, if folks managed to

switch into funds that performed better than the ones they leave behind. The problem is that they don't, and much of the reason can be attributed to the folly of herd investing. That's because fund hoppers are generally playing a financial version of follow the leader. Unhappy with the lagging performance of their current investments, they pour their cash into other funds that have posted strong recent returns or whose assets have been growing by leaps and bounds thanks to a rush of other investors. Typically these funds have recently received favorable recommendations from a research service such as Morningstar or from any number of personal finance publications or programs.

The trouble is, when you chase after strong past performance, the trend is very often *not* your friend, for two reasons. First, a fund's record often looks best just before its investment strategy stops working (remember the phenomenon of regression to the mean that we discussed in the introduction?). Consider, for example, the gangbuster performance of mutual funds that invested in shares of Internet stocks. Had you jumped on that bandwagon in the late 1990s—as many investors did—you would have received quite a jolt when the so-called dot-com bubble burst. That leads us to our second point: Unless you're among the first in line, chances are you're investing at a time when the prices of the stocks or bonds in which your new fund invests have already enjoyed a steep climb. So you're investing with the herd, only you're at the end of the pack. Result: Many investors take their money out of poor-performing funds just before they begin to rebound and put their dough into zooming funds just before they stall. Then they repeat the cycle all over again.

Are we contradicting what we said earlier when we urged readers not to sell their winners too quickly and hang on to their losers too long? Not at all. The "average" winner is unlikely to be the type of "flavor of the month" investment we are discussing here—one that has been run up excessively and is thus headed for a steep fall. Thus an investment that has been doing well during the time you've owned it shouldn't be sold simply because you're nervous about not locking in the profit you've made. If it's a sound investment, there should be more gains on the way. Note that the information you receive about such investments (the sound performance and solid investor confidence that is reflected in the rising price) is quite different from the type of information you receive about the latest "hot" investment (the frenzied interest you've heard about secondhand). It is no contradiction to say that you should be more swayed by the former than the latter.

More than anything, it's this sell-low, buy-high approach that keeps shareholder returns below that of the funds in which they invest. Consider this example, courtesy of then–*Money* mutual fund columnist Jason Zweig (now with the *Wall Street Journal*). In 1997, Zweig—along with *Money* reporter Malcolm Fitch and former Securities and Exchange Commission economist Charles Trzcinka—analyzed the total returns reported by more than one thousand U.S. stock funds for 1996 and more than eight hundred funds for the three years that ended in December of that year. Among their findings, the average shareholder at more than a dozen *profitable* U.S. stock funds actually *lost* money in 1996. And many more investors, who weren't quite so unlucky as to lose money while their fund was profiting, nonetheless fared far worse than they might have expected.

Zweig illustrated his point back then with the case of PBHG Core Growth, an aggressive stock fund that had more than $50 million in assets at the beginning of 1996.

In the first three months of the prior year, while the benchmark S&P 500 index of stocks rose 5.4 percent, PBHG Core Growth zoomed an even more impressive 18.2 percent. Indeed, for the entire year the fund returned a whopping 32.8 percent, compared with better than 28 percent for the S&P 500. The problem, though, was that most people who invested in PBHG Core Growth that year missed most of the good stuff. Here's the math: At the end of March, the fund had just $31 million in assets. But after its eye-popping performance in the first quarter—duly noted in the press and in the fund's ads—a pack of fund hoppers pounced into the fund: In May and June, they added more than $200 million to PBHG Core Growth's assets. Too bad, since in the second half of the year the fund lost 3.8 percent. So even though the fund gained more than 32 percent over the year, its average shareholder *lost* 3 percent.

RUNNING WITH THE BULLS

It may seem that we're just stating the obvious. Even the most inexperienced investor knows that money can be lost by running headlong with the bulls into a dubious investment. That was painfully obvious when global stock markets collapsed in unison in 2008, and even more classically during the so-called dot-com bubble of the late 1990s and early part of this century. In what can only be described as a mania of sorts, investors smitten with the promise of the Internet and fearful of getting left behind while others grew rich, bid up the share prices of any companies that even sounded like they were connected to Web technology. But not as many people remembered that herds move both ways, causing many people to abandon perfectly fine investments. We suspect—in fact, we're betting on it in our own retirement portfolios—

that a decade from now many investors will look back at some of the prices now being paid for shares of excellent companies and scratch their heads at having missed the chance to make so much money. But that's the rub with paying too close attention to the herd; you can't hear anything else. We included an illustrative example of this in an earlier version of this book, and it bears repeating. It concerns some herd behavior that was witnessed soon after Bill Clinton was elected president and began his much-ballyhooed efforts to reform the nation's health care system. Given the size of the task—the health care industry in all its incarnations accounted for roughly one-seventh of the United States economy at the time—and the difficulty of even conceiving of a reasonable way to implement change, investors were concerned about the future of health care companies.

This concern tended to manifest itself as pessimism—understandably so, when you consider that the implied goal was to cut the rising levels of health care costs. That could only hurt the profits of health care providers, especially pharmaceutical makers, whose impressive stock price growth over the previous decade had been fueled by the firms' immense drug profits. That's what the "smart money" said, and that's what drove down prices of all health care companies, including such blue-chip companies as pharmaceutical giant Johnson & Johnson. Indeed, professional stock pickers began selling their J&J shares in early 1992, followed quickly by a horde of individual investors. One woman explained her reasons for dumping her J&J shares in early 1993 and pretty much summed up the general feeling of her investing peers: "I don't know how health care reform is going to turn out, but if Washington gets involved, it's not going to be good." As a result of such widespread sentiment, J&J's share price plummeted 30 percent over an eighteen-month period.

But there was one flaw with the market's reasoning, and it wasn't even that health care reform never materialized. It was the fact that if investors had been paying attention to Johnson & Johnson's business fundamentals, they would have noticed that (1) J&J manufactures lots of other things besides drugs, such as baby shampoo, contact lenses, and Band-Aid adhesive strips; and (2) the company's profits were continuing to rise even as health care costs in general were stagnating. Instead, too many investors paid heed to what other investors thought of the company's prospects under health care reform. The cost? After bottoming out at $36, J&J's stock almost doubled by the end of 1997.

THE MADDING CROWD

Using the dot-com bubble and investor overreaction to the possibility of health care reform is a bit like shooting fish in a barrel. Both examples are so extreme as to be parodies of the genre. But we dredge them up for a reason different from the ease with which both confirm our thesis. Despite their disparate story lines, both the Internet boom and the health care reform saga were chronicled extensively in the media during the periods in which we examined their investment performance. This fact is extremely important if you are to understand how investing trends start and how you might avoid falling victim to them. But first a little background.

Through the years, a variety of social mechanisms have been identified as the major causes of (or catalysts for) uniformity of behavior—that is, there are a variety of different ways that people learn to conform to the actions of others, learn to *want* to conform, and learn to decipher the clues that dictate how that conformity should manifest. One mechanism might be called "sanctions": Children learn that temper tantrums are frowned upon when they are sent for a "time-out." Adults learn that assault is unacceptable when they are arrested for it, and they learn that removing money from a tax-deferred retirement account is a no-no when they are levied with a 10 percent early-withdrawal penalty. The flip side of sanctions is positive reinforcement: Behaving in class brings praise from teachers, just as keeping your lawn manicured earns the approval of neighbors. Such enforcement can be obvious (the government encourages people to save for retirement by offering tax breaks) or implied (some people seem to think you're "hip" when you wear the latest fashions, so you keep wearing them).

Whatever the mechanism, though, the desire or tendency to conform—to follow in the footsteps of others—is enhanced when people are in a state of uncertainty or con-

ALL THE WORLD IS NOT A STAGE

In the late 1990s, Tom and some colleagues at Cornell explored one reason why we try so hard to conform. It's called the "spotlight effect," and it is humbling and instructive. A typical experiment went like this: Tom's crew researched which current entertainer's image would be considered especially unhip to wear on a T-shirt. (The "winner": Barry Manilow.) A volunteer was then asked to put on the shirt before joining a group of other students filling out questionnaires. After a minute, the volunteer was pulled from the room and asked to guess how many people had noticed his T-shirt. On average, T-shirt wearers guessed that nearly half the other students had noticed; in fact, only one in five had. The key lesson is not that fewer people are paying attention to you than you think; it's that you're paying more attention to what you think people are thinking about you than is warranted. The point is crucial, since so many of your money decisions are influenced by your thoughts about who will be paying attention to what you bought.

fusion. If you throw an otherwise self-confident corporate chieftain into unfamiliar territory—say, a climbing expedition up Mount Everest—she is probably more likely to do as the Sherpas do than as she would in the executive dining room. Any alternative looks appealing in a vacuum: When you don't have any idea what to do or how to behave— particularly in times of crisis or anxiety—the fact that a lot of other people seem to have a plan is a very compelling reason for mimicking them.

That's especially relevant in any discussion of money and investing. As an increasing number of people become involved in the stock market—say, by dint of retirement plans at work—they are often thrown into situations about which they know very little and about which they are subjected to various and competing sorts of advice. Doing what everyone else does is not an unreasonable alternative in that situation, and it has a bonus allure: If your decision turns out to be unwise, you can at least comfort yourself with the knowledge that a lot of other people made the same decision (some of whom may even be famous). It's not so much that misery loves company as that misery loves to dodge blame.

In any event, the more uncertain people are—and the higher the stakes involved—the more vulnerable they are to the sort of cue taking that leads to herd behavior. That's why teenagers are presumably more likely to succumb to peer pressure than adults. They have less experience to draw upon when evaluating the pros and cons of conforming, and the stakes are higher: Going one's own way really does have greater consequences for a seventeen-year-old than for a thirty-seven-year-old. But the stakes are pretty high even for adults when the issue is money, a fact that often leaves investors in a highly vulnerable state of mind: They're desperate for guidance, ripe for taking cues from almost anyone.

This heightened sensitivity to the actions of others dovetails neatly with a notable theory about fads, trends, and crowd behavior. In a 1992 paper in the *Journal of Political Economy,* economist Sushil Bikhchandani, along with finance professors David Hirshleifer and Ivo Welch, described a phenomenon they called "information cascade." Their work sheds light on one of the great puzzles of finance and economics: Why do investors consistently "overreact," paying too much for securities that later fall in price (and too little for investments that turn out to be worth far more)?

Essentially, their theory posits that large trends or fads begin when individuals decide to ignore their private information and focus instead on the actions of others, even if that action conflicts with their own knowledge or instincts. Think about a traffic jam on a freeway and how you might be tempted to follow a driver who abruptly veers onto a little-used exit, even if you doubt that it will save you any time. The actions of a few people lead others to mimic their behavior, which in turn leads even more people to imitate

POP! GOES THE BUBBLE

It's worth noting that the faster a herd-induced bubble inflates, the more quickly it's likely to burst. Not too long ago, Jonah Berger and Gaël Le Mens of the Wharton School of Business looked at the first names that parents in the United States give their kids. What they found was that, adjusting for overall popularity (James is consistently more common than Anton) the faster a newly fashionable name becomes popular, the more quickly it loses its appeal. If Madison became hot more quickly than Brittany, chances are that Madison won't remain popular as long. It appears that the faster a trend develops, the more likely people are to suspect it's a fad or a bubble and try to get out while the getting is good.

that behavior, and so on. What's especially interesting about the theory is that it showed that even the smallest bit of new information can lead to rapid and wholesale changes in behavior. As they wrote: "If even a little new information arrives, suggesting that a different course of action is optimal, or if people even suspect that underlying circumstances have changed (whether or not they really have), the social equilibrium may radically shift." In other words, it doesn't take much for the terrain to shift dramatically.

This observation rings especially true in financial markets, where new information arrives by the second. That's why the dot-com bubble and health care reform narratives are illustrative. Both situations were heavily monitored by the news media, which offered regular bits of new information (some important, some not) that caused those who follow the minute-by-minute movements of stock prices to take action. Their action subsequently led to even more investors following suit. This only reinforced the apparent wisdom of the initial investors, leading them to repeat their actions.

Think about it this way: You sell (or buy) a stock, which causes its share price to fall (or rise). This leads other investors to sell (or buy) their shares, which causes the price to fall (or rise) even more, which leads you to repeat your actions. That's how a stock market crash—and, in the opposite direction, a stock market bubble—gets started. But what's even more important to understand about all of this is that very often the forces that move markets and investment prices, at least in the short run, are not directly related to the true worth of the underlying assets or companies. Powerful information cascades lead people to sell simply because other people are selling, or to buy because other people are buying.

• • •

Remember that one of the basic principles of modern economics is that the market is efficient. That is, stock prices reflect all the knowledge and experience of investors, so it's useless to try to pick stocks because the market knows better than you. You'd do just as well throwing darts at the stock listings of the newspaper.

This may or may not be true over time. But numerous studies have shown that investors are notoriously off the mark when assessing the worth of companies on a day-to-day, or even a year-to-year, basis. Partly due to information cascades—because people are prone to go with the flow—investors often overreact to both good and bad news, causing the prices of favored companies to rise too high and prices of tainted companies to fall too low. A good example of this phenomenon turns up in a study published in the *Journal of Finance* in 1985, authored by behavioral economics pioneer Richard Thaler and finance professor Werner De Bondt.

Thaler and De Bondt, known for their exploration of securities' price movements, analyzed the performance of stocks listed on the New York Stock Exchange (NYSE) that had either risen or fallen in excess of the average ups and downs of share prices in general. They examined six-year and ten-year blocks of time, which they divided in half. Then, using returns from the first half of each period—what they called the "formation period"—they came up with separate portfolios of winners (stocks whose gains were above average) and losers (shares whose drops were steeper than average). Finally, they examined how the winners and losers performed over the second half of the study periods (the "holding period," in their words). Their findings: "Extreme returns of stocks listed on the New York Stock Exchange were found to be subsequently followed by significant price movement in the opposite direction. Using ten-year blocks of time, loser portfolios earned from the beginning to the end of the five-year holding periods an average of 30% more than the winner portfolios. Using the same procedure with six-year blocks of time, losers outperformed winners by almost 25% during the three-year holding periods."

Let's restate that in simpler terms. Thaler and De Bondt showed that when investors react in extremes—remember, they looked at stocks whose prices bounced up or down in excess of the movements of the typical NYSE share—their reactions will likely be reversed over time. Although the term *information cascade* had yet to be coined, Thaler and De Bondt effectively demonstrated how such overreaction offers a tremendous opportunity to make money, like the

THE HERD IS SMALLER THAN YOU THINK

During a recent market plunge—when news reports mentioned that billions of dollars had been lost in a few days—a friend claimed that he could make a bundle if only he knew "where all that money was going." His logic: The money taken out of stocks had to be invested somewhere else. This common misconception is due largely to the fact that many people don't understand how stocks are priced and how the actions of a relatively small number of investors can seem like a stampede. Specifically, stock prices are set at the margins of shareholder ownership. If one hundred people own shares of Belsky & Gilovich Inc. stock worth $100 a share, the total market value of the company is $10,000 (100 times $100). Gary's mom decides to sell her share, but because there are no buyers at $100, she sells it to Tom's wife for $90. In the next day's paper, B&G Inc.'s stock price is listed at $90—the most recent sale price—so the company's market value is now $9,000 (100 times $90), a whopping 10 percent less than the day before. While some money has "left the market"—Gary's mom has $90 in her pocket—it's far less than the $1,000 loss in market value.

one that presented itself when investors overreacted to the potential for health care reform to harm Johnson & Johnson. When pessimistic investors dampen a company's stock price, odds are it will bounce back. Conversely, when overly optimistic buyers inflate a firm's share price, odds are it will fall back. It's an example, once again, of regression to the mean—the idea that extremes tend to revert back to something closer to the average. But it's also a reminder that the crowd is often wrong.

Now, we're not suggesting you make investing decisions based solely on which stocks (or bonds or mutual funds) happen to be out of favor when you open the newspaper. Nor are we recommending that you sell your winners and hold on to your losers in the hope that regression to the mean will rescue you from your poor investment decisions. Such a strategy could be a recipe for disaster, inasmuch as the market is sometimes right on target. After all, Enron's shares tumbled once management's fraud was revealed, but that was hardly a reason to buy the company's stock.

Nonetheless, an entire school of investing is based on the premise that over short periods the market is often misguided but over the long run true value will win out. This school—called value investing—counts among its "graduates" some of the best investment minds in history, including Benjamin Graham, Warren Buffett, and John Neff. Over decades as investment managers and teachers—Graham was a legendary finance professor at Columbia University in New York City—these pros and others have demonstrated an uncanny knack for identifying companies that are out of favor with investors for any number of reasons, none of which has to do with their core business prospects. And over time those investors have been rewarded with market-beating investment returns. But even if you aren't confident enough (or foolish enough) to think that you can prospect for diamonds among lumps of coal, the lesson of this chapter is hardly diminished: If you insist on going along with the herd, you could very well find yourself heading straight for the slaughterhouse.

NO NEWS IS GOOD NEWS

One final word about the herd before we get to our advice section. We want to stress, as we have elsewhere in this chapter and book, that it's perfectly reasonable to take cues from others when trying to resolve your decision dilemma. But oftentimes we don't even know which cues we're taking, and once they're taken, we generally don't know what to do with them. That's especially true in the realm of investing. In some of their more recent research, Terrance Odean and Brad Barber, whose work informed earlier parts of this book, examined how investors solve complex investment decisions, which pretty much all of them are. In essence, Odean and Barber demonstrate that the typical investor, consciously or not, tries to simplify the whole process by focusing on what they call "salient" options—that is, shares that stand out from the sea of stocks available: usually because they were exceptionally strong (or poor) performers in the prior day's market close or because there was a lot of trading in those shares or because the underlying companies were in the news. Makes sense, right? With so much information out there to digest, we tend to focus on the outlier facts and trends; it's simpler.

Unfortunately, it's also misleading when it comes to investing. Often, the "salient" information is not remotely relevant. That's why we're of the strong belief that investors who tune in too closely to financial reports probably fare worse than those who tune out the news. Psychologist Paul B. Andreassen demonstrated this in the 1980s by comparing the performance of four groups of mock investors. Using the stock prices of real companies and real news reports, two of the groups made simulated investment decisions about a relatively stable stock—its share price didn't vary much over the course of the experiment. But one group was subjected to constant news reports about the company, while the other received no news. A similar test was given to two other groups, although the stock in question was subject to wider price swings than the shares of the other company. The results: Investors who received no news performed better than those who received a constant stream of information, good and bad. In fact, among investors who were trading the more volatile stock, those who remained in the dark earned better than *twice as much money* as those whose trades were influenced by the media.

HOW TO THINK AND WHAT TO DO
Warning Signs

You may be prone to following the herd if . . .
- you make investment decisions frequently.
- you invest in "hot" stocks or other popular investments.
- you sell investments because they're suddenly out of favor, not because your opinion of them has otherwise changed.
- you're likely to buy when stock prices are rising and sell when they are falling.
- you make spending and investment decisions based solely on the opinions of friends, colleagues, or financial advisers.
- your spending decisions are heavily influenced by which products, restaurants, or vacation spots are "in."

Life would be a whole lot simpler if we could tell you to ignore any and all investment trends and fads, but that would be a mistake. Sometimes the crowd knows best. Millions of Americans have moved into the stock market over the past twenty years or so, and following them would have been the right thing to do: A lot of money has been made by a lot of people as a result. Unfortunately, a lot more money might be in folks' pockets if they had managed to stick to a sound and simple investing strategy rather than following others blindly. Knowing when conventional wisdom is on target and when it is misguided is not easy, but the following suggestions should help you chart a safe and steady course of your own.

Hurry up and wait. When you're tempted to rush headlong into an investment trend, remember that financial fads are a lot like buses: There's no sense running after one, since another is certainly on its way. This is our way of saying that patience is paramount. Take the time and effort to thoroughly research any large-scale financial endeavor. Yes, there's a chance you might miss the boat. But there's as good a chance that you already have. If you're not sure, we urge you to remember the first rule of poker: If you look around the table and can't figure out who the sucker is, it's you. In any event, investment ideas that are worth their salt have staying power. A lot of people, nervous about taking their money out of banks and putting it into the stock market, missed most of the great run-up in stock prices during the 1980s. But many still made bucket loads of money when they finally started dipping their toes into the market a decade later.

Avoid hot investments. That's particularly true with mutual funds, which relentlessly advertise their recent records as a way to lure investors. But funds often rack up their gains in short bursts of a few months or a year. By the time you sign up, the fun could be over. That's one reason we advise investing in index funds. But if you nonetheless choose to invest in actively managed mutual funds, you should concentrate on less trendy portfolios whose performance records are consistently good, not recently great.

Don't date your investments, marry them. We have already explained how some people have a problem letting go of their losing investment, which is true enough. But too many investors have the opposite problem: They view their relationship with a stock, bond, or mutual fund as nothing more serious than a Las Vegas quickie wedding, bouncing in and out as they chase one investing fad or another. That's why it's crucial that you assemble a portfolio of a half dozen to a dozen major investments (fewer if you invest in funds, more if you buy individual stocks) and stay with them for the long term—at least five years and preferably longer. Pay no more attention to the latest investment trend than you would to a waitress at Hooters or a dancer at Chippendales: nice to look at, but hardly someone you'd bring home to meet your mom. One way to help maintain your investing fidelity is to follow our next bit of advice.

Tune out the noise. During the early part of Gary's tenure at *Money,* the magazine would periodically poll Americans to see how savvy they were about investing. Among other questions, respondents were sometimes asked to choose among several numbers to find the one closest to the recent level of the benchmark Dow Jones Industrial Average. Increasingly, though, as the magazine's writers and editors began to understand more about behavioral economics, they began to understand that *not* knowing where the Dow was could just as easily be a sign of investing intelligence as investing ignorance. That's because the best investors often ignore the majority of what passes as important financial news these days.

We suggest you do the same. Unless you need your money quickly—in which case you should probably have your cash tucked away in safe money market accounts or funds—you're probably better off disregarding most financial news. Warren Buffett, chairman of Berkshire Hathaway and one of the wisest investors ever, explained this attitude in his company's 1993 annual report. Wrote Buffett: "After we buy a stock, consequently, we would not be disturbed if markets closed for a year or two. We don't need a daily quote on our 100% position in See's or H. H. Brown (companies wholly owned by Berkshire Hathaway) to validate our well-being. Why, then, should we need a quote on our 7% interest in Coke?"

This may seem reckless—ignoring most financial news, including changes in share prices—but it's not. Long-term investors need not concern themselves with yesterday's closing price or tomorrow's quarterly earnings reports. After all, the investor who bought Johnson & Johnson stock in 1990 and didn't look at it until recently would be very happy with the stock's appreciation and would be none the worse for having missed all the speculation about health care reform. It's a simplistic example, yes, but it's also true.

Rely on rules. We've said this before and we'll doubtless say it again in the conclusion to our book: One of the best ways to tame our most costly biases is to deal with them before they come into play, and the best way to do that is to establish rules of conduct for certain situations before encountering them: rules for how much you will spend when traveling with friends (so you won't try to impress by conforming); rules for how to react when the stock market shoots up or plummets down (so you don't buy too late or sell too early). Few people love rules, but many people find them comforting in the face of decision dilemmas. Try setting up a few, and writing them down, and it won't be long before you extol their virtues, too.

Finally, look for opportunities to be a contrarian. Again, we're not suggesting that you blindly invest in every loser stock out there. That would be silly and contrary to our belief that you should have most of your money invested in index funds. That said, to whatever extent you do choose to take an active approach to investing, you could do a lot worse than beginning your search for appropriate investments by focusing on those investments that the general public has turned its back on. As we've already mentioned, many of the most successful investors in history followed just such an approach. Although this book is not an explicit how-to investment guide, we'd be foolish if we didn't note that one of the smartest ways to evaluate stocks—if you're determined to do so—is to focus on those with below-average price-to-earnings ratios, or P/Es.

A P/E is simply the ratio between a stock's price per share and its profits per share. It allows every company to be measured on an equal basis, regardless of size or business. So if Consolidated Steel is selling for $10 a share and has earnings per share of $1, the stock's price-to-earnings ratio is ten to one. Similarly, if Amalgamated Steel is selling for $100 a share but has earnings per share of $20, the stock's P/E is five to one. Two steel companies, one whose stock sells for $10 and one whose stock sells for $100. Yet the $100 stock is actually cheaper, a better bargain: For every $1 of Amalgamated profits, you must pay $5; $1 worth of Consolidated profits will cost you $10.

The reason investing in low P/E stocks can be considered a contrarian approach is this: P/Es reflect how much of a premium other investors are willing to pay to own shares of a given company. The higher the P/E, the higher the premium—and, therefore, the more popular that stock is. Low P/E stocks, on the other hand, reflect diminished investor enthusiasm. By way of example, in 1991, before Johnson & Johnson fell out of favor with investors as a result of concerns about health care reform, the company's average P/E was 20.5. By 1994 J&J's P/E ratio had slipped to an average of 14.8 (it's around 13 at this writing). Investors were wrong in that case, and as a general rule, you can make a lot more money buying out-of-favor stocks with low P/Es than crowd-pleasing stocks that may be too highly priced and ripe for a fall.

Of course, it's not easy discerning worthwhile stocks with low P/Es from those that are justifiably ignored by most investors and thus valued at bargain-basement prices. One of the best screens to use when analyzing such out-of-favor companies is to invest only in those with sound balance sheets—in other words, not too much debt, a lot of cash in the bank, and profitable operations. But, frankly, it's probably not worth the effort. The real contrarian approach to investing is to rebel against your instinct for believing that you can make sense of balance sheets, stock reports, economic conditions, industry trends, and a dozen other factors that influence stock prices. As we'll argue again in our book's conclusion, you'll likely be a lot richer if you cast your lot with a few mutual funds and forget about everything else but making regular contributions to them for the next ten, twenty, or thirty years.

8

EMOTIONAL BAGGAGE

Imagine for a moment that you're back in high school. Try to remember that time in your life as vividly as you can, specifically an instance when you felt excluded by other students. It doesn't matter whether you were on the football team or the chess team, a prom queen or a wallflower. Just try to recall a situation when everyone else who mattered to you socially was "in" and you were "out." It may take a few moments, so we'll wait. [Undetermined pause.] Come up with something? Good. Think about if for a minute or two. Now estimate the temperature of the room in which you are sitting.

A few chapters back we observed that we wouldn't have been misguided had we written this book as one long essay about loss aversion, the bedrock principle of behavioral economics explored by the renowned research psychologists Daniel Kahneman and Amos Tversky. In many ways, we could just as honestly make the same observation regarding the subject of this chapter, which we'll loosely describe as the role of emotion in decision making in general and financial choice in particular. The book wouldn't have read the same—our chapters and paths of reasoning would have taken different forms and shapes—but we would have reached much the same conclusions and offered similar advice.

That's because emotions are partners in all the decision-making processes that we've been discussing; aiders and abettors, if you will, in the rules of thumb that our brains employ to make choosing and understanding the world faster and less complicated. We'll gladly refund the price of this book to any reader who can honestly contend that he or she has never regretted a decision with words to this effect: "I would have done it differently if I hadn't been so [emotional state here]!"

And like most of the judgment and decision-making biases we've been discussing, emotions often exert their influence on us in the shadows; even if we expect our moods and outlook to inform our behavior in certain ways, we may miss how they determine our actions in others. Consider, as just one example, the effect of the weather on stock markets. We refer not to what is undoubtedly a significant connection between rainfall, corn production, and the stock price of Kellogg's. Rather, we're talking about the effect of weather on mood, and mood on investment decisions. Exhibit A: An examination of stock markets in twenty-six countries over a fifteen-year period revealed that the amount of sunshine on a given day is, as academics like to say, positively correlated with market performance. That is, the market tends to rise more often on sunny days and fall more often on gloomy days, a result that researchers, finance professors David Hirshleifer and Tyler Shumway, argued was due to investors incorrectly attributing their sunshine-induced good spirits to positive economic circumstances.

This study doesn't presume to prove that the prices of particular stocks over the years are affected by the moods of investors—over the long run, they reflect nothing so much as the underlying values of the businesses they represent—only that how we feel affects how we act on any given day. Recall again the words of the legendary finance professor Benjamin Graham, who described the stock market as a weighing machine in the long run but a voting machine in the short run; sometimes how we vote is determined by how we feel when we're at the polls. Likewise, how we spend, save, and borrow is tied to our dispositions. Understanding how requires a Cook's tour of the human brain. What we hope to show you over the next few pages is that your emotions "help" you make decisions in life in a manner that is sometimes quite useful but can also be highly counterproductive. Which brings us back to the exercise at the beginning of this chapter. We adapted it from a study by Canadian psychologists Chen-Bo Zhong and Geoffrey Leonardelli that asked thirty people to recall an experience in which they had been socially excluded, and another thirty to remember a time when they basked in the inclusive arms of others. Immediately after, the researchers asked the participants to guess the temperature of the room in which they were sitting (ostensibly to help the maintenance staff solve a heating and air-conditioning problem). Curiously, the average guess from members of the group that thought about exclusion was three degrees colder than the average guess of group members who recalled being included. In remembering a time when they were metaphorically frozen out, they physically felt a little colder. Our point here is not to suggest that feeling ostracized will make you more likely to buy a sweater, although it might. Rather, we mean to emphasize again that how you *feel* can affect how you *think*. This idea is both patently obvious and incalculably mysterious, as is the difference between thoughts and feelings themselves.

THINKING, FEELING, AND EVERYTHING IN BETWEEN

If you consider the subject for a moment, there's probably a very good reason why our brains evolved to equate the mental feeling of exclusion with a physical feeling of coldness. A long time ago in human history, being shut out from a clan or tribe or village had far more serious consequences than being excluded from a high school clique. The latter leaves you without a date or study partner. The former might leave you on your own in a hostile environment, without shelter, food, companionship, or protection from predators or the elements. Feeling a little chilly already, aren't you? And possibly a little more willing to compromise and get along with the group. Which makes sense: We are the descendants of those who understood the benefits of inclusion, not those who didn't.

Indeed, this is as good a time as any to discuss a field of study that, like emotions and decision making, has grown in prominence since we first wrote this book. That field is generally called "neuroeconomics," and it's essentially the exploration of how the structures and functions of the brain affect our decisions, financial and otherwise. In fact, you might reasonably say that if behavioral economics is a study of the mind's role in financial decision making, neuroeconomics is a study of the brain's role in the same arena. Not surprisingly, neuroeconomics is in many ways a bridge between the study of the role of emotions in choice and the broad collection of heuristics that has come to define behavioral economics. And while this may sound a little complicated, it's really not that hard to grasp. You just need to understand two basic ways the brain processes information and makes decisions, a duality that is at its core a function and manifestation of the physical structure of the gray matter that sits inside all our skulls.

The idea that the brain operates in two different ways, we imagine, isn't entirely new to most readers. Exaggerated images of "left-brain" people (emotional, creative) and "right-brain" people (analytical, logical) penetrated popular culture quite some time ago. But as the financial writer Jason Zweig writes in his excellent book *Your Money & Your Brain*, "Right and left have less to do with it than above and below." Essentially, the brain's architecture can be described in broad terms as one in which the parts that we think of as more emotional or instinctual sit below the parts we think of as more analytical. The location is not as important as the distinction, for our purposes, but the instinctual parts of the brain are situated where they are mostly because they came first. Our brains, we might say (with apologies to all the neurobiologists out there), were built from the ground floor up. That's because if our ancestors were going to evolve higher functions, they first had to survive, and those who did were those blessed with lightning-fast reflexes and thinking processes that maximized access to scarce resources and minimized vulnerability to danger situations. From these parts of the brain, composing what is sometimes called the "reflexive system," spring emotions like fear and disgust (which help us react to immediate dangers), or greed (which prods us to quick action when valuable resources seem ripe for the taking). They are what some might call basic or even pri-

DRAW YOUR OWN CONCLUSIONS

One way to understand the influence—and value—of emotions on decision making comes from research involving people with damage to areas of the brain that control the ways we "mark" emotional consequences of certain actions. In a study comparing neurologically impaired people with undamaged participants, a team of researchers led by neurologists Antoine Bechara and Antonio Damasio had both groups play a game. The goal: Earn as much money as possible by turning over cards that specified wins and losses of varying amounts. But the decks that contained cards with the biggest payoffs also held even bigger losses. Eventually, all the players realized that the safer play was to draw from the decks that had smaller individual payoffs but more modest losses as well. But the neurologically impaired participants never applied this lesson; they continued drawing from high-reward, high-risk decks until they went bankrupt. They did so not because they didn't understand the difference between the decks—they did—but because they couldn't translate that understanding into smart decision making. Intellectually they understood the dangers, but emotionally they were incapable of translating that knowledge into practical behavior. They didn't "feel" it.

mal emotions, and they occupy some of the lower rungs of our unconscious thought ladder, only slightly above the automatic processes that control functions like breathing. When we think of these emotions and processes, in fact, we often use metaphors of the body: "gut instinct," "from the heart," "hair-raising." They are stealthy, quick, and powerful.

The other parts of the brain, housing what is often called the "reflective system," are where more reasoned thought takes place. They are the parts that allow us to write and do long division, to negotiate and to analyze. Although quiet, they are not as stealthy; although quick by most measures, they are more deliberate; and, of course, they are what made us the dominant species on the planet.

Needless to say, the two systems and their respective functions operate magnificently but also messily—sometimes independently, sometimes redundantly, and sometimes in concert. Many of their mechanisms and processes remain to be discovered and understood. That's where neuroeconomics enters the picture. Sometimes almost literally: Advances in technology (such as functional magnetic resonance imaging) now allow researchers to identify specific parts of the brain that are activated when we contemplate various financial problems and make certain choices. We're choosing to write about this topic now, and here, because for years much of behavioral economics research seemed to focus on the reflective system—on conscious, reasoned judgment and decision making. We say "seemed" because many of the field's leading lights never truly ignored the brain's duality, often anticipating much of the focus on emotions and other reflexive processes that would come later. For example, in his acceptance speech upon receiving his Nobel Prize, Daniel Kahneman, speaking about his early days of collaboration with Amos Tversky, wrote, "In the terminology that became accepted much later, we held a two-system view, which distinguished intuition from reasoning."

In any event, emotions have become an area of greater interest in recent years to many of the people who study behavioral economics. And so throughout this chapter, which in many ways is really the beginning of the end of our book, we're going to focus on intuition over reason, reflex over reflection. We do this because we believe that if you are to consciously absorb some or all of what we've been writing about, and if you are to use it to get more satisfaction from your money and your life, you need to understand the ways your less deliberate faculties might affect the ways in which you form judgments and make decisions. And it's highly probable that you understand less than you think you do, in much the same way investors are probably clueless about the extent to which a sunny or rainy day can affect their trading habits. We could, of course, write an entire volume about this topic; many have. Instead we'll try to avoid the obvious and center our thoughts on a few key ideas that might surprise you. First we'll look at the ways our current emotional states can affect our financial decisions—and the reasons why we have such a hard time understanding those causes and effects. Then we'll look at the way we make choices based on our forecasts about how we'll feel in the future, and how those projections are often wildly inaccurate.

SECONDHAND EMOTION

You need only watch one episode of *Sex and the City* to understand how widespread is the cultural understanding that the reflexive system can affect financial decisions. Actually, you need only look in the mirror. Who among us doesn't own at least one shirt or piece of furniture or consumer electronic device that was purchased because we were depressed? And how many of us have bought extra life insurance because we just heard about a friend who died suddenly, leaving his wife and young children in financial straits? For that matter, who hasn't bought some extra liability insurance when renting a car, not quite sure if our own policy covers it but suddenly terrified by the prospect that we'll get into a terrible accident and wind up liable for millions of dollars in damages? These are examples of the reflexive system in action: gut feelings that lead us to outcomes we might not choose if our reflective system were in full control. (That said, life is full of instances when it doesn't matter that your rational mind knows that your emotional mind is holding too much sway; people who fear heights understand that there's no real chance that they'll plummet to the sidewalk from a penthouse apartment, but just try getting them onto the terrace.)

Of course, you might see it as perfectly reasonable for folks to buy extra insurance in situations like these, or even to try to buy their way out of a funk with a new recliner. Even if they came from a reflexive process, the decisions taken have a perfectly logical connection to the emotions felt. And you'd be correct. What's more relevant to this discussion is how our current emotional states can affect our decisions in less defensible and more surprising ways—that is, when the mood and decision in question are not connected. Amos Tversky and Eric Johnson explored this idea in a seminal paper published in 1983. Specifically, the two researchers examined the ways that "incidental affective states" influence people's assessments of risk. In other words, they sought to find out whether people are more likely to, say, buy extra insurance (to use the above hypotheticals) if they are more anxious or fearful than normal, *regardless of the cause of that fear and anxiety*. In their study, Tversky and Johnson asked participants to rate the journalistic quality of news stories depicting anxiety-provoking, depressing, uplifting, or neutral events. Then they had those same folks estimate the number of people who die each year as a result of such things as traffic accidents, leukemia, and homicide. Result: Those who'd read the anxiety-provoking or depressing articles provided significantly higher estimates than those who read either neutral or uplifting stories.

The implications of this study and other similar research are profound. (Recall the sunshine-and-stocks example from earlier.) Most people intuitively understand that feelings connected to an issue or decision can affect our thoughts and choices; we know we are vulnerable coffin buyers. But few people are truly cognizant that their feelings about, say, a favorite sports team might affect their judgments and choices about insurance or credit cards or investing. And we're not just picking a random topic from thin air. Consider a study by finance professors Alex Edmans, Diego Garcia, and Oyvind Norli, who found that stock market returns drop when a country's soccer team is eliminated from a prominent tournament such as the World Cup, and that similar dips occur in countries following losses in other sports that are popular there (like cricket, rugby, and basketball). That's how powerful the reflexive system can be: When we feel bad—

WHY SO TENSE?

To the many causes of stock market turmoil you can add another: stress. Not too long ago, psychologists Anthony Porcelli and Mauricio Delgado wanted to see the level of financial risk people were willing to take depending on whether they were calm or stressed. Working with students, some of whom were forced to keep one of their hands in ice-cold water, the researchers orchestrated a gambling game in which participants could choose between, say, an 80 percent chance of losing 75 cents and a 20 percent chance of losing $3. Similar propositions were available on the positive side: Participants could choose between, say, an 80 percent chance of winning 75 cents and a 20 percent chance of winning $3. What Porcelli and Delgado discovered was that stressed-out students were likelier to take more risk when facing the prospect of a loss, and likelier to be more conservative when deciding between large and small gains. It's not hard to see how this tendency might contribute to sudden market plunges: When anxiety is high, losses are large and our reflexive brains are in fifth gear.

anxious, fearful, depressed—about one thing, significant or not, it can color our view of all things at that moment.

Of course, there is more to emotion than feeling bad or good. Some emotions, notably anger, are not necessarily one or the other; you can be angry for perfectly good reasons, producing a rather satisfying state that can even prove productive. Investors who were swindled by the notorious Bernard Madoff, for example, have doubtless channeled some of their anger into a healthy suspicion of money managers who promise consistently impressive returns regardless of the overall performance of financial markets. More dangerously, though, anger often is attached to feelings of certainty. This should make intuitive sense: If emotions evolved as survival tools, anger would have been more helpful to our ancestors if it went hand in hand with surety, while fear would naturally come with uncertainty.

These associations have been demonstrated in a number of studies. In one, researchers found that participants who'd been asked to think about events from their lives that made them angry (providing, in theory, a condition of high certainty) gave lower estimates of the likelihood that they would suffer various maladies than those who had been asked to think about events that made them afraid (low certainty). In a notable extension of this finding, a national sample of Americans was contacted two months after the 9/11 terrorist attacks on the World Trade Center and the Pentagon. Some of the respondents were led to focus on fear-inducing elements of the attacks; others on anger-inducing elements. The angry participants gave lower estimates of the likelihood of both future terrorist attacks and other, unrelated risks.

But anger, and its accompanying feeling of certainty, doesn't just affect risk perception. Other studies have found that people who were led to feel angry relied more on the source than the content of a persuasive communication to evaluate its merits than did those led to feel worried or surprised. In other words, the feeling of certainty associated with anger gives people the sense that they have a better handle on things, which in turn leads them to rely on relatively superficial cues, such as who is pitching the message. This, of course, is an example of how the reflexive and the reflective systems can mix, and how a fundamental principle of behavioral economics can intersect with a core principle of the study of emotions: The sense of certainty that comes with anger might easily remind some of the overconfidence bias we discussed at length in Chapter 6.

It's worth noting, by the way, that anger isn't the only emotion that springs from and leads to feelings of certainty. Contentment is another such emotion. And, again, this makes sense when you think about emotions as survival tools. Being satisfied with your lot, after all, will likely lead you to decisions of complacency and inaction, since having what you need means that you can rest rather than expend valuable time, energy, and resources. But as with anger, in today's world a sense of certainty resulting from feelings of contentment or joy can lead to a dangerous willingness to rely on superficial information in decision making, especially information that reinforces those feelings. So, for example, investors will react reflexively and positively to the shares of companies that change their names to edgier, hipper-sounding alternatives. Zweig, in *Your Money & Your Brain*, gives the example of investor reaction to the announcement a few years back that Computer Literacy Inc. had changed its name to fatbrain.com: The share price went up 33 percent in one day of trading. Likewise, the willingness of investors to act based on meaningless cues was demonstrated in a study that examined the relationship between the name of a company newly listed on the stock exchange and its performance. Stocks in companies with easy-to-pronounce names (say, Belden or Accenture) performed better the day after and one week after they were listed than companies with hard-to-pronounce names (Magyar Tavkozlesi, for instance, or Inspat International). Those who were initially swayed by the sound of a stock's name suffered for being so, as the prices of easy-to-pronounce stocks were not higher six months later. Eventually, the performance of the company, its profitability, not its name, carried the day.

There are other examples of the tricky ways in which current emotional states can affect our decisions, regardless of their relevance. They are countless, really. But we'll explore two more, if only because research into the effects of moods touches upon another bedrock principle of behavioral economics, the endowment effect. You'll recall that this is the tendency to value a good more if we own it than we would if we don't. It was the focus of a fascinating study a few years back by the behavioral economists Jennifer S. Lerner, Deborah A. Small, and George Loewenstein. In their paper (cleverly titled "Heart Strings and Purse Strings: Carryover Effects of Emotions on Economic Decisions"), the researchers were considering the effect of two primal emotions—disgust and sadness—on unrelated economic decisions. To achieve those desired moods, as well as a third neutral state, the researchers showed short clips from three films to study participants: *The Champ* (in which the death of a boy's mentor was meant to spark feelings of sadness), *Trainspotting* (where a particularly graphic toilet scene was used to induce disgust), and a *National Geographic* special (about the Great Barrier Reef, which was meant to have very little or no emotional influence).

After their little film festival, study participants were enrolled in an auction of sorts: Half of them were given (or "endowed") with a set of highlight markers that they were asked to price for sale while the other half was asked to bid on the same markers. The researchers predicted that the recently disgusted people on both sides of the auction would devalue the markers, since disgust puts us in a rejecting mood. And that's what happened: Offers and bids by potential sellers and buyers were dramatically lower than those from the neutral group. Although the disgust induced was from a prior, irrelevant situation, it affected the way all parties valued an object. Likewise with sadness, which the researchers theorized would create what they called a "reverse endowment effect." Essentially, because sadness sparks in us a desire for change, Lerner, Small, and Loewenstein predicted that potential sellers in the sad group would lower their asking price relative to the neutral crew, while potential buyers would raise the prices they would be willing to pay. And, again, that's what happened.

Think about this the next time you go to the mall after learning that you didn't get that new job, or go online after hearing that you were passed over for promotion at work. Chances are your thresholds for spending and borrowing will have temporarily changed without your conscious knowledge.

RESISTING TEMPTATION

Suppose you roll a die, agreeing that if it lands on six you will pay a fine of $10. How likely does it seem that a six will come up? Now suppose you're playing Russian roulette with one bullet in a six-chambered revolver. How likely does it seem that this game of chance will end in disaster?

We're guessing that, like most people, you recognize that in the italicized scenarios above the chances of a bad outcome are the same for each, but that the odds "feel" less favorable in the latter.

Have you ever gone through a stack of mail, decided to throw away one of the many solicitations for charity that funds disease-related research, then reached into the garbage can to retrieve that same pitch letter because you've decided to donate? Technically, the dice/gun thought experiment and our charity hypothetical illustrate the way in which emotions can influence probability assessments. That is, our feelings about a possible outcome can affect our judgment of the likelihood of that outcome actually happening. So we come across a solicitation for, say, a charity that's researching a cure for ALS (Lou Gehrig's disease) and our reflexive brain kicks in with such force that any rational assessment of our likelihood of getting the disease is not really possible (though of course there are other—indeed better!—reasons for donating than a concern about contracting the disease oneself). What's curious, though, is that if someone asks you five minutes before encountering a letter from an ALS charity how worried you are about your chances of contracting that disease, you'd likely answer, "I'm not really worried at all." But when the possibility of making a choice in relation to those odds comes into play, our reflexive brain gets to work, generating the rule of thumb that tells us it's not wise to "tempt fate." That heuristic developed because we know that a negative outcome will be experienced as especially negative if we're not able to shake the thought that, accurate or not, we did something to bring it about. In many ways, this feeling is a close cousin of the regret aversion we discussed in Chapter 3. Getting rained on feels bad, but getting rained on after deciding not to carry an umbrella feels worse because we might have avoided it; the end of a winning streak feels bad, but having it end after calling attention to the streak feels worse. Tom and a former doctoral student, Jane Risen, have conducted research indicating that it's the very negativity of imagined negative outcomes that follow fate-tempting actions that makes them especially accessible, thus making them seem especially likely to occur.

A related phenomenon was wonderfully explored in a 2008 paper by a team of Israeli scientists, "Action Bias Among Elite Soccer Goalkeepers: The Case of Penalty Kicks." The researchers, led by business professor Michael Bar-Eli, analyzed 286 penalty kicks (a one-on-one confrontation between an offensive player and a goalkeeper) and found that 94 percent of the time goaltenders quickly dived to their left or right, despite the fact that their best chance of stopping the ball was to stay in the center of the goal crease as long as possible. In speculating why this might be—it's remarkable because people are generally thought to favor inaction when faced with tough problems—the academics focused on the desire of goaltenders to look like they're doing something in the face of dire circumstances. Or rather, their desire to *not* look like they're doing nothing. The researchers went on to theorize that this kind of thinking could play out in financial crises as well. Everyone from CEOs to shareholders may be tempted to do something in times of high tension and consequence so as to avoid appearing (to themselves and to others) like stewards on a sinking ship who were manning their posts when they should have been bailing water, plugging holes, or launching lifeboats.

HERE TODAY, GONE TOMORROW

In a certain light, a goaltender's decision to dive to one side of the net as opposed to staying centered can be viewed solely as a prediction, specifically as to how he might feel after either choice should a goal be scored. Basically, what most goaltenders say to themselves, albeit unconsciously, probably sounds like this: "If I dive and she scores, I'll feel bad. But if I stay put and she scores, I'll feel bad and look bad, which is twice as bad." As it happens, this line of thinking probably sounds reasonable to most people. After all, the phrase "Don't just stand there, do something" is a cliché because the thought itself is so ingrained in our collective consciousness. There's nothing wrong with that approach; it has served us well over the years, particularly when situations feel dangerous or otherwise urgent. Remember, both choices in the fight-or-flight dichotomy involve action.

The problems come when we follow these calls to action—or, for that matter, calls to inaction—based on our notions of how we think we'll feel in the future. That's because we're often surprisingly clueless when trying to anticipate how we'll feel down the road. This was notably demonstrated by Daniel Kahneman and David Schkade in 1998, in a paper that might have been called "The Grass Is Always Greener in California Even Though It's Not." (In reality, it was titled "Does Living in California Make People Happier? A Focusing Illusion in Judgments of Life Satisfaction.") In their research, the two psychologists found that students at Midwestern universities thought they would be happier in California, and students at California universities believed they would be less happy in the Midwest. In actuality, though, there was no difference in self-reported happiness of respondents living in the two areas.

But it's when we look ahead that our misconceptions about what makes us happy or unhappy come most into play. Research has shown that across a variety of objective circumstances (body weight, say, or income) people expect future changes to affect their happiness much more than they actually do. A persuasive exploration of this idea was a 1998 study led by psychologist Daniel Gilbert, outlined in a paper titled "Immune Neglect: A Source of Durability Bias in Affective Forecasting." That title says it all! No, really: "Affective forecasting" is a fancy way to say predicting future moods; "durability bias" describes the tendency for people to assume that their moods, especially negative ones, will last longer than they do; and "immune neglect" is a major cause of the durability bias—the tendency to ignore or discount our capacity to adapt (or make ourselves immune) to unpleasant occurrences down the road. In six experiments, participants overestimated the duration of their unhappiness in connection with six "negative events": the end of a romantic relationship, the death of a child, the failure to achieve tenure, the electoral loss of a preferred candidate, unflattering personality feedback, and rejection by a prospective employer. When something bad happens, or when we anticipate it happening, we can't help but imagine that our unhappiness will last longer than it usually does.

Durability bias, we should note, is hardly the only way in which we're bad at predicting our future moods. Another, called "focalism," is particularly interesting as it relates to financial decisions. Focalism helps to explain why the death of a child turns out to be less devastating over the long run than many parents assume. When imagining such an occurrence, or its aftermath, people tend to focus on the specific event and not all the other circumstances in their life that will come into play. That is, when imagining how we'll feel if a child dies, we may only be capable of imagining life without our absent child, period. We can't imagine the joy and distraction we will get from our job, friends, spouses, other children, hobbies, travels, and so on. We're understandably too focused on the horrific event to be realistic appraisers of how we'll actually cope or, perhaps, thrive.

So, too, with financial decisions. Conservative investors may shy away from appropriate investment risks because they imagine only how they'll feel if their gamble fails—and not on how they might benefit from having tried. A clothes-horse might focus on the disappointment that may come from not wearing the latest outfit at a party—and not on the joy to be had by creating a "new" ensemble out of old clothes or the satisfaction to be gained from having money in the bank.

HOW TO THINK AND WHAT TO DO
Warning Signs

You may be prone to reflexive financial thinking if . . .
- you spend money in impulsive bursts.
- you shop when you're feeling blue.
- you tend to buy extended warranties or extra insurance policies, just to be safe.
- you feel extraordinarily anxious when stock prices fall, even if you don't need your invested money for years to come.
- you tend to hold on to winning investments well beyond the price you think the security is worth.
- you routinely spend more for goods and services than you planned to.

Take a look once more at the warning signs listed above.

If you're being honest, you can probably answer in the affirmative to almost all of them, or could have at some point in your life. That's because we're all emotional thinkers to some degree or another. And that's fine: Sometimes the best recipe for lifting your mood is online shopping; sometimes the peace of mind we get from providing our loved ones with extra financial support in some possible world tomorrow equates to much-needed emotional peace in the actual world today. But to the extent that our reflexive system can lead us to decisions we wouldn't otherwise make, it's important to understand how these processes control us and how we might control them. As we mentioned earlier in this chapter, we are beginning the windup to our little book, and so we'll center our final advice stage on some broad principles connected to emotional thinking. As much as any chapter in this book, the advice in this one might easily apply to your life as a whole. So, too, will our recommendations sometimes sound a little Buddhist in their orientation. Which makes sense, since Eastern religions are fundamentally less about deities and more about taming both the reflexive and reflective parts of our brains.

One of the best ways to explain the power of the reflexive system over our more rational thought processes is through sex. Not by having it, but rather by detailing an experiment by renowned behavioral economists Dan Ariely and George Loewenstein. In their study, the researchers asked participants to answer a number of questions on a laptop computer loaned to them for the purpose. Some participants answered in their normal, (presumably) not-intensely-aroused state. But others answered the research queries after complying with instructions to begin masturbating while viewing erotica. Aroused participants reported that they would be less likely to use a condom during intercourse, that they would be more likely to lie to obtain sex, and that they found practices such as S&M, anal sex, and sex with a wider age range of partners more appealing. What's crucial about these findings is that aroused participants knew better; they were no less likely than nonaroused participants, for example, to agree with the statement "If you pull out before you ejaculate, a woman can still get pregnant." But the heat of the (vividly imagined) moment had a pronounced effect on their inclinations to engage in behavior that more dispassionate participants viewed as highly questionable. In other words, we might know it's impulsive to sell our stock holdings in a falling market or buy a camera when we stumble upon a going-out-of-business sale, but we still may find it challenging to stop ourselves.

Our point here is simple: Sometimes knowledge isn't enough to overcome our visceral or emotional thinking. Sometimes you need a system, a default plan for helping you navigate the push-pull of your brain. Here are some ideas that we've found to be helpful over the years—some more so than others, of course, depending on your issues and approach to making decisions.

Voice your reason. More than a quarter century ago, the psychologist Norbert Schwartz conducted an experiment in which someone claiming to be from out of town called students at a Midwestern university and asked them questions about their state of mind. Some calls were made on sunny days, others on gloomy days. As you might have guessed after reading this chapter, the folks who picked up the phone reported that they were significantly happier and more satisfied with their lives if they were called on a sunny day. Well, almost all of them said that. There was one sure way to erase the effects of weather on people's assessment of their happiness levels: by asking them about the weather. Indeed, half the respondents were asked, before the life-satisfaction questions, "By the way, how's the weather down there?" And doing this negated the impact of the weather on people's responses. Think of it like those special boron rods that are put into heavy water at some power plants to control nuclear reactions. The weather question almost certainly didn't influence people's moods, but it did affect what they understood their moods to signify about their lives. Without the question, survey participants interpreted their feelings as indicative of their overall happiness levels; with the question, they did not.

The idea here is that sometimes we need to eviscerate our gut reactions with reasoned processes, like speaking. Gary has a Post-it note on his computer that reads, "Say it out loud." Sometimes he ignores it, but oftentimes he'll use it as a prompt to voice a desire or thought that feels impulsive. And in so doing, in calling on his reflective system, he will undercut his reflexive instincts.

Use checklists. In the annual report for Berkshire Hathaway, company chairman (and superinvestor) Warren Buffett lists six criteria he uses for buying a company. We don't know that Buffett uses that checklist every time he mulls an acquisition, but we wouldn't be surprised. Not so much because the criteria are sound, though they are, but because Buffett's partner, Charles Munger, is a longtime fan of behavioral economics. (In fact, he reviewed an early draft of this book.) And both men understand the need to build a structure of discipline into major financial decisions, which removes the destabilizing effects of emotion. Having a set of rules or criteria or questions that you train yourself to run through before any purchase or investment of, say, $500 or

$1,000 can be a simple way to curb some of your more reflexive impulses.

One thought, though, about your checklists: Keep them short, and reasonable. Life is meant to be lived, chances are meant to be taken, money is meant to move. More important, if you set up checklists that you know to be onerous or time-consuming, you'll quickly get in the habit of "forgetting" to use them.

Play decision chess. Many of the more reflexive responses in our financial lives result from a version of the so-called startle reflex, among the most visceral of our operating system's rules of thumb. Essentially, this heuristic allows us to quickly—and with a supreme sense of urgency—raise our level of awareness and defenses, to protect us from attacks of all kinds. It's a valuable trait to have, but it can get in the way of rational thinking. That's why one of the best strategies for avoiding impulsive or emotional responses in money decisions is to try to anticipate the worst-case scenarios. We call it "decision chess," whereby like a grand master in the game of kings, you play out the various ways a situation might unfold. So, for example, before meeting with a stockbroker, car salesman, insurance rep, or real estate agent, you should first ask yourself what your goals and limits are—that's obvious—but you might also ask yourself what you'd do if presented with a proposition that deviates from your preconceived boundaries, in both positive and negative ways. This is hard. We know. But so is thinking several moves ahead in chess, and those who think ahead are better players. So as hard as it may be, get in the habit of thinking ahead and thinking of alternative scenarios when making financial decisions. This is useful not so much because you can anticipate every situation that might arise, but because you'll be anticipating *some* unplanned-for situations that might arise, and in planning to be surprised in certain ways, you can often mitigate the effects of surprise in all ways, leaving you a more reasoned thinker.

Mind your pros and cons. This advice, like a lot of the suggestions in this section, has a dual purpose. We'll get to the primary one in a bit, but the secondary agenda is shared by almost all of our recommendations: It takes some time. And time can be your best friend in winning the battle of emotions vs. reason (see below). We're hardly the first to note this. In fact, more than two centuries ago, one of our favorite thinkers made that point when advising a friend on how to make a tough decision. The thinker was Benjamin Franklin, and in advising his associate, the Founding Father recommended what was then a fairly sophisticated decision-making tool: a pro-and-con list. But before you move to the next paragraph because you know this already, consider Franklin's advice after recommending that his friend divide a piece of paper in two, putting "Pro" at the top of one side and "Con" atop the other. He continued: "Then, during three days or four days of consideration, I put down under the different heads short hints of the different motives, that at different times occur to me, for or against the measure. When I have thus got them all together in one view, I endeavor to estimate their respective weights; and where I find two, one on each side, that seem equal, I strike out the two." Franklin goes on to acknowledge that his "moral or prudential algebra" is not perfect, but he extols the virtues of the problem nonetheless. We can't help but agree. Note first that this system takes some time. Plus, if you take it seriously, the strategy requires you to anticipate various scenarios and deliberate upon them. Finally, the strike-out aspect of the advice helps to simplify the decision-making process. Once pros and cons of equal weight are eliminated, you can rest assured you've considered those attributes without getting bogged down by them. Best of all, this system turns out to be surprisingly enjoyable, almost gamelike, but with the added advantage that you finish the game with a very real sense of peace of mind.

Don't just do something, stand there! We might just have fairly called the final piece of advice in this chapter the "twenty-four-hour rule." That's because this kernel of counsel, essentially the flip side of our "hurry up and wait" suggestion in the previous chapter, speaks to the reflexive desire to rush to action in a crisis. But in today's world, where information overload is the norm, *perceived* crises far outnumber actual ones. Stock markets fall, home prices drop, clothing and shoes and laptops and cell phones go on sale—these are the normal ebbs and flows of economic life. But most people respond to these events with reflexive actions that spring from the most basic of instincts. Greed is one such emotion, and it's why stores and Web sites increasingly flash discounted prices at us: They know that our subconscious minds will experience these signals as a chance to get fat at little cost, prompting a fast and emotional response. These signals—falling prices, falling markets—are hard to resist, and perhaps you shouldn't. But if they are meaningful and necessary, they'll still be so tomorrow, which is why we recommend a waiting period for any major purchase or financial move. In the same way that letting found money sit in the bank for a few weeks may turn it from gift money to *your* money, coming back to a purchase or a stock sale the next day can help you overcome your reflexive system. Gary has another Post-it note on his computer, which reads "Do it tomorrow." Rather than a call to procrastination, it's a reminder to breathe. Sometimes Gary ignores his own instructions, but more often than not he'll defer an online purchase or stock trade until the next day, when just as often as not the seeming urgency of the transaction turns out to have been fleeting. As with most things, time is a great equalizer.

NOW WHAT?

When we decided to revise and update this book, one of the first things we did was read what we wrote last time, hoping to make an objective judgment about the quality and value of our previous effort. Objectivity was probably a naive goal, but when we reviewed our ideas and advice we felt confident that we had prepared readers for the tough job of making financial decisions in a world that gets more complicated every day. If nothing else, our maxim that any funds needed within five years should be taken out of the stock market doubtless saved many people considerable anxiety and money. Likewise, our advice that the smartest investment moves are often those that run counter to the herd should have proven profitable to readers who invested some of their sidelined savings back into the market when the bottom fell out. Or so we hope.

Those were two of the important ideas we were trying to

communicate last time around, and our job now would be a lot simpler if we could summarize all the concepts presented in this book with a set of prescriptive nuggets—say, "The Top Ten Mental Money Secrets" or "The Seven Habits of Financially Effective People." Unfortunately, there are no easy fixes for many of the issues we've touched upon. Change is often hard won. There's a reason why the majority of Weight Watchers members have been through the program before. Actually, the Weight Watchers analogy is particularly apt for the challenge you face in trying to give order to your financial decision-making processes. One of the tough challenges in trying to change one's diet is that—unlike, say, smoking—you can't just stop cold turkey. You have to eat something. Similarly, you can't stop spending or investing or saving while you rethink the way you make financial decisions. You have to change course in flight.

It is also difficult to alter many of the behavioral-economic habits we've discussed in this book because, although they cost you money, they reflect psychological tendencies that bring great benefits in other ways or in other areas. Almost all of these habits have a flip side that's beneficial, and it is these benefits that have made them so ingrained. The tendency to weigh losses more heavily than gains, for example, is doubtless a beneficial trait overall because an organism that cares too much about possible gains and too little about potential losses runs too great a risk of experiencing the kinds of losses that threaten its survival. The sunk cost fallacy is likewise connected to a predisposition with beneficial effects, a predisposition nicely captured by the injunction "Waste not, want not." A person who is too cavalier about previous spending might be too cavalier in other ways as well, and too wasteful. And as we discussed earlier, both the tendency to set up mental accounts and the predisposition to follow the herd can serve a person well.

The barriers that exist between certain mental accounts can compensate for problems with self-control, and a tendency to look to others for guidance allows a person to take advantage of the information that others really do possess. It would be nice if we could take all of the benefits of these general tendencies and bear none of their costs, but it doesn't work that way. Not without a lot of effort, at any rate. What we're asking you to do is shed those parts of these general tendencies that exact a financial cost to you.

A second difficulty in summarizing and synthesizing the ideas in this book is one we hinted at in the introduction. Many behavioral-economic principles appear to conflict with one another, and appearances in this case are not deceiving. We can tell you in good conscience that people routinely overestimate their own abilities and knowledge, and we can follow that with an earnest discussion of the ways in which people blindly follow the actions of others. Both are true. So what should you do? Should you dismiss the crowd and always trust your instincts? Or should you recognize that you probably know a lot less than you think you know and put your faith and finances in the hands of others? The answer, not surprisingly, lies somewhere in the middle.

With these difficulties in mind, our next-to-last chapter approaches the concepts in this book from two angles. First, inside out: the overarching ideas that inform behavioral-economic theory and how they affect your day-to-day and lifelong financial decisions. We've labeled this section "Principles to Ponder." Second, outside in: things you can do now and the behavioral-economic reasons you might not already be doing them. We call this section "Steps to Take." Not very clever, but to the point—as we hope this summation will be. In fact, we almost called the second section "Tom and Gary's Rebate Plan," because following these tips should return the cost of this book many times over.

PRINCIPLES TO PONDER

Every dollar spends the same. The term *mental accounting* is meant to describe the way people tend to treat money differently depending on where it comes from, where it's kept, or how it's spent. It can be a useful habit when it leads you to treat savings for college or retirement as sacred. But it can be dangerous when it causes you to spend money from some sources—such as gifts or bonuses—more quickly than you might otherwise. Conversely, treating some money as *too sacred*—an inheritance, for example, or even long-term savings for a home, education, or retirement—can lead people to choose overly conservative investment strategies that avoid the ups and downs of the stock market but leave them exposed to the ravages of inflation. Whatever the case, how you label and treat different mental accounts is often the difference between amassing significant savings or finding your bank account wanting just when you need money most.

That's why it's important that you learn to view all money equally—salary, gifts, savings, even lottery winnings. One way to help this process along is to park "found" money in a savings or investment account before you decide what to do with it. The more time you have to think of money as savings—hard earned or otherwise—the less likely you'll be to spend it recklessly or impulsively. Conversely, to the extent that you *need* to have mad money, consider putting a small portion of your savings—say, 5 percent—in a special account designed for speculation or gambling or shopping sprees. If you can't kill the beast, tame it.

Losses hurt you more than gains please you. One of the central tenets of prospect theory—a bedrock principle of behavioral economics—is that people are "loss averse." The pain people feel from losing $100 is much greater than the pleasure they experience from gaining the same amount. This helps explain why people behave inconsistently when taking risks. For example, the same person can act conservatively when protecting gains (by selling successful investments to guarantee the profits) but recklessly when seeking to avoid losses (by holding on to losing investments in the hope that they'll bounce back and become profitable). Loss aversion causes some investors to sell *all* their investments during periods of unusual market turmoil. Although comforting in the short run, such efforts at timing the market don't work in the long run. This "asymmetry" between losses and gains can also work to your advantage. Saving money through a payroll deduction plan is relatively painless because the reduction in your paycheck is experienced as a foregone gain (passing up a bigger check) rather than an outright loss (paying into savings "out of pocket").

Money that's spent is money that doesn't matter. The "sunk cost fallacy," one of the most common behavioral-economic mistakes, results in decisions that are based on previous investments or spending. This tendency is harmful for the simple reason that past mistakes shouldn't lead you to make future ones. The past is past, and what matters is what is likely to happen from now on. So a person who turns down an offer for a house because the bid is lower than the original purchase price may be following one blunder (paying too much in the first place) with another (not getting out while the getting is good). The sunk cost fallacy can sometimes be helpful—say, if you keep going to your gym because the annual membership dues were so expensive. But it can be harmful, too, helping to explain why people stay in unhappy careers or why individuals (or governments) continue to spend money on useless or wasteful projects. That's why it's important to remember that once money is spent, it's generally gone. About the only choice a previous outlay should influence is the decision to ask for a refund.

It's all in how you look at it. Another basic principle of behavioral-economic theory is that the way you frame decisions—particularly the way you "code" losses and gains—profoundly influences the choices you make. The same set of options might lead to a different decision depending on whether you view your choice as one of rejection or one of selection, or whether you view it as protecting a gain or avoiding a loss. That's why it's wise to view decisions from all sides—not just the pros and cons, but the ways in which a decision might be framed in your mind. For example, a person deciding among several different investment options in a retirement plan might assume that she already owns all or several of the available choices. The decision then becomes one of rejection ("Which investments am I uncomfortable owning?") rather than selection—and perhaps brings hidden considerations to light.

Too much choice makes choosing tough. Although we have been conditioned to view unlimited options as something to be desired, in reality a surfeit of options can leave us anxious and unable to decide. In fact, "choice conflict" and "decision paralysis" are major contributors to financial mistakes—say, the inability some people have to move money out of a conservative retirement fund; or the difficulty others have in refinancing their mortgage. But this challenge pervades almost every aspect of life, from deciding on a mate to choosing a wine to picking out shirts. That's why it's often a good idea to limit your own choices, which is easier than it seems. One smart way is to find "trusted screeners" whose judgment you like—and whose honesty you can rely upon—to pare down or even make your choices for you. Independent rating services or media entities like *Consumer Reports* often do the research for you, then identify the top three selections among a jumble of products or services. That will leave you in control of your final choice while also limiting your options to a number that won't inspire paralysis. An alternative strategy is to ask a colleague, friend, or relative with expertise in the subject to pare your options to a manageable few.

All numbers count, even if you don't like to count them. Throughout this book we've demonstrated the ways in which small numbers can add up to big costs. For example, the tendency to dismiss or discount small numbers as insignificant—what we call the "bigness bias"—can lead you to pay more than you need to for brokerage commissions and mutual fund expenses. And this can have a deleterious effect of surprising magnitude on your investment returns over time. Similarly, the bigness bias and mental accounting allow people to bury small expenditures in bigger ones, while the money illusion leads people to ignore the harmful effects of inflation. Over time these incremental expenses and price hikes can be the difference between financial freedom and just scraping by.

You pay too much attention to things that matter too little. The tendency to weigh certain facts, figures, and events too heavily—to give too much importance to them—can be explained by a number of behavioral-economic principles. "Anchoring," for example, explains how people fixate on a specific dollar amount and base subsequent decisions on that figure, often mistakenly. People also tend to place too much emphasis on especially memorable or unusual events, not realizing that memory is much less reliable than they think. For example, many people still recall the stock market crash of 2008 with anxiety and forget that stocks have offered the most consistent investment gains over time. And many people became house poor (or just plain poor) by stretching to buy the largest home they could afford under the false belief that home prices are a better-than-average investment. In fact, although home prices soared in the late 1970s and the early part of this century, in most parts of the country they have roughly kept pace with inflation.

Separately, a failure to fully grasp the role that chance plays in life leads many investors to be overly impressed with short-term success and other random or unusual occurrences. Thus, many investors pour money into mutual funds that have performed well in the recent past on the often mistaken belief that the funds' success is the result of something other than dumb luck.

Your confidence is often misplaced. Nearly everybody falls prey, at one time or another, to an overestimation of his or her knowledge and abilities. This hubris, tough to admit but nonetheless very common, leads people into all manner of financial mischief. The most important example of it is the belief that with a little knowledge or homework you can pick investments with better-than-average success. Overconfidence is a particularly seductive trap when people possess special information or personal experience—no matter how limited—that leads them to think their investment strategy is especially savvy. In reality, however, there is little reason for even the most sophisticated investor to believe that she can pick stocks—or mutual funds—better than the average man or woman on the street. That's why Jason Zweig, in his book *Your Money & Your Brain,* recommends a strategy he describes as "Embrace the Mistake." Rather than trying to forget past investing errors or spending goofs, review them, write them down, and keep them close at hand. Not to make yourself feel bad, but to keep yourself humble—and calibrated.

It's hard to prove yourself wrong. This sounds basic, but we're talking less about pride and more about a subconscious inclination people have to confirm what they already know or want to believe. This "confirmation bias" makes it hard for you to break patterns of thought and behavior because it leads you to find support for even the most questionable ideas and policies. Subsequently your ability to make sound spending and investment decisions is weakened because you don't evaluate relevant information with an even hand. Once again, then, it's important to temper your own self-confidence by sharing financial decisions with others—seeking not only specific advice, but also critiques of your decision-making process.

The trend isn't always your friend. The challenge in taking counsel from others is not to abandon completely your own instincts, common sense, and reason. "Herd investing" is just one example of the tendency to base decisions on the actions of others. In the long run, conventional wisdom is often on target—as it has been over the past twenty-five years in the trend away from fixed-income investments and toward stocks. In the short run, though, the vagaries of crowd behavior—particularly "information cascades," which result in dramatic shifts in tastes and actions—frequently lead to costly overreactions and missed opportunities. That's why the most successful investors and spenders are those who view trends and fads skeptically and cautiously.

You can know too much. Knowledge is power, but too much information can be destructive. Studies have shown that investors who tune out the majority of financial news fare better than those who subject themselves to an endless stream of information, much of it meaningless. In part, that's because the oblivious investor is unlikely to be swept up in information cascades or other herd-investing tendencies. Similarly, the less frequently you check on your investments, the less likely you'll be to react emotionally to the natural ups and downs of the securities markets. For most investors, a yearly review of your portfolio is frequent enough.

Your emotions affect your decisions in more ways than you imagine. Advances in the study of emotion and the blossoming of a new field of inquiry called "neuroeconomics" have yielded valuable insights into the ways in which our most primitive instincts affect our more reasoned thought processes. Even unrelated factors, like the weather or an especially emotion-laden movie, can influence our decisions about money. As a result, we often make spending and investing decisions that don't serve our true well-being or long-term goals. That's why it's often helpful when money is involved to have a few basic rules of play that you can refer to without investing too much time or effort. Brevity is crucial, since a book full of rules will likely remain unheeded on the shelf.

But a few self-imposed guidelines—say, enough to fill one side of an index card—might be accessible enough to use and eventually memorize. Examples of guidelines that could prove highly useful: implementing a cooling-off period of

twenty-four hours before making any major financial decision, allowing you time to let your emotions be countered by
more reasoned or deliberative thought; vocalizing your in-
tentions and your reasons for having them; arguing against
your intention by asking three probing questions. Whatever
your guidelines, this kind of preparation for big decisions is
always wise, because, as you'll read in a moment, we often
misinterpret why we can't achieve our goals or control our
behaviors, financial and otherwise.

You're not very good at predicting your future. Studies show that in many
ways people are not adept at forecasting their future levels
of satisfaction, joy, or contentment. These "affective forecasting" errors exist in part because, as mentioned above,
we often don't know what's making us happy or sad today,
but also because we underestimate our ability to adapt to
life's challenges and overestimate the improvement in mood
or satisfaction that imagined riches or better circumstances
will bring. As a result, we let fear or greed dictate our financial decisions to an extent that leaves us with less money
than we want and more anxiety than we need. One way to
overcome surprises in the future is to imagine a spectrum
of outcomes and ask yourself how you would react to each.
The answers, which may be naively optimistic or cautiously
pessimistic, are not nearly as important as the process. If
you mean to take an impulsive action, you may not be dis-
suaded. But research suggests that contemplating unpleasant
or surprising outcomes will make you less likely to overreact to at least some of them. Likewise, it's helpful to develop
a routine when contemplating long-term financial decisions,
like buying or selling a home, starting a business, lending
money to friends or family, deciding on graduate school,
evaluating insurance of any kind. Some ideas for that rou-

tine are contained above, but one that isn't—asking someone who's already been through the experience or decision in
question—applies specifically to our problems with predicting the future. We can't stress enough the value of what we
like to call a "back to the future" perspective. It sounds obvious, and in some cultures tapping the wisdom of older or
more experienced friends and relatives is built into decision-
making habits. But in many other cultures and social cir-
cles, a determined focus on newness and youth has led many
people to ignore what you might call the wisdom of years.
Which is a shame, since there are few better teachers than experience, in part because experiences are so often repeated.
Google the lyrics of Cole Porter's "Anything Goes," written in 1934, to see what we mean. Or, as a friend of Gary's
likes to say about TV, "There's nothing new under the sun,
there are just remakes of *Candid Camera* and *I Love Lucy*
episodes." Think of it this way: Having a personal board
of advisers that includes more experienced counselors is like
studying with seniors for your freshman chemistry test. They
may very well already have the answers.

Small tweaks can have big results. Although it's far from easy to overcome emotional and cognitive biases, we can sometimes
act in subtle ways to achieve profound change. The power
of these adjustments—called "channel factors" by the pio-
neering psychologist Kurt Lewin—was illustrated notably in
1965 by researchers at Yale University. As part of an effort to
prod college seniors to get tetanus shots, a group of students
was given a lecture meant to educate them about the dangers
of tetanus and the importance of getting inoculated against
it. A large majority of those students reported that they were
convinced and planned to get their shots, but in the end only
3 percent got them. But another group of students, who were

presented with the same lecture, had a 28 percent inoculation rate. The difference? The second group was given a map of the campus and asked to plan their route to the health center and pick a date and time to go. Sometimes, you see, motivation isn't our problem. Rather, we need to identify life's everyday mental obstacles—regret, fatigue, overconfidence, fear, to name just four—and put ourselves into position to hurdle them. Some governments understand the power of small tweaks. Consider organ donations, a habit that if widespread could improve or even save the lives of millions of people around the world. So in certain countries, rather than presume their citizens don't want to donate their organs at death, government assumes the opposite—that all things being equal, people would choose to help save others' lives. A citizen in these countries can choose not to give by filling out a form or checking a box, but otherwise he'll be considered a willing donor when he dies. The results are impressive. Donation rates in Spain, for example, are 40 percent higher than they are in the United States. Are Spaniards more altruistic or civic-minded than Americans? Doubtful. It's just that their government made the decision to donate organs easier with a small tweak in public policy.

Think about this the next time you think you're not motivated to exercise. Promise yourself that if you go to the gym and change into your workout gear, you can leave without breaking a sweat. If you're not on the treadmill five minutes after changing, we'll run your miles for you. In financial decisions, the channel factor might be something as simple as automatic and regular account transfers between checking and savings accounts. Both are especially useful if loss aversion makes it difficult for you to save by writing a check or actively transferring money to a savings or investment account. By funneling money automatically into long-term savings, small amounts of cash that you might have used for incidentals are mentally accounted for as sacred savings—and are less likely to be frittered away. Almost any fund company or bank will help you set up such automatic withdrawal or transfer plans. Likewise, shoppers who have a tough time adhering to spending limits can simply leave their credit and ATM cards at home when they go to a store. It's basic, but so are the impulses that drive many of our worst money decisions. After all, the best way to stop snacking at night is to stop keeping snacks in your house.

STEPS TO TAKE

Raise your insurance deductible. The tendency to overweight memorable events and the failure to understand the odds of many potential hazards lead people to overestimate the likelihood that they'll have to file a claim against their life, health, and auto insurance. As a result, they buy insurance policies that include needlessly low deductibles and pay an excessively high price in the process. By hiking deductibles from, say, $100 or $250 to $500 or $1,000, you can often cut your premiums by 10 to 25 percent or more, enough to make up for the extra expense in the unlikely event that you'll have to file a claim.

Self-insure against small losses. The sensitivity to experiencing losses also leads people to take out insurance policies they do not need and that are not in their best interests. On average, insurance is a bad gamble for the consumer. Because insurance companies must pay agents and appraisers, employ a large clerical staff, and return a nice profit to shareholders, the amount they charge policyholders considerably exceeds the amount that policyholders get back in the form of claim reimbursements. Also, insurance companies have to allow for people in their "pool" who may be far more likely to file a claim than you, and that drives up your rates as well. As a result, you should have insurance only against losses that you cannot cover yourself. If your car was bought on credit, for example, by all means take out a collision and comprehensive policy to insure against damage. If you paid cash for it, however, you're better off just paying for liability coverage. If disaster strikes your car, you can have it repaired or buy another—either out of pocket (if yours are that deep) or with an auto loan. In the end, the odds are you'll come out ahead. Thus, whenever possible—that is, when you *can* cover the loss—be your own insurance company and pocket all the overhead costs that insurance companies would pass on to you.

Pay off credit-card debt with emergency funds. This sounds reckless, but it's not, and it can save you big bucks. Here's the math: A lot of people have money stashed for a rainy day. By treating that money as untouchable, however, they typically keep it in ultrasafe bank accounts or money market accounts. These days such savings are likely earning less than 2 percent a year, or less than $20 for every $1,000 invested. Yet many of these same people have credit-card balances in the thousands, which costs them about 16 percent a year, or $160 for every grand. Simply by paying off your debt with emergency funds, you will save $120 for every $1,000 in borrowing. And don't worry about not having money for rainy days; credit-card companies will happily lend you money if you're laid up, laid off, or need a new bed to lay your head on.

Switch to index funds. This is one of the most important lessons of this book. A failure to understand the odds against beating the market—and overconfidence about their abilities to do so—causes many investors to pick their own stocks or actively managed mutual funds. But the wiser course for most people is to pair their fortunes with those of the market averages by investing primarily in index funds. Index funds are portfolios that attempt to do no more than mirror the benchmark stock and bond averages in different investment categories. The idea is to guarantee that you will at least keep up with the typical investor—but, in fact, you'll likely do better than all those brave souls who think they can beat the law of averages. That's because high transaction and management expenses, not to mention faulty psychology and the law of averages, often burden actively managed portfolios. Index funds, as a rule, take much of the emotion out of investing. If you must take a more active hand in selecting investments, limit your exposure to your psychological weaknesses by devoting no more than 10 percent of your assets to this approach.

Diversify your investments. Most investors who are still working should have a large portion of their assets invested in the stock market, which has historically offered the best returns over time. Retirees also should invest in stocks with money that they'll need ten years or more down the road, while money they will need for current living expenses should be invested in safer securities such as money market instruments or short-term bonds. As a general rule, subtracting your age from one hundred will tell you the amount of your long-term (five years out) savings that ought to be in stocks. But whatever the primary thrust of your portfolio allocation, diversifying at least partly among stocks (ideally stock index funds), bonds (bond index funds), money market funds, and real estate (real estate investment trusts) has two huge and related advantages. First, diversification allows you to benefit when a decline in the value of one asset is offset by a rise in the value of another. More important, the extent to which your overall portfolio shows steady growth rather than wild swings up and down could be the difference between you staying the course over the long run or pulling your money out of the markets when stocks hit a rough patch. You'll be less likely to succumb to loss aversion and other behavioral-economic tendencies that might lead you to do something drastic.

Review your assets. Diversification works only if you can view individual components of your portfolio in the context of your overall wealth. In order to do that, you have to know what you are worth. That's why it's important to take stock of all your assets: retirement plans, real estate, savings accounts, art, and other collectibles. You need not know your worth to the penny, and you shouldn't undertake this exercise more than once every three months, but you should have some idea if your investments and other holdings balance out or leave you vulnerable.

Max out your retirement plan. Each year millions of Americans fail to contribute the maximum amount allowed to their retirement plan at work or don't contribute at all. If *you* don't max out, you are putting too great a value on what is yours—your salary today—and too low a value on what *could* be yours: matching contributions from your employer and decades of tax-free investment gains. So contribute as much as you think you can to your 401(k), 403(b), or 457 plan at work, then contribute a little more! If that seems unpleasant, you may be viewing the idea of savings for tomorrow as a loss today. One smart strategy for overcoming that feeling is to commit a portion of an upcoming raise to your retirement plan. You won't feel too much pain of a loss from money you don't have yet.

Finally, keep track. If you're determined to be an active investor in individual stocks or bonds, you might first try practicing a little when there's nothing at stake but your pride. Portfolio tracking software available at any number of Web sites, financial and otherwise, allows you to experiment as an investor with virtual portfolios. At the very least you'll come to understand your bad habits and you'll have a record of your true investing acumen that won't cost you anything but time. If you're one of those lucky souls who can follow a budget, good for you. If not, one of the best ways to understand the behavioral-economic factors that affect the way you view and handle money—especially the ways in which the bigness bias leads you to pay too little attention to small numbers and amounts—is to track your spending. It sounds annoying, and it is. That's why we recommend that you try it for just one month, any month. If you can pull it off—writing down every expenditure, big and small—you'll no doubt see patterns in your spending habits that will explain why you do not feel completely in control of your finances. And that's the first step in mastering your money.

PSYCHIC INCOME

Among the many fascinating insights we have encountered since first updating this book, the most startling may be one that overturns a supremely hackneyed cliché about wealth. It turns out, you see, that money can buy happiness! In fact, a casual review of recent research suggests that there are four ways money can actually make people happier: (1) If you're so poor as to not be able to afford food and shelter, an increase in income that can provide such basics has been shown to increase reported well-being; (2) if you truly worry about finances, the removal of concern over things like hospital bills and mortgage payments can lessen stress to such an extent that it increases reported happiness—provided the getting and keeping of your newfound wealth doesn't create new stresses; (3) if you give to charity, research suggests that you're more likely to report a higher level of happiness then less generous types; and (4) people who spend money on experiences—vacations, scuba lessons, concerts—report higher levels of happiness than people who just buy things.

So if in writing and revising this book we've offered up useful ways to increase your wealth, we're thrilled. More money in your pocket just might equal more happiness in your life. And, ultimately, that's why we have invested so much time in this project over the years. Sure, we hoped to make some money. Yes, we believe that the ideas upon which this book is based—the principles of behavioral economics—deserve a hearing before the widest possible audience. And certainly we want to pay homage to the many economists and psychologists whose creative and intellectual labors have for the most part gone unheralded among the general public—particularly Amos Tversky and Daniel Kahneman, true pioneers.

Mostly, though, we hope this book can help ease your mind. We think we have offered insights and advice that will aid you in dealing with one of the most complicated and critical areas of life—your finances. Although some people are no doubt motivated by gathering wealth as an end unto itself, we believe that most folks think of money as a tool, a way to achieve goals and live a meaningful and enjoyable life. The paradox, of course, is that money is often a great cause of angst and frustration, a battle between great aspirations and base realities. That's why we want to end this book with two pieces of advice.

First, pick your fights. Even if you subscribe fully to everything we've explored in this book—even if you believe you now understand the causes of your financial missteps and the ways you can go about correcting them—the task ahead of you is daunting. And it's not always worth fighting. Trying to extract every last dime out of your financial decisions is likely to incur significant social and psychic costs. As you've no doubt noticed, not everyone likes a person who's obsessed with money. And even if everyone did, an insistence on always making *the* best financial decision in a given situation can lead to excessive worry and anxiety. Think of those annoying entreaties to switch your Internet service provider (or your phone service or electricity provider or your natural gas service). You might lower your bill a bit by fully contemplating the pitch, but do you really want to? Is it worth it? Not always. Nevertheless, it is our hope that knowing about some of the principles we've discussed will allow you to discard some bad habits and adopt a few good ones and thereby significantly improve your financial prospects.

With that in mind, you may find it easier (and more rewarding) if, rather than trying to incorporate all you've learned into your day-to-day decision-making process, you choose a couple of areas in which you'd like to effect change and attack those first. Certainly we'd like you to adopt all the advice we dispensed along the way that's relevant to your habits, especially the steps outlined in the previous chapter. But maybe a more realistic approach would be to consider the behaviors that are costing you the most money or anxiety and concentrate on them.

Second, go easy on yourself. However you choose to use the information and advice we've served up, be prepared to experience successes and failures. We make no promises about the ratio of one to the other, only that both will likely occur. But the extent to which you remain optimistic and patient—the extent to which you recognize that sea changes in behavior and attitude come infrequently and stubbornly—will largely determine your ability to persevere and experience real progress. Don't expect miracles or overnight transformations. Expect instead to learn some things about yourself, some things about the ways in which you make decisions in general and about money in particular. Like all knowledge, such awareness of self should translate into real wisdom and, with luck, wealth.

ACKNOWLEDGMENTS

We won't bore you with bromides about the many people who contributed in one way or another to this book; we'll just bore you with a list of those people. Gary's thanks come first, then Tom's. Both of us, of course, are especially thankful to the people upon whose research this book stands.

G.B.:

To Elaine Pfefferblit, the first to suggest a book to me about behavioral economics. I admire her prescience.

To Jane Dystel, all you'd want in a literary agent, and then some.

To the smart folks at Simon & Schuster, who have always seemed to understand the value in what we had to say about this subject.

To Judy Feldman, for her diligence.

To Clint Willis, the first to write about behavioral economics at *Money* magazine. I could do worse than follow in his footsteps. Thanks also to Kevin McKean, who led *Money*'s early exploration of the topic; Frank Lalli, the magazine's editor at the time; and Jason Zweig, whose early reading of this manuscript improved it considerably.

To Russell Roberts, who taught me most of what I know about economics, and much about many other things. His comments on an early version of this manuscript were keen and kind, much like his friendship.

To friends and colleagues whose support has been invaluable: Dan Ain and Alana Joblin, Morty Ain and Hallie Geller, Lesley Alderman and Steve Koepp, Meredith Berkman, Alan Blum, the Borow Brothers, Therese and Dave Courtney, Harold and Rene Denlow, Scott DeSimon and Christine Egan, Beth Fenner, Lynne Goldner, Stephanie Greene, Sarah and Danny Grover, Caroline and Peter Friedman, Jimmy and Lynn Harris, Allie Jacobs, Kevin Jacobs, Patty Kelly, David Kingsley, Sinai and Veevee Knopp, Joe and Jill Lazarov, Jill Neiberg, Brendan O'Connor and Emily Loreto, Debi Pomerantz, Andy Regal and Jennifer Friedman, Patrick Reilly and Suzanne Grua, Ron Reisler and Ilana Sultan, Erin Richardson, Kathy Ritchie, Sharon Roberts, Saul Rosenberg and Esther David, Suzy Ross, Karina Scalise, Aliyah Schneider, Deborah Schneider, Beth and David Shaw, the Sklar Brothers, Larry Smith and Piper Kerman, Frank Sommerfield, Jay Susman, Nikki Weinstein, Ana Wilson, and Craig Winston. If we are judged by the company we keep, I've gotten the better of the deal.

To Laura Dave—who makes the world a better place with almost every thought—for her wise counsel; in general, and when I needed it most.

To Karen Schad and Annie Santoro, generous supporters in spirit and substance.

To the good souls at Urban Pathways, the creative souls at the New York Neo-Futurists and the flexible souls at the Laughing Lotus—inspiring in countless ways.

To the fantastic editors, writers, designers, researchers, and operation and production crews at *ESPN The Magazine*. I am especially grateful to Catriona Ni Aolain and Siung Tjia, who make me look better than I should every two weeks; Linda Ng, for her patience; and Chris Berend, who catches almost every ball I drop.

To Gary Hoenig, Keith Clinkscales, John Walsh, and John Skipper, bosses worth having. If I'm half the friend to Gary that he's been to me, I have accomplished something.

To the Montclair Mafia: David and Kimberly Cummings, who opened their extraordinary family to me; Peter and Karen Keating, who don't miss a thing; and Chad and Stacey Millman, who deserve each other (which is saying something).

To Neil Fine, Robbyn Footlick, and Sue Hovey, for their friendship and support. I write books and other things with Neil sometimes, and he is a collaborator unlike any other.

To Lisa and Jason Ablin, Mark and Linda Eisner, David and Jodi Kahn, and Leslie Koren and Juan Pablo Lombana. I count my blessings.

To my mom (Irene), my sister (Barbara), my brothers (Howard and Jonathan), my brother-in-law (Larry Nudelman), my nephews and nieces (Ari, Emily, Elly, Yirmi, Shara, Adir, Sam, Zevvy, Anielle, Noa, and Maayan), my cousins (Chad Chervitz, Daren Chervitz, and Keri Sugel) and my aunt and uncle (Annabelle and Kenny Chapel). You don't choose your family, but I would have.

And, finally, to my sister Rhona, for her vigilance; and my brother-in-law Myron, for his grace under pressure. I am grateful always for the example.

T.G.:

To Amos Tversky and Daniel Kahneman, who have so greatly advanced what is known about the psychology of judgment and decision making, and, in the process, have made the study of psychology so much more rewarding, and so much more fun. To have had the privilege to work with both represents more good fortune than anyone could hope to have in one professional lifetime.

To Dick Thaler and Bob Frank, who gave me my education in economics, and taught me that even that can be a playful experience. I am also indebted to both for their pivotal roles in creating the Cornell Center for Behavioral Economics and Decision Research. I have benefitted enormously from the intellectual contributions of all of the center's many distinguished members: my dear friend Dennis Regan, Rob Bloomfield, Simona Botti, Dave Dunning, Eric Eisenstein, Melissa Ferguson, Bob Gibbons, Ori Heffetz, Ben Ho, Alice Isen, Bob Libby, Mark Nelson, Ted O'Donoghue, David Pizarro, Jeff Rachlinski, Valerie Reyna, Jay Russo, Dave Sally, Bill Schulze, Kathleen Valley, and Vivian Zayas.

To Karen Dashiff Gilovich. The only reason I can have the chutzpah to write about judgment and decision making is that the most important decision of my life was, without doubt, the wisest. But of course it was not driven by wisdom, and it was also the easiest I've ever made.

INDEX

Accenture, 221
action bias, 224, 225
"Action Bias Among Elite
    Soccer Goalkeepers: The
    Case of Penalty Kicks"
    (Bar-Eli et al.), 224
advisers, 150–51
affective forecasting, 226, 245
Africa, 140–41
ALS (Lou Gehrig's disease),
    223
American Express, 176–77
anchoring, 132, 137, 138–44,
    146, 163, 241–42
    on "buy side," 145
    experience and, 145, 151–52
    investing and, 132, 146–47,
        149, 152–53
    by numbers in product's
        name, 147

in real estate market, 140,
    142–45
on "sell side," 145
suggestions for, 150–53
warning signs of, 149
Andreassen, Paul B., 202
anger, 219–20
annuities, 3, 60, 125
antiques, 146
"Anything Goes," 246
Applied Materials, 173–74
appraisers, 152
Ariely, Dan:
    on concern for public image,
        185
    on deadlines, 102
    sex and reflexive system
        study of, 228–29
    on trade-off contrasts, 88
Arizona, 51

Arkes, Hal R., 61–63, 64–65
Asch, Solomon, 184–85
AT&T, 175
ATM cards, 248
Attila the Hun, 139
auto insurance, 116
automobile-related deaths, 11–12
availability, 36–38
averages, 126–27

Baby Bells, 175
"back to the future" perspective, 246
balance sheets, 207
banking, 3
Bank of Israel, 31
Barber, Brad:
    on perils of trading stocks often, 169, 170
    on salient options, 200
    on selling winning stocks, 56–57, 169
Bar-Eli, Michael, 224
base rate, neglecting, 112–16, 128–29
basketball, 116–18
Bechara, Antoine, 214
behavioral economics, 2, 4, 13
    contradictions of, 17–18
    creation of, 9
    significance of, 14–15
    see also anchoring;
        confirmation bias;
        endowment effect;
        mental accounting;
        overconfidence
Belden, 221

Belsky, Gary, 36–37
    "Do it tomorrow" sticker of, 234
    mental accounting by, 28–30
    "Say it out loud" sticker of, 230
    sunk cost fallacy of, 64
    "trusted screener" of, 101
Benartzi, Shlomo, 58, 176
Berger, Jonah, 196
Berkshire Hathaway, 175, 205, 230–31
Berra, Yogi, 52
bidding, 95
bigness bias, 106, 122–24, 241
Bikhchandani, Sushil, 196–97
Black Monday, 37
Blumer, Catherine, 62–63, 64–65
Boeing 747s, 157, 162–63
Bond, Samuel D., 181
bonds, 3, 26, 70, 72
    average return of, 153
    frequent trading of, 123
    individual, 252
    municipal, 90, 92
    mutual funds of, 67, 84, 127, 168, 187–88, 251
    as safe, 60, 114
bonuses, 26–27, 30, 32, 33, 42, 238
borrowing, 2, 15
    anchoring and, 132
    confirmation bias and, 132
Boston, Mass., 164
Boston Celtics, 34
brain, 211, 212–13, 214–15
brand loyalty, 137–38, 149

Buddhism, 228
Buehler, Roger, 163, 171
Buffett, Warren, 69, 175, 177,
    200, 205, 230–31

Cambria Investment
    Management, 49
cameras, 88–89
Candid Camera, 246
capital gains, 74
Capon, Noel, 121–22
Carlson, Kurt A., 181
cash, 70, 72, 85, 114
casinos, 21–23
Centers for Disease Control, 45
Central Artery/Tunnel Project,
    164
certainty, 220
    see also overconfidence
certificates of deposit, 70, 84
Champ, The, 221
channel factors, 246–47
charity, 5, 223, 253
chat rooms, 151
checklists, 230–31
children, death of, 226–27
chocolate, 83
choice, 51, 131–54
    anchoring and, 132, 137,
        138–47
    confirmation bias and, 132,
        134–35, 137–38, 148–50
choice under conflict, 78–80,
    240–41
    see also decision paralysis
Clinton, Bill, 192
Coca-Cola, 175
coincidence, 106
coin flips, 120

college savings, 25, 67, 70, 165,
    238
"come back" investments,
    56–57
commodities markets, 114
comparison shopping, 151
compound earnings, 123
compound interest, 125, 128
computer chips, 173–74
Computer Literacy Inc., 220
confirmation bias, 132,
    134–35, 137–38, 148–50,
    243
    warning signs of, 149
conformity, 184–86, 193–95,
    206
consistency, 5–6, 8
Consolidated Keyboards,
    184
Consumer Reports, 241
contentment, 220
Cornell University, 15
cost-consciousness, 29
counterfactual thinking, 99,
    115
credit cards, 17
    compound interest on, 125,
        128, 249
    for emergency money, 40
    emergency money for, 249
    mental accounting and,
        33–34, 38
    minimum payment
        requirements, 153
    overspending with, 3, 248
    for taxes, 41
Critcher, Clayton, 147
"Crossroads" (song), 77
crowd behavior, 196

Damasio, Antonio, 214
deadlines, 18, 86, 102–3
De Bondt, Werner:
  on information cascades,
    198–200
  on mutual fund
    performances, 121
debt, 17
decision chess, 231–32
decision paralysis, 78–89, 96,
    240–41
  endowment effect and,
    92–96
  regret aversion and,
    96–100
  status quo bias and, 90–92,
    93, 97, 98
  suggestions for, 100–104
  warning signs of, 100
deductibles, 115, 125, 248
deflation, 107–8
Delgado, Mauricio, 218
Della Vigna, Stefano, 158
depression, 216
diamond industry, 141–42
dice/gun thought experiment,
    222–23
disconfirmation disinclination,
  see confirmation bias
discount packages, 180
disgust, 221–22
disposition effect, 59
diversification, 67–68, 126,
    250–51
divisions, money-losing, 3
"Does Living in California
  Make People Happier?
  A Focusing Illusion
  in Judgments of Life

Satisfaction" (Kahneman
  and Schkade), 225–26
"Doing Better but Feeling
  Worse" (Iyengar, Wells,
  and Schwartz), 82
dot-com bubble, 189, 191, 193,
    197
Dow Jones Industrial Average,
    37, 55, 111, 127, 204, 205
dread disease insurance, 115
Dunkin' Donuts, 175
durability bias, 226–27

eBay, 95
Econometrica, 46
economics:
  behavioral, *see* behavioral
    economics
  core assumptions of, 5–6, 8
  history of, 4–5
economic stimulus plans, 27,
    42
Edmans, Alex, 218
e-filing, 41
elections, 226
emergency money, 40–41, 249
emotions, 214, 215, 217–22,
    244–45
  endowment effect and,
    221–22
  probability assessment
    influenced by, 222–24
  see also reflexive system
endowment effect, 46, 92–96,
    104, 137
  emotions and, 221–22
  and real estate, 167
engagement rings, 141–42
Enron, 176, 200

entrepreneurs, 159
Epley, Nick, 26, 27, 42
evolution, 12–13, 97, 213
Excel, 71
expense ratios, 123–24, 129,
    136–37
experiences, 254
experts, 104
extended warranties, 30, 227
extremeness aversion, 88–89

Faber, Mebane, 49
fads, 196–97
fashion industry, 8
fatbrain.com, 220
feature fatigue, 82
Federal Deposit Insurance
    Corporation, 84
Fidelity Magellan mutual fund,
    175
fight-or-flight dichotomy,
    225
financial markets, upheaval in,
    1–2
Fischhoff, Baruch, 172
Fitch, Malcolm, 190
"Five Whys" approach, 180
five years, law of, 85, 99–100,
    235
fixed-income investments, 60,
    243
fixed-rate loan, 128
flight insurance, 115
focalism, 226–27
forecasts, 160–61, 172–73
formation period, 198
For Sale By Owner (FSBO),
    166–67, 177
found money, 30, 31, 32

401(k) accounts, 3, 25, 36, 84,
    85, 94, 95, 176, 251
403(b) accounts, 36, 84, 94,
    251
457 plans, 36, 84, 251
frame of reference, 103
framing, 18, 106, 240
    of pricing, 51
    of school taxes, 51
    of similarity, 51–52
    of sunk costs, 73–74
    see also mental accounting;
        prospect theory
Franklin, Benjamin, 232–33
"Freewill," 77
French Canadians, 161
FSBO (For Sale By Owner),
    166–67, 177
functional magnetic resonance
    imaging, 215

Galton, Francis, 9
gambler's fallacy, 113
gambling, 21–23, 24, 39, 49
Garcia, Diego, 218
Garmin, 146
Genghis Khan, 138, 139
Georgia Institute of
    Technology, 181
gifts, 26–27, 30, 39, 41, 238
Gilbert, Daniel, 226
Gilovich, Tom:
    on anchoring, 147
    on confirmation bias, 150
    on herding, 194
    on hot hands, 117
    on randomness, 120
    regret aversion research of,
        99–100

Gilovich, Tom (*cont.*)
  savings study of, 50–51
  on tempting fate, 224
Glaser, Markus, 170
glasnost, 161
GM, 176
gold, 70
Gorbachev, Mikhail, 161
Graham, Benjamin, 75, 200,
  211
Great Depression, 35
greed, 233
Griffin, Dale, 160, 163,
  171
groceries, 29
Guah, Rahul, 137
*Guinness Book of World
  Records*, 118
gyms, 158, 247

Hall, Monty, 118–20
Hamilton, Rebecca, 82
happiness, 225–26, 229–30,
  253–54
health care system, 192–93,
  197, 200, 205
"Heart Strings and Purse
  Strings: Carryover Effects
  of Emotions on Economic
  Decisions" (Lerner, Small,
  and Loewenstein), 221–22
Hebrew University, 9
heights, fear of, 217
herding, 17–18, 183–208, 235,
  243
  benefits of, 186, 201, 237
  causes of, 193–95
  information cascades in,
    199–200, 243–44

investing and, 8, 184,
  187–93, 197–208
with music downloads, 186
overconfidence and, 184
salient options and, 201–2
in shopping, 186
in stock market, 8, 184,
  187–93, 197
suggestions for, 203–8
warning signs of, 202
heuristics, 7, 12–14, 213
  "availability," 36–38
  judgmental, 12–13
  obsolete, 13–14
  "representativeness," 13–14,
    112
  on tempting fate, 223–24
H. H. Brown, 205
hindsight bias, 171–72
Hirshleifer, David, 196–97,
  211
Hoch, Stephen J., 142
holding period, 198
homesbyowner.com, 166
hospital bills, 253
hot hands, 116–18
house, purchase of, 12, 41, 83,
  110–11, 238
  down payment on, 25, 36,
    70
  loss aversion and, 56
  see also real estate
house, sale of, 166–67
housing bubble, 110
Huberman, Gur, 85, 174,
  175
humbleness, 153–54
hurry up and wait, 203,
  233

Idson, Lorraine Chen, 26
I Love Lucy, 246
Immaculate Conception, 155, 156
immune neglect, 226
"Immune Neglect: A Source of Durability Bias in Affective Forecasting" (Gilbert), 226
incidental affective states, 217
income, 26–27, 74, 95, 96
index funds, 18, 65–66, 71, 104, 126–27, 168, 177, 188, 204, 206, 250–51
Individual Retirement Accounts (IRAs), 3, 25
inflation, 60, 106, 107–9, 110–11, 123, 125, 127–28, 238, 241, 242
information cascades, 196–97, 199–200, 243–44
inheritance, 35–36, 39, 41, 238
Innumeracy: Mathematical Illiteracy and Its Consequences (Paulos), 106
Inspat International, 221
insurance, 26, 145, 152, 165, 217, 227
  deductibles, 115, 125, 248
  life, 30, 145, 152, 216
  and neglecting the base rate, 114–16
insurance policies, deductibles on, 4
integrating losses, 29–30, 75
Internal Revenue Service, 41, 57

International Association of Financial Planning, 164–65
Internet, 151, 189, 191, 193, 255
investing, 2, 5–6, 11, 14, 15
  anchoring and, 132, 146–47, 149, 152–53
  confirmation bias and, 132, 136–37
  diversification of, 67–68
  as early as possible, 122–23, 128
  endowment effect and, 46
  fixed-income, 60, 243
  focalism and, 226–27
  herding in, 187–91, 197–208
  in individual stocks, 66, 178
  loss aversion and, 55, 56–57, 59–60
  luck and, 121–22
  mental accounting and, 26
  overconfidence and, 164, 165, 167–70, 173–82, 184
  paying attention to, 75–76
  reflexive thinking and, 228–29
  status quo bias and, 46, 90–92
  strategy for, 71–72
  trading costs and, 129
  turning losses into gains in, 74
  value, 200–201
  in what you know, 174–76, 177
  see also index funds; mutual funds; stocks, stock market

investments, diversification of, 67–68, 126, 250–51
IRAs, 3, 25
Israel, 31–32
Iyengar, Sheena, 80–81, 83, 85

jams, 80–81
Jaws, 114
Jiang, Wei, 85
Johnson, Eric, 217
Johnson, Robert, 77
Johnson & Johnson, 192–93, 200, 205, 207
Journal of Economic Behavior and Organization, 97
Journal of Finance, 198
Journal of Marketing Research, 87
Journal of Political Economy, 196
judgmental heuristics, 12–13

Kahneman, Daniel, 10, 12, 14, 15, 254
   on anchoring, 140–41
   on happiness, 225–26
   on loss aversion, 54, 60, 210
   on neglecting the base rate, 112
   on prospect theory, 45–46, 47, 54, 60
   on regression, 9
   on representativeness, 13
   on two-system view, 215
Keeney, Ralph L., 181
Keillor, Garrison, 158
Kent, Robert J., 142

Keynes, John Maynard, 5
Kruger, Justin, 99

"Lake Wobegon effect," 158–59
Landsberger, Michael, 31
Langer, Eileen, 173
laptops, 132
Las Vegas, Nev., 21–23
law of five years, 70–71, 85
left-brain people, 213
"Legend of the Man in the Green Bathrobe," 21–23
Le Mens, Gaël, 196
Leonardelli, Geoffrey, 211
Lepper, Mark, 80–81, 83
Lerner, Jennifer S., 221–22
Let's Make a Deal, 118–20
Lewin, Kurt, 246–47
Lexus, 183–84, 187
liability insurance, 216
life insurance, 30, 145, 152, 216
Lin, Sabrina, 160
lines, 11, 12
liquidity, 126
List, John A., 104
locking in profits, 56–57
Loewen Group, 89
Loewenstein, George:
   on anchoring of prices in real estate, 140
   on emotions and economic decisions, 221–22
   sex and reflexive system study of, 228–29
loss aversion, 46, 77–78, 94, 209–10, 239, 247, 251
   benefits of, 54–55, 236

downside of, 55–60
savings and, 58
sunk cost fallacy and, 46,
  60–61
warning signs of, 65
losses, integrating, 29–30, 75
lottery, 112–13
Lou Gehrig's disease (ALS),
  223
Lynch, Peter, 175, 177
Lynn, Michael, 6

Madoff, Bernard, 14, 219
Magyar Tavkozlesi, 221
Mak, Dennis, 26
Malmendier, Ulrike, 158
Manilow, Barry, 194
marginal propensity to
  consume, 30–31
marginal propensity to save,
  31
Mary, 156
maximizers, 81–83
media, 161, 197
medical insurance, 116
Medvec, Victoria, 133
Meloy, Margaret, 133
memberships, 158, 180
mental accounting, 21–43,
  238, 241
  as absent from traditional
    economic theory, 24
  benefits of, 25, 39, 43,
    236–37
  bigness bias and, 123
  of bonuses vs. rebates,
    26–27, 42
  credit cards and, 33–34
  devaluing of, 35

downside of, 26–27, 28,
  29–32, 33–41
as encouraging
  conservativeness, 35–36,
  39
Gary's radio purchase and,
  28–30
in "Legend of the Man in the
  Green Bathrobe," 23
loss aversion and, 59
of savings vs. winnings,
  39–40
of small vs. large amounts,
  30–32
spending justified by, 32
suggestions for, 38
upside of, 43
warning signs of, 38
mere-measurement effect,
  135–36
Merrill Lynch, 176
message boards, 151
microwaves, 87–88
Mill, John Stuart, 4
Miller, Dale, 99
Millers, Lawrence, 89
minimum payments, 153
mirror-image effect, 54
Money, 15, 101, 204–5
money illusion, 106, 107–9,
  241
  danger of, 109–11
money managers, 168–70
money market mutual funds,
  27, 42, 67, 84, 205,
  251
Moore, Don, 161
Morningstar, 189
mortgage payments, 253

Mother Jones, 65
motivation, 103, 247
Munger, Charles, 230–31
municipal bonds, 90, 92
music market, 186
mutual funds, 26, 43, 55, 67,
    84, 101, 208
  average returns on, *124*
  buying and selling of,
    187–89
  expense ratios of, 123–24,
    129, 136–37
  index, 18, 65–66, 71
  luck and, 121–22, 125–26
  past performance of, 3, 11,
    121–22, 125–26, 204

National Geographic, 221
Neale, Margaret, 144–45
Neff, John, 200
neglecting the base rate,
    112–16, 128–29
neuroeconomics, 212–13, 215,
    244
neurologically impaired people,
    214
news, 202–3, 217, 244
New York Stock Exchange
    (NYSE), 198–99
New York Times, 117
Nixon, Richard, 172
Norli, Oyvind, 218
Northcraft, Gregory, 144–45
nuclear energy, 65
Nudge (Thaler and Sunstein),
    14

Obama, Barack, 14
objectivity, 235

obsolete heuristics, 13–14
Odean, Terrance:
  on perils of trading stocks
    often, 169, 170
  on salient options, 201
  on selling winning stocks,
    56–57, 58–59, 60, 169
opportunity costs, 94, 101–2
organ donation, 247
*Organizational Behavior and
    Human Decision
    Processes,* 61–62
overconfidence, 17–18, 149,
    154, 155–82, 220, 242–43
  of failures, 173–74
  herding and, 184
  high and low estimates and,
    157
  hindsight bias and, 171–72
  investing and, 164, 165,
    167–70, 173–82, 184
  and lack of information,
    165–66
  and "Lake Wobegon effect,"
    158–59
  of personal knowledge, 160
  planning fallacy and,
    163–64, 171
  of predictions, 160–61,
    171–72
  unpreparedness and, 164–65
  as unwarranted optimism,
    158
  warning signs of, 177
overconfidence discount,
    179–80

Parade, 118
pari-mutuel pools, 113

Paulos, John Allen, 106
payroll deduction plans, 43
PBHG Core Growth, 190–91
Peale, Norman Vincent, 16
peer pressure, 195
Persian rugs, 95
personality feedback, 226
pharmaceutical makers,
    192–93
Philadelphia 76ers, 117
pilots, learning methods of, 9,
    10
planning fallacy, 163–64,
    171
Plato, 5
Porcelli, Anthony, 218
Porter, Cole, 246
portfolio allocation theory, 67
portfolio review, yearly, 76
"Power of Positive Thinking,
    The" (Peale), 16
Predictably Irrational (Ariely),
    88
predictions, 160–61, 172–73,
    245–46
preferential bias, *see*
    confirmation bias
Prelec, Drazen, 34
Price of Everything, The
    (Roberts), 7
price-to-earnings ratio (P/E),
    206–7
pricing, 51
*Principles of Political
    Economy* (Mill), 4
probability, 106, 111–22
    emotions and assessment of,
        222–24
    suggestions on, 125–27

products, failing, 3
pros and cons list, 232–33
prospect theory, 45–76, 77–78,
    239
    disposition effect and, 59
    suggestions from, 66–76
    Weber's law, 49–50
    see also loss aversion; sunk
        cost fallacy
"Prospect Theory: An Analysis
    of Decision Under Risk"
    (Kahneman and Tversky),
    46
"Psychology of Sunk Costs,
    The" (Arkes and Blumer),
    61–63
public works, 164
pundits, 161
punishments, 9, 10

Quicken, 71

rationality, 5–6, 8, 12
real estate, 26, 67, 70, 72,
    109–10, 242
    anchoring in, 140, 142–45
    comparison market analysis
        in, 151
    drop in, 233
    endowment effect and, 167
    see also house, purchase of
real estate investment trusts,
    67, 251
rebates, 26–27, 30, 42
record keeping, 18
reflective system, 214–15
reflexive system, 213–14, 215,
    216–17, 218, 223, 228–29
    suggestions for, 229–34

reflexive system (*cont.*)
see also emotions, *specific emotions*
refunds, 30
regression, 9–10, 200
regret, 78, 210
regret aversion, 96–100, 101, 223
religion, 228
representativeness, 13–14, 112
restaurants, 131–32, 133–34
restitution payments, 31–32
retirement accounts, 4, 38, 68, 121, 122, 194, 195, 238, 250, 251–52
decision paralysis and, 84–85
SMarT plan for, 58
stock of own company in, 176
tax-deferred, 85, 95, 96
rewards, 9, 10
riders, 30
right-brain people, 213
Risen, Jane, 224
risk tolerance, 48, 49, 66, 91
Roberts, Russell, 7
romance, 226
Ross, Lee, 160, 171
Rule of 100, 71, 129
Rush, 77
Russo, J. Edward, 133, 139, 162
Rust, Roland, 82

sadness, 221–22
salary, 24
Salganik, Matthew, 186
"salient" option, 201–2

sample size, 10–12
Samuelson, William, 90, 91
sanctions, 193–94
S&P 500 index fund, 127, 191
Sasser, James, 64
satisficers, 81, 82–83, 104
savings, 2, 15, 27, 50–51, 239
anchoring and, 132
confirmation bias and, 132
loss aversion and, 58
mental accounting and, 26, 29, 43
overconfidence and, 165
savings accounts, 3, 27, 38, 42, 43, 84, 98
Schkade, David, 225–26
school taxes, 51
Schwartz, Barry, 82
Schwartz, Norbert, 229–30
securities, 3
See's, 205
self-control, 25, 237
self-esteem, 16
self-help books, 15
self-insurance, 248–49
self-interest, 5–6, 7, 8
semiconductors, 173–74
SEPs, 25
September 11, 2001, terrorist attacks of, 12, 219
service contracts, 30
sex, 228–29
Sex and the City, 216
Seyhun, H. Nejat, 55–56
Shafir, Eldar:
on choice under conflict, 79–80
on deadlines, 86

on decision-making, 52–54
on money illusion, 107, 108–9
shark attacks, 114
Shefrin, Hersh M., 59
Shiller, Robert J., 110
Shoemaker, Paul, 162
Shumway, Tyler, 211
Simester, Duncan, 34
similarities, 51–52
Simon, Herbert, 81
Simonsohn, Uri, 140
Simonson, Itamar, 87, 88
Simpsons, The, 105–6
Six Sigma, 180
"slush fund" accounts, 29
Small, Deborah A., 221–22
small numbers, 123
SMarT (Save More Tomorrow), 58
smart-cart technology, 186
Smith, Adam, 5
Soman, Dilip, 42–43
Soros, George, 177
Soviet Union, 161, 172
Spain, 247
spending, 2, 15
  anchoring and, 132
  confirmation bias and, 132
  endowment effect and, 46
  mental accounting and, 26, 38–39
  status quo bias and, 46
spending rate, 30–32
spotlight effect, 194
Stanford University, 160
startle reflex, 231–32
statistical regression, 9–10

Statman, Meir, 59
status quo bias, 46, 90–92, 97, 98, 101, 103
  as measure of satisfaction, 93
Stewart, Neil, 153
stockbrokers, 153–54
stock market crashes:
  of 1929, 35
  of 1987, 114
  of 2008, 242
stock reports, 207
stocks, stock market, 3, 26, 70, 72, 178
  anchoring and, 146–47
  average return of, 70, 153
  bubbles in, 197
  crashes in, 197
  drop in, 233
  efficiency of, 198
  fixed-income investments vs., 60
  frequent trading of, 123
  herding in, 8, 184, 187–93, 197
  individual, 66, 178, 252
  loss aversion and, 55
  overconfidence and, 164
  regret aversion and, 96–97
  selling winners in, 56–60, 169, 189–90, 200
  stress and, 218
  volatility of, 49, 68, 111
  weather's effect on, 210–11, 217
  see also index funds; mutual funds
stress, 218
subscriptions, 180

sunk cost fallacy, 46, 60–66,
　72–73, 77–78, 94, 239–40
　causes of, 62–63
　warning signs of, 65
Sunstein, Cass, 14
supermarkets, 186
Sweden, 158
Sydney, Australia, 164

taxes:
　credit card payments for, 41
　investment losses and, 57–58
tax rebates, 27
tax refund, 24, 28, 38, 39, 41,
　75
television, 78–79
temperature, 209, 211–12
tempting fate, 223–24
Tennessee-Tombigee Waterway
　Project, 64
tenure, 226
Terrell, Dek, 113
tests, 99
tetanus shots, 246–47
Tetlock, Phil, 160–61, 172
Thaler, Richard, 14
　on endowment effect, 93–94
　on information cascades,
　　198, 199–200
　on mental accounting, 23, 46
　on probability, 112
　on regret aversion, 97–98
　SMarT created by, 58
theses, 163
Third Unit Target
　Merchandising system, 89
Thompson, Debora Viana, 82
ticket purchasing, 23–24
tipping, 6–8

TQM, 180
trade-off contrast, 87–88, 89
trading costs, 129, 177, 178
traffic jams, 196
Trainspotting, 221
treadmills, 165–66, 181
Treasuries, U.S., 24, 60, 84,
　90, 91, 92, 109
trends, 196–97, 243–44
trusted screeners, 82, 101,
　241
Trzcinka, Charles, 190
Tversky, Amos, 12, 14, 15, 215,
　254
　on anchoring, 140–41
　on choice under conflict,
　　79–80
　on deadlines, 86
　on extremeness aversion, 88
　on hot hands, 117
　on incidental affective states,
　　217
　on loss aversion, 54, 60, 210
　on neglecting the base rate,
　　112
　on prospect theory, 46, 47,
　　54, 60
　on regression, 9
　on representativeness, 13
　on sample sizes, 10–11
　on trade-off contrast, 87
Twain, Mark, 100
twenty-four-hour rule, 233–34
Tykocinski, Orit E., 115–16

uncertainty, 106
underpreparedness, 164–65
United Nations, 140–41
United States, 247

vacation, 52–54
vacation allowance, 25
Vallone, Robert, 117, 160
value investing, 200–201
vos Savant, Marilyn, 118–20

Wall Street Journal, 190
Wansink, Brian, 142
wealth, democratization of, 84
weather, 210–11, 217, 229–30, 244
Weber, Ernst, 49
Weber, Martin, 170
Weber's law, 49, 74–75
wedding insurance, 115
Weight Watchers, 236
Welch, Ivo, 196–97
Wells, Rebecca, 82

Whittier, John Greenleaf, 99
Williams-Sonoma, 88
wills, 165
Wirtz, Derrick, 99
Wittink, Dick R., 137
Wood, Joanne, 16
World Cup, 218
World War II, 31

Yale University, 246–47
Yeltsin, Boris, 172
Your Money & Your Brain (Zweig), 213, 220, 243

Zeckhauser, Richard, 90, 91
Zhong, Chen-Bo, 211
Zweig, Jason, 101, 190, 213, 220, 243